CAPTIVES

OF

THE SOUTHWEST

Captives of the Southwest
ISBN-10: 1-941184-13-8
ISBN-13: 978-1-941184-13-4

© December 2016 Fletcher & Co. Publishers LLC.
All photography © Noël Fletcher (unless otherwise attributed).

Cover and graphic design by Zita Steele
Cover photo of Sandia Mountain foothills by Noël Fletcher.
Image of Dr. Carlos Montezuma (1881), courtesy of the National Archives and Records Administration. Montezuma had been a captured Native boy named Wassaja (Beckoning), who was bought from the Pimas for the $30 (the price of a pony) by Italian photographer Carlo Gentile. Gentile adopted, renamed, and raised the child as his son. An Apache, Montezuma became a medical doctor and prominent Native American activist. Image of a woman (a white captive married to an Apache) in Sonora, Mexico (1900), by DeLancey Gill, courtesy of The Smithsonian Institution. As nomads, the Apaches frequented New Mexico, Texas, Arizona and Mexico.

All rights reserved. No part of this publication may be reproduced, distributed, or transmitted in any form or by any means, including photocopying, recording, or other electronic or mechanical methods, without the prior written permission of the publisher, except in the case of brief quotations embodied in critical reviews and certain other noncommercial uses permitted by copyright law. For permission requests, see: www.fletcherpublishers.com.

Cataloging-in-Publication data for this book is available from the Library of Congress.

Library of Congress Catalog Number: 2016915767

Fletcher & Co. Publishers LLC
www.fletcherpublishers.com

First Edition
Printed in the United States of America

CAPTIVES

OF

THE SOUTHWEST

Noël Fletcher

Fletcher & Co. Publishers
www.fletcherpublishers.com

Contents

Chapter 1: *Distant Relative Kidnapped by Navajos* — 8

Chapter 2: *Indian Raids & Captives* — 12

Chapter 3: *Charley McComas* — 23

Chapter 4: *Santiago (James) McKinn* — 29

Chapter 5: *The Comanches* — 35

Chapter 6: *Santa Fe Trader Rescues 3 Captive Women* — 39

Chapter 7: *Sarah Horn & Mrs. Harris* — 40

Chapter 8: *Scalping Survivors: Robert McGee & Josiah Wilbarger* — 50

Chapter 9: *Rachel Plummer & Cynthia Parker* — 52

Chapter 10: *Comanches Slaughtered at Texas Peace Council* — 68

Chapter 11: *Indian Taos Fur Trapper Rescues Texas Boy* — 74

Chapter 12: *Comanchero Traders & Captives* — 79

Chapter 13: *Propaganda & Jane Adeline Wilson* — 91

Chapter 14: *Hispanic Captives* — 116

Chapter 15: *From Andres Martinez to "Andelle" the Kiowa* — 129

Chapter 16: *Methodist Missionary to the Indians: John Jasper Methvin* — 147

Chapter 17: *Indian Captives* — 163

Chapter 18: *Native Captives under the U.S. Military* — 177

Chapter 19: *Wilson Graham: Captive Arapaho Boy Found in Circus* — 185

Chapter 20: *The Tragedy of Apache May* — 188

Chapter 21: *Pease Ross: Comanche Boy Named after a Murder Site* — 195

Chapter 22: *Maria the Navajo Baby: A Short Convent Life* — 201

Chapter 24: *Carlos Montezuma: An Apache Warrior of a Different Type* — 214

Chapter 25: *Geronimo's Cousin Nah-thle-tla: A Determined Mother* — 228

Conclusion — 237

About Noël Fletcher — 238

Acknowledgements

I am thankful to the following people and organizations for their assistance in bringing this important part of Southwestern history to life.

- John B. Phillips, director, Oklahoma Digital Maps Collection, Edmon Low Library, Oklahoma State University, Stillwater, Okla.
- Marlea D. Leljedal, operations clerk, U.S. Army Heritage and Education Center, Carlisle, Pa.
- Sarah McReynolds, director, Old Fort Parker, Groesbeck, Texas.
- Dee Ann Smith, executive director, Bucks County Civil War Library and Museum, Doylestown, Pa.
- Sara Good, collections manager and archivist, Bucks County Historical Society, Doylestown, Pa.
- Robert Craig, newsletter editor, Hightstown-East Windsor Historical Society, Hightstown, N.J.
- Irisha Corral, library associate, Thomas C. Donnelly Library, New Mexico Highlands University, Las Vegas, N.M.
- Dr. Mike Adler, executive director, Southern Methodist University-in-Taos Program, (formerly Fort Burgwin) in Taos, N.M.
- Laraine Daly Jones, collections manager, Arizona History Museum, Tucson, Ariz.
- The Oklahoma Historical Society, Oklahoma City, Okla.
- The Huntington Library, San Marino, Calif.
- Fort Union National Monument, Watrous, N.M.
- John Slaughter Ranch Museum, Douglas, Ariz.

Chapter 1: Distant Relative Kidnapped by Navajos

The town of Cubero, N.M. (1867). Photo by Alexander Gardner, in "Across the Continent on the Kansas Pacific Railroad: Route of the 35th Parallel."

Each of the three cultures in New Mexico during the mid-1800s (Caucasian, Hispanic, and Native American) were actively involved in kidnapping each other. As competition and fighting occurred between the three races, cruelty and violence were rampant on all sides. Yet, some captives found kindness among their captors.

After the Conquistadors settled in New Mexico, the Natives and Hispanics periodically raided each other, during which times women and children were stolen. Most kidnap victims never returned to their families. Instead they became servants of their captors. Some married and integrated with their new people.

Instances of Hispanics being kidnapped by Indians were more common than most people realize. As a child, I heard old timers talk about their relatives or acquaintances who had been kidnapped by Natives. Someone usually knew the story of a parent, grandparent, relative, friend or villager who had been kidnapped by Natives. My family was no different. I had a distant relative, on my Candelaria grandfather's side, kidnapped as a child by Navajos.

At 9 years old, Manuel Antonio Candelaria was abducted while playing near his home in Cubero, N.M. At that time, Cubero was a small Spanish ranching community near the sloping plains of Mount Taylor, an 11,300-foot-high stratovolcano in the San Mateo Mountains, some 70 miles west of Albuquerque. That area bordered Laguna Pueblo to the south and Navajo country to the west. During his 10 years of captivity, Manuel Antonio became the property of Apaches from Arizona, who won him in a gambling match.

Photo of Manuel Antonio Candelaria, a distant relative, who was kidnapped by Navajos at age 9 and returned to his family a decade later after living with the Apaches.

He was raised by the wife of an Apache leader. He lived with Native Americans during his formative years, even participating in raids with the Apaches. At 19 years old, Manuel Antonio left the tribe while helping a captive Spanish girl escape. He recognized her as someone who also lived in Cubero. Manuel Antonio encountered difficulties when returned in the 1850s to his family because his mannerisms and appearance were more Indian than Spanish. Eventually, the girl he rescued helped the community accept him, and he married a local woman in Cubero.

He moved with his family to Arizona, where he became a prominent sheep rancher. Throughout the rest of his life, he remained on good terms with the Apaches and stayed in contact with his adoptive Apache mother. Under protection of the tribe, his family wore a designated bandana around their heads to avoid being attacked by Apache war parties, who left them unharmed. When he died in November 1889, *The St. Johns Herald* newspaper in Arizona called him "one of the oldest and most highly respected citizens of Apache County."

When I was a teenager, I heard another tale of a Spanish man kidnapped as a youngster by Navajos in the 1800s. He and his adoptive Navajo mother loved each other dearly. As he was about to mature into manhood, his Navajo mother grew fearful that he would be killed if he remained. So she put him on a horse, told him his Spanish surname, instructed him where to find the town where he had been abducted, and told him to get there as fast as he could. This story was told by his son, an elderly gentlemen, who became friends with one of my relatives.

A Native youth in Arizona watches the arrival of emigrants (1877). Photo by Enoch Conklin, courtesy of the Library of Congress.

Although I was already familiar with the topic of such kidnappings, what surprised me during my research for this book was the enslavement of Native Americans. Growing up in New Mexico among my Hispanic relatives, I had heard stories throughout the years about Native Americans kidnapping Anglos and Hispanics. No one ever mentioned anything about captured Natives. I had to find it out while preparing to write this book.

After the United States claimed New Mexico as a Territory in 1846, more and more American settlers and U.S. officials began to arrive. Tensions arose. The Army declared war on nomadic Native tribes whose traditional homelands were being invaded by homesteaders, miners, land grabbers, and other opportunists. Kidnappings increased during reprisals and raids. Native women and children taken from battlefields by the military rarely returned to their tribes. Instead the Natives found themselves placed into servitude in Hispanic and American homes. One military wife wrote about a Native boy's difficulties integrating into her family after he had been placed in a circus.

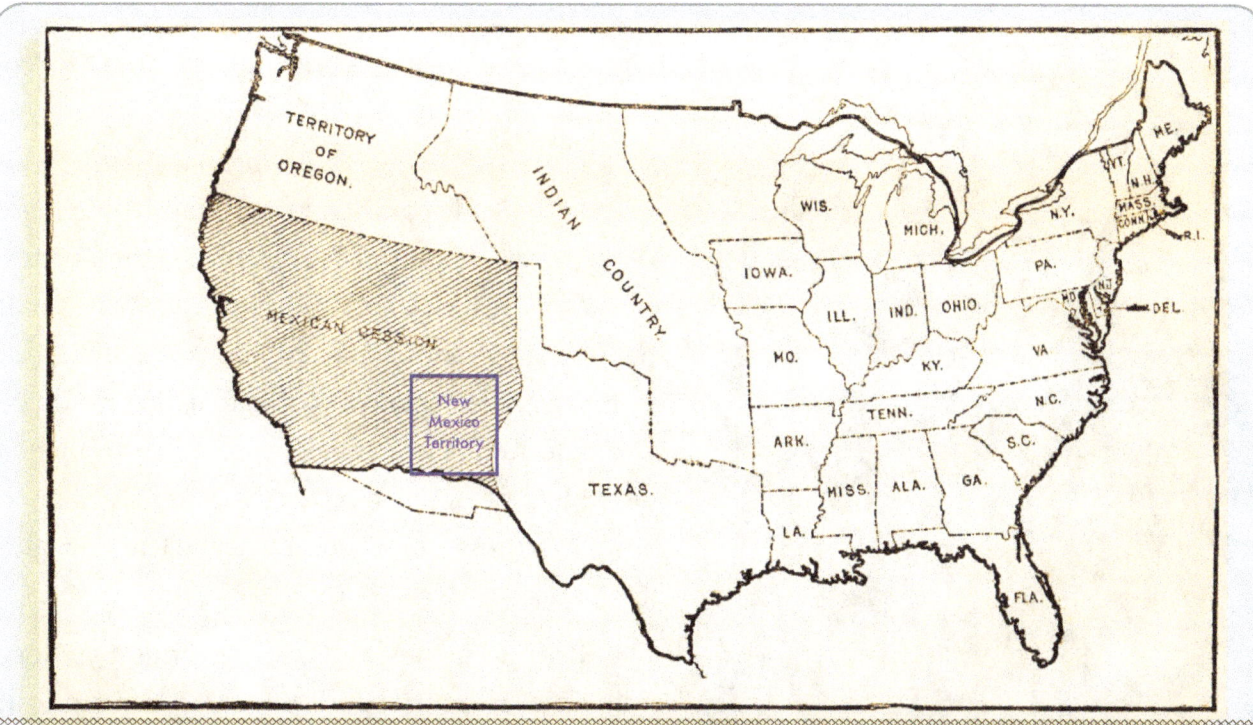

A 1901 U.S. government map showing 1848, with New Mexico and California ceded to the United States by Mexico on payment of $15 million and assumption of $3.25 million in claims by American citizens against Mexico. Courtesy of the Edmon Low Library at Oklahoma State University, Oklahoma Digital Maps Collection, McCasland Collection.

I read through squiggly handwriting in report after report from military officers to superiors detailing results from marches, expeditions, and campaigns. Over and over, I found statistics about the numbers of Indian women and children taken by the Army after killing this or that many Native warriors. Occasionally, a report discussed a tribe coming to negotiate for the return of their women and children taken captive by the military after a particular battle. More often than not, though, no further mention was made about the fate of the prisoners. I wondered to myself what happened to these people? After months of digging, I learned the ugly truth, which also is addressed in this book.

Chapter 2: Indian Raids & Captives

During the 1800s, the primary tribes who took Hispanic and Anglo captives in New Mexico were the nomadic Apaches, Comanches, Kiowas, Navajos, and Utes. Different tribes had their own territories, which could overlap. If settlers or travelers were in a particular area, they could be subject to raids from tribes whose ancestral lands had been there long before Europeans laid claim to various territories of what became the United States of America.

Cultural clashes and kidnappings by those victorious in battles had occurred throughout the centuries in New Mexico between the Native Americans and the Spanish, when the area was seized for Spain in the 1500s and passed over into Mexico. Despite differences, both sides engaged in trade with each other and pursued their individual livelihoods.

Two prospectors and a dog at a turquoise mine in a rocky canyon in New Mexico (circa 1875). Photo courtesy of The Smithsonian Institution.

Hostilities, however, reached a much higher level after the 1850s when American military forces took possession of the area and polarized the existing Indian and Hispanic inhabitants. Anglo settlers descended into the land seeking to enhance their fortune.

Young, old, single, and married, Americans began traveling in greater numbers into New Mexico. Travelers wanted to reach California after the Gold Rush. Some people wanted to start new lives in various places out West. Businessmen sought to exploit New Mexico's rich

Remnants of Fort Craig (active from 1854–1885) in southern N.M. Soldiers from there fought many battles against famous Apache leaders. Photos by Noël Fletcher.

natural minerals near mountains. Families took over land for new homesteads. Assimilation with prevailing Native American or Hispanic cultures, deemed inferior, was out of the question for most newcomers. American military authorities governed with the threat and use of violence to protect the interests of the government in Washington and its American adventurer citizens.

The military presence created an environment that gave rise to an increase in Indian raids and people being taken captive. Also, American newspapers that began setting up presses throughout New Mexico seized on both real and fabricated attacks, and kidnappings by Indians to sensationalize the public and incite lawmakers. One such example is a Nov. 1, 1879 article from Santa Fe by *The New Mexican* newspaper entitled *"How Indian News Is Got Up."* It describes how a Hispanic man, with a bullet wound to his head, rode wildly into Fort Craig in the southern part of the territory seeking assistance to combat a large group of Indians attacking a train. A nearby detachment of cavalry was dispatched. It returned soon after learning the man was accidentally shot by people riding a wagon on the way to attend court in Socorro. "The above is a fair specimen of material out of which sensational Indian news is manufactured. We will be surprised if some Eastern journal does not soon reach us, announcing with stunning

Armed Apaches on a hillside (1886). Photo by Camillus Sidney Fly, courtesy of the Library of Congress.

headlines, the massacre of the garrison at Fort Craig, and the post itself reduced to ashes, not excepting even the adobes," the newspaper stated.

Despite such misrepresentations, the news media did report on cases of captives who escaped or were rescued from Indians. A few former captives wrote books about their experiences. The stories I have included share commonalities that lend credibility to these accounts, which happened to people who were either in New Mexico when they were abducted or snatched elsewhere and rescued in New Mexico.

Apache Grievances Lead to War

Apache tribes considered their homelands to be in areas in southern Arizona and New Mexico well before American newcomers arrived. In fact, famed Apache leader Mangas Coloradas (Spanish for red sleeves) lived near Pinos Altos, and signed a peace treaty in 1846 with U.S. forces after their victory over Mexico.

Americans in that area gained infamy for their brutal treatment and murder of Apaches, which infuriated previously peaceful Apaches to the point of hatred and declarations of war on outsiders. Three outrages against respected Apache leaders resulted in decades of bloodshed throughout New Mexico and Arizona.

No hostilities occurred until a fateful encounter in 1851 with a group of American miners in southwestern New Mexico that marked the first outrage. It was during the early years of the California Gold Rush, which beckoned 300,000 people, half of whom who journeyed there crossing the land from the U.S. East Coast to the West.

Seeking riches, the group of miners set up a camp in Pinos Altos (tall pines in Spanish) in the Gila Mountains, a rugged range whose elevations span from meadows at 4,200 feet in elevation to deep canyons and peaks at 10,900 feet. Eagles, mountain lions, elk, deer, and bear are among the ample wildlife there. The mountains also are home to a 700-year-old ancient Indian community called the Gila Cliff Dwellings.

Major John C. Cremony, (1873). Photo courtesy of Wikimedia Commons.

This area around Pinos Altos and a town that would be called Silver City was the base for Mangas Coloradas and his group. To trick them to leave his homeland, Mangas met several times with a group of miners to tell tales of riches elsewhere. Eventually the miners realized his scheme and humiliated him when he came to their camp. The miners tied Mangas to a tree and beat him. Afterwards he sought revenge. The miners "were shot at from the cover of trees and rocks, their cattle and horses were driven off, their supply trains robbed and destroyed." This account was detailed by newspaperman and military officer Major John C. Cremony, in *"Life Among the Apaches,"* published in 1869. Cremony knew Mangas and other Apache chiefs, became fluent in their language, and wrote a book about his experiences. "Mangas desired their utter extirpation. He wanted their blood; he was anxious for their annihilation, and feeling himself unable to cope with them single-handed, he dispatched emissaries to [his brother-in-law] Cochise, the most famed warrior of the Chiricahua tribe, to come and help him oust the Americans."

The second major outrage by Americans against the Apaches occurred 10 years later. It involved a captive rancher's boy and famed Apache leader Cochise in an incident that became known as the "Bascom Affair"—which sparked a decade-long escalation in Apache hostilities.

The incident began at Fort Buchanan, then a part of New Mexico territory. A few years later, the area was split into two territories and Fort Buchanan became the first U.S. military post established in Arizona. Located

Illustration of the Butterfield Overland Mail stagecoach in *The San Francisco Call* newspaper on Jan. 23, 1898.

in rolling grass hills in southern Arizona, the fort had gained a bad reputation because of the continuous sickness of soldiers and nearby stagnant water. "The troops are badly quartered, astonishing as it may seem, after nearly three years' occupation of the country. The houses are build of upright posts of decaying timber, and daubed with mud; the roofs are flat, and covered with dirt and grass, now in a state of decomposition; the rooms are very low, narrow, and without ventilation; the floors are of mud, and in the rainy season covered with water," noted Dr. William J. Sloan, Army Surgeon and Medical Director, in an inspection report to the military Medical Director's Office in Santa Fe in July 1859. "There is no real protection from the sun or rain, in a climate where it is essentially necessary for well men, and especially so for the

Jason Betzinez (1906), author and businessman, was a cousin of Geronimo. He wrote about his life on the run with the Apaches. Photo by DeLancey Gil, courtesy of The Smithsonian Institution.

restoration to health of those who have suffered from repeated attacks of fever." Fort Buchanan was a key military post in Apache country near the Butterfield Overland Mail Line, an important stagecoach line carrying U.S. mail and passengers to San Diego and into California.

In October 1860, a rancher named John Ward came to Fort Buchanan seeking assistance against Apaches who has stolen three horses, two mules, and his 12-year-old adoptive stepson, a half-Irish, half-Hispanic boy, who would become a famous Indian scout called Mickey Free. A detachment under Lieutenant George N. Bascom was sent in January 1861 to the stronghold of Cochise—then at peace with the Americans—to retrieve the captive boy and property.

A native of Kentucky, 25-year-old Lt. Bascom, of the 7th Infantry Regiment, had graduated from West Point less than three years earlier. He was ordered to travel 150 miles north to Apache Pass, where Cochise was known to winter near an important freshwater spring in the desert. When the young Army officer asked for the captive and livestock, Cochise had no knowledge of the incident but offered to help. A cousin of Geronimo, with him when he surrendered, affirmed the fact. Jason Betzinez, in his autobiography *"I Fought with Geronimo,"* written in 1959, declared that Cochise knew nothing of the kidnapping because a different band of Apaches (the San Carlos) had taken the boy.

"Not expecting any trouble and not being conscious of having committed any offense against the [U.S.] government, Cochise and his subchiefs prepared to go to the meeting,"

Mickey Free, who was captured as a child and scouted Apaches on behalf of the U.S. Army, (1881). Photo courtesy of The Smithsonian Institution.

Betzinez said. "They had their women give them a good scrubbing, comb their hair, paint their faces, and otherwise make them presentable."

According to a history of Arizona, published in 1884 under authority of the territory's legislature, "Next day Bascom invited Cochise and a number of his warriors to a 'big talk.' They came at the appointed time, among them being the chief's younger brother. When all were seated, a cordon of soldiers, with fixed bayonets, surrounded the tent, and the lieutenant informed his dusky guest that he should hold them as hostages, until the property he was in search of, and the boy, were delivered up."

Betzinez said the Apaches called this infamous event "Cut through the Tent." Only three warriors were able to escape after the Americans attacked because Cochise "reacted more quickly than the others for he sprang to the side of the tent, slashed it open with his knife, and with two others dashed out into the brush," Betzinez said.

Despite a wound to the knee, Cochise grabbed a hostage during the escape.

"Cochise went out, captured the neighboring stationman, a white man who had been his friend, put a rope around his neck, and in plain sight and hearing of Bascom told him that this man would be hung unless he surrendered his friends. Bascom hung his [Cochise's younger brother and] friends, and their bodies remained there for years. While out in that country, a man told me he had slept under the skeletons as the safest spot, because the Apaches would not go near that point.

"Cochise had a rope around the man's neck, attached to the pommel of his saddle and choked the man to death. That was the beginning of the war," stated General Oliver Howard during an 1873 meeting of the U.S. Board of Indian Commissioners. General Howard had met with Cochise in Arizona in 1871 and heard the chief's version of events while brokering a peace treaty to end hostilities. The captured Apaches were executed by Bascom and hung. However, there is a discrepancy between General Howard's account about the skeletons under the tree and Betzinez, who claimed the skeletons were Americans hung by Cochise, who reclaimed the Apache bodies and left American corpses there after the event.

This indignation caused so much outrage among Apaches that even those in distant bands in different locations even heard about it, remarked Betzinez.

The third outrage took place two years after the Bascom Affair. On Jan. 17, 1863, Mangas Coloradas was near Pinos Altos during U.S. military expedition. At that time, the Apache leader was 70 years old and interested in discussing peace with the American forces, who wanted to rid the area of Apaches to protect mines in Pinos Altos.

Mangas Coloradas Jr., whose father was captured under a flag of truce and murdered by soldiers (circa 1884). Photo courtesy of the Library of Congress.

Calling it "the greatest wrong" ever done to Native Americans, Geronimo discussed this in his autobiography, *"Geronimo's Story of His*

Life," which he dictated in 1906 while living as a prisoner in Oklahoma.

Geronimo said Mangas and three warriors went to New Mexico to a place called Apache Tejo near Silver City to discuss peace with citizens and the military in a belief of being treated better there than in Arizona.

"They (the American citizens and military) told him that if he would come with his tribe and live near them, they would issue to him, from the government, blankets, flour, provisions, beef, and all manner of supplies. Our chief promised to return to Apache Tejo within two weeks. When he came back to our settlement he assembled the whole tribe in council. I did not believe that the people at Apache Tejo would do as they said and I opposed the plan," stated Geronimo, noting that a decision was made for half of the tribe to accompany Mangas.

Geronimo, (1887). Photo by Ben Wittick, courtesy of Wikimedia Commons.

Geronimo was to remain in Arizona in charge of the others. If all went well, he would bring the others to live in peace in New Mexico. "We gave almost all of our arms and ammunition to the party going to Apache Tejo, so that I case there should be treachery, they would be prepared for any surprise. Mangas Coloradas and about half of our people went to New Mexico happy that now they found white men who would be kind to them, and with whom they could lie in peace and plenty," he added.

Under a flag of truce, Mangas was escorted to Fort McLane, N.M., to meet Colonel Joseph

> HEADQUARTERS DEPARTMENT OF NEW MEXICO,
> SANTA FE, N. M., June 22, 1863.
>
> *Capt.* NATHANIEL J. PISHON, *Company D, First California Cavalry, Fort Craig, N. M.:*
>
> CAPTAIN: I send you a map of New Mexico, on which I desire that you will trace your route to and from the new gold fields, in obedience to orders to go as an escort to Surveyor-General Clark.
>
> Have great care taken of your animals. When you arrive at the new diggings, I want each of your men to prospect and wash, and I want you to report the exact time they severally work, and the amount of gold each one obtains in return for his labor during that time. Much reliance will be placed upon these statistics. The people must not be deceived, nor inveigled into that distant country without knowing well what they may expect to find.
>
> If the country is as rich as represented—and of this I have no doubt—there will, on your return, be a revolution in matters here which no man now can ever dream of. I have written to the authorities at Washington that if the country is as rich as reported, on your return I shall send two companies of California troops to establish a post in the heart of the gold region. Your company may, perhaps, be one of them, so you will have an eye to the best location of a post for one company of infantry and one of cavalry.
>
> In returning by the Whipple route to Albuquerque, mark the country well for the whole way from the gold region. Take your best men with you, and things to wash with. Send me a few specimens for the War Department on your return. Wishing you good fortune,
>
> I am, Captain, very respectfully your obedient servant,
>
> JAMES H. CARLETON,
> Brigadier-General Commanding.

James H. Carleton, commander of the military forces in New Mexico, wrote this letter to a subordinate in a southern fort located some 160 miles from Pinos Altos. Advocating lethal force against the Indians, Carleton issued in 1866 the following Special Order No. 28: "All Navajo and Apache Indians large enough to bear arms who can be found will be killed on sight."

Rodman West, of 1st California Infantry Regiment. Once in Army custody, Mangas was told he would spend the rest of his life in captivity. Mangas was ordered to spend the night in a tent or be shot if he tried to escape.

"In the early morning, the soldier on guard in the rear of the tent saw Mangas rise up from the tent and start to run. He raised his carbine, fired, and the Indian fell dead," noted Ralph Emerson Twitchell, a former mayor of Santa Fe, in a 1917 account of New Mexico's history. "It has been stated that a solider of the command, not on guard duty at the time, thrust a bayonet through the tent into the Indian's thigh, causing him to jump and run out of the tent." A few soldiers who witnessed the murder of Mangas attributed it to a directive by Colonel West, later promoted to Brigadier General, who wanted Mangas punished for past offenses. Soldiers desecrated the body of Mangas, who was scalped and tossed in a ditch.

Shortly after his death, Army surgeon Capt. D.B. Sturgeon thought it would be useful to analyze the remains of the Apache leader because of his large size at 6-feet, 6-inches in height. Capt. Sturgeon excavated the body, decapitated Mangas, boiled his head, and sent his skull for examination to N.Y. phrenologist Orson Squire Fowler. Later Fowler made two drawings of the skull and wrote about it for three pages in a lengthy book in 1880 about his theories on phrenology. The skull of Mangas eventually disappeared in time.

Unsatisfied with executing Mangas, Colonel West sought to kill more Apaches. In the days that following the murder of Mangas, the 1st Cavalry under Capt. William McCleave took a nearby Apache camp by surprise, killed 9, wounded "many more," and destroyed the community. Then soldiers went to Pinos Altos, where the band of Mangas knew nothing of his fate. The Apaches approached the soldiers when they saw their leader wasn't among the group. At once, the soldiers "were ordered to attack them, which was done" — 11 Apaches were killed and the wife of Mangas sustained injuries, according to a U.S. War Department report from 1864.

Joseph Rodman West (circa 1870) ordered the murder of famed Apache leader Mangas Coloradas, lured under a flag of truce and killed while held hostage in a tent. West was promoted to Army General and U.S. senator. Photo courtesy of the Library of Congress.

Geronimo recalled how his tribe "vainly waited for the return of Mangas Coloradas and our kinsmen. No tidings came save that they had all been treacherously slain." Afterwards, Geronimo was elected tribal chief to replace Mangas. These American betrayals and executions of Apaches would have lasting repercussions to unknowing settlers, who found themselves victim to raids and kidnappings, particularly in around Pinos Altos and Silver City, where Mangas had lived.

Attracted to this area of New Mexico were two families whose children would forever be linked to notorious kidnappings.

Chapter 3: Charley McComas

Judge McComas and his family were attacked by Apaches in a canyon 18 miles from Lordsburg, N.M., which was their destination. This photo of Main Street in Lordsburg was taken about the same time period (circa 1882–1883). Photo courtesy of The New York Public Library.

A constant state of war continued by various Apache leaders against U.S. forces and settlers in Southwest, including New Mexico, for 20 years following the death of Mangas Coloradas.

With the passage of time, Americans continued getting on with their lives after the Civil War ended in 1865. U.S. military forces, adventurers, homesteaders, and immigrants from Europe came closer and closer to New Mexico with greater ease as each new mile of railroad track from both the East and West was hammered into the ground.

While Santa Fe remained the capital of the Territorial government and military headquarters, a town in the southern end of the area, called Silver City, was undergoing rapid development during the 1870s–80s due to mining in the area. The discovery of gold in 1860 near Pinos Altos, less than 10 miles from town, brought thousands of prospectors to the area. In 1881, $25,000 worth of gold (equivalent today to $500,000) was produced from there.

In 1870, prospectors began in earnest to mine for silver. Spanish explorers had operated some mines there centuries earlier before abandoning them due to problems with local Indians. As mines yielded large quantities of high-grade ore, the economy boomed. From 1,000 to 2,000 prospectors at any given time established camps in the mountain areas around Silver City, where zinc, iron, copper, and turquoise also could be found. Some political leaders of New Mexico sought to attract outsiders to populate areas where few settlers had lived before.

In an 1897 annual report, N.M. Governor Miguel Otero wrote: "The streets of Silver City are broad, smooth, and lined with shade and ornamental trees, which furnish ample protection in winter and cool, refreshing shade in the summer time. Unlike the average Western town, our business houses are built of brick or stone, with plate-glass fronts and ornamental copings that would do credit to modern Eastern cities." Otero was the first governor who was actually born in New Mexico. Other U.S. presidents had appointed governors for four decades before him who came from elsewhere to rule over the area. Otero's report continued: "The sociological

A Silver City advertisement in a New Mexico business directory for 1882, when Judge H.C. McComas lived in that mining town before being murdered by Apaches.

conditions of Silver City are unsurpassed, and it may be said in truth of her that she is strictly an American town. She has a population of about 3,000 souls, and her numbers were drawn principally from the intelligent and refined cities of the East and South. Here you will find people of high-born social attainments, and business men and women of the modern school."

A buckboard wagon from the 1800s in Corrales, N.M. Photo by Noël Fletcher.

This same area, once home to Mangas Coloradas, attracted a prominent judge named Hamilton C. McComas. In the past decade, he had moved his family every five years to improve their fortune. In 1876, he opened up a law partnership in Fort Scott, Kansas until a plague of Rocky Mountain locusts wreaked economic havoc there. Next McComas relocated to St. Louis, Mo., where he stayed for another five years until lured by an opportunity to enrich his finances through precious metals in New Mexico.

Dissolving his law partnership, McComas left behind the safety and refinements of St. Louis society and relocated his family—wife Juniata, two daughters, and young son Charley—over 1,300 miles to the wilds of the Southwest in an area where Apache raids were the fiercest. He set up his attorney shingle in Silver City, the focal business point in the capital of Grant County, the legal hub of mining. Within a year of their settlement there, the McComas family would never be the same.

Illustration of Charley McComas in *Harper's Weekly*, April 28, 1883.

Although still spring, Silver City's weather in March 1883 felt more like summer. Officers in nearby Fort Bayard already had recorded a high of 82 degrees when McComas set out on March 28 with his wife and Charley in a rented buckboard wagon to Lordsburg, 44 miles south. The daughters remained in Silver City. Before leaving on what was described as a pleasure trip, McComas telegraphed the Lordsburg operator to expect his arrival the next evening.

They were last seen alive at 9 a.m. by a passing stagecoach bound for Silver City. When the McComas party came within 18 miles of their destination, they stopped at noon in Thompson Canyon where their dirt stagecoach route entered a valley beneath an area characterized by cliffs and mountains near the Continental Divide. No doubt the family felt safe in the valley, because they stopped before the heat of the day to picnic there. Suddenly they were attacked by a band of 25 Apaches, allegedly led by famed sub-chieftan Chato.

At that time, the government had rounded up various Apache bands (some at odds with each other) from their different homelands and placed them in the San Carlos Reservation in southern Arizona, where they were totally dependent on the U.S. military. Capt. John Bourke, of the 3rd Cavalry, described the reservation as "malaria-reeking flats…where the water is salt and the air poison, and one breathes a mixture of sand blizzards and more flies [than imaginable]." General George Crook, in 1885 testimony to Congress, explained that some Apaches feared remaining on the reservation due to bad treatment there, and they mistrusted authorities. Therefore, some Apaches decided if they were going to die it would be as a warrior on their own terms.

The Apaches behind the McComas murders came upon the family accidentally after being driven into New Mexico while fleeing U.S. military forces in Arizona. The Apaches were riding in a roundabout direction to hide out in Mexico when they stumbled across the McComas family resting under the shade of a walnut tree, noted a Sept. 6, 1883 report by N.M. governor Lionel Sheldon.

Six-year-old Charley was kidnapped, while his father died from multiple gunshot wounds and his mother slain with a bludgeoned head. Both bodies were stripped. McComas was found mutilated a short distance from his wife. Their buckboard wagon was described as "broken to pieces."

N.M. Territorial Governor Lionel Sheldon (of New York), courtesy of Wikimedia Commons.

A *Silver City Enterprise* newspaper reporter returned from the massacre site and gave the following account: "One horse was shot and dropped dead near the wagon, Mrs. McComas was lying on her face near the dead horse, with her skull mashed in and perfectly nude. From her appearance she was not shot but had her head crushed by a rock or something of that character. Judge McComas was found about 400 or 500 feet from Mrs. McComas, shot through both legs and in the left side, and his right arm was shot above the elbow. The blood on the ground coming from McComas could readily be followed by moonlight to where the Judge was found. He was perfectly naked too…An empty cartridge box was found near Judge McComas' left hand. He was evidently making a running fight at the time he fell dead."

A stagecoach, traveling at night on its run to Lordsburg, found the bodies, which had blistered in the hot sun until discovery of the murder scene hours later. "Besides stripping Mrs. McComas of everything she had on, even her hair was pulled down," declared the reporter,

Chato poses with a rifle (1888) by George Ben Whittick. Chato surrendered and lived on the San Carlos Reservation for several years, but became concerned with his fate there and left for a life on the run. Five years before this photo was taken, he surrendered to General George Crook and became a scout who helped capture Geronimo. Photo courtesy of The Smithsonian Institution.

whose article was republished in New Mexico on April 7, 1883 by the *Lincoln County Leader*.

The McComas massacre became the talk of America as newspapers kept alive its details and the ensuing military search for little Charley.

A year later, U.S. officials received word from Apaches in Mexico, which indicated that Charley McComas died in captivity.

Although the case of the double murders of the prominent McComas parents and the kidnapping of their child had been discussed far and wide—even to the halls of government in Washington, D.C.—the kidnapping of another little boy in the same area a few years later went unnoticed.

Chapter 4: Santiago (James) McKinn

Old farm equipment abandoned in a field in Moriarty, N.M. Photo by Noël Fletcher.

When the sun rose on a typical hot, dry summer's day in mid-September 1885 on the chicken farm of John McKinn, the family had no idea that a band of marauding Apaches would swoop down into their homestead in the fertile valley nestled between the convergence of two small creeks fed by the Mimbres River, some 50 miles southeast of Silver City. Farms throughout most of New Mexico would be harvesting the last crops of corn, squash, pinto beans, apples, melons, and green chili during the final lazy days of an Indian summer. Families who settled around the Mimbres River established successful farms in plots of land cleared for cultivation.

An Irish immigrant, John McKinn married a Hispanic woman from New Mexico named Lucetia. They had sons Martin and James (called Santiago in the Spanish version of his name), and a daughter Mary. Accounts vary about whether John had experience dealing with Indians. Some say he previously served in the U.S. military in the West. However, others who lived near the McKinn family during the same time period provided oral histories in the 1930s contending that the McKinn family took no safety measures against possible Apache attacks.

Charlie Nickolie, a neighbor who recalled events when he was six years old: "Mr. McGregor was going around to the settlers and warning them to gather at the Mill Post Office on the Mimbres River. When he came to the head of Bear Canyon, a Mexican by the name of Montoya was herding the horses and stock. He was surprised when he saw McGregor coming to warn of the Indians, but before he could get the stock away from there, the Indians were seen in the distance, so they left the stock and made for the Mill Post Office. McGregor was unable to warn the McKinn family of their danger, and the family was scattered all over the place, some at work, others reading," he stated.

G.B. Hudson, who worked on a nearby cattle ranch, described the kidnapping in the June 1928 issue of the *Frontier Times*. "There was no telephone or telegraph near than [Fort Bayard, 25 miles away], and when news of an Apache raid came in, the people for miles around would assemble at some particular ranch and maintain a lookout until the scare was over, and then return to their homes and try to forget the bloody Apache." A sunrise raid surprised everyone. "A band of 12 or 15 Apaches killed George Polock near Cooks Peak, took all the plunder they could find, set fire to everything else, and threw Polock's body in the flames. Later they killed George Horn on Cold Spring canyon, mutilating the body horribly," he said. Later the same day, the Apaches found the McKinn boys.

> **Murdered by Apaches.**
> SAN FRANCISCO, Sept. 18 — The Call's Santa Fe, N. M., special says: During the last ten days the Apaches have murdered six citizens in Grant County, a ranchman named Brady Pollock. near El Macho; Evaristo Abeytia, a Mexican, near San Lorenzo; two sons of Jean McKennon, on a ranch near Gallinas Creek; George Horn, a woodchopper near Georgetown; a Mexican sheepherder near Lake Valley, name unknown. They also destroyed McKapt & Keith's ranch houses near Lake Valley.

> The newspaper account above was among the first breaking news stories about the raid involving the McKinns. *The Las Vegas Daily Gazette* in New Mexico reprinted this article Sept. 19, 1885 a day after it appeared in *The Call* newspaper from San Francisco. In the early confusion, reporters wrote the wrong name "Jean McKennon" for John McKinn and declared that both of his sons were murdered.

While John McKinn was away from the ranch, his boys were out in the field. The eldest, 17-year-old Martin, was with the herd at a distance from 10-year-old Santiago, who was apparently reading in a tree, when the Apaches approached. They questioned him if any men were in the house and asked if the family's horses were tame or not. The boy answered that he horse herd was a mixture of both. Santiago was placed on a horse and gathered with the Apaches to ride off. In the distance, he heard his brother shot. Hours later, when Martin was discovered dead face down in the dirt, Santiago, the herd of horses, and the warriors had all vanished.

A few days later, news broke of the Apache raid involving the McKinn boys and other settlers who had been attacked. McKinn, Hudson, and Nat Hicks for 2 days followed the trail of the Apaches, who traveled near the Florida Mountains, a small jagged mountain chain, with deep canyons, that rises for 12 jagged miles from flatlands in the Chihuhuan desert only 33 miles away from the Mexican border. The Apaches had used that area in the past to hide while driving stolen livestock into Mexico. Often merely crossing the border into Mexico provided Apaches with a refuge from U.S. forces, which were prohibited from trespassing across the border without a specific U.S.-Mexican government agreement.

Hudson remarked, "At their last raid, the Indians had taken along a woman's corset, for what reason no one was ever able to figure out. On the third day, we ran across a dead horse which had apparently been killed by

Santiago McKinn was captured 150 miles southwest of this mountain chain outside Bosque del Apache (Spanish for Woods of the Apaches), N.M., traditional Native campgrounds next to the Rio Grande, where wildlife is abundant. Photo by Noël Fletcher.

the Indians after it had become to tired to proceed…Well, we found the woman's corset tied around the dead horse's neck, and indications were that the Indians had held a war dance around the dead horse and its corset decoration." At that point, McKinn wanted to return home because "if the Indians had not killed his boy by that time, he [Santiago] would probably be spared if the Indians were not pursued. So we rode back down the canyon, got a drink, watered our horses, and started for home."

With Santiago missing, McKinn "seemed to care for nothing," noted Bill Rawlee, in another oral history from the 1930s. McKinn said he didn't mind losing his property and Martin being killed if he only knew what happened to Santiago and where he was. "He tried to find him [Santiago] every way that was possible, but all efforts were useless." Soon after the trail of the Apaches went cold, news interest waned. The McKinns were poor. There would be no military generals seeking Santiago, no interest in his whereabouts in Santa Fe, much less on Capitol Hill. Those who knew John McKinn, aged 49 at the time of the raid, remarked later in the press about how he lost his mind after the incident and died prematurely a decade later. Not knowing the fate of his youngest son preyed upon his thoughts and placed a significant strain on his health.

Geronimo (second from left) is seen in the midst of peace talks with General George Crook (right) in 1886. C.S. Fly captured this image before the one of Santiago in the Apache camp. Capt. Gregory Bourke, seated on the left of Crook, is shown with three interpreters. Among the Apaches gathered was Nana (next to Geronimo), a chief and warrior who married Geronimo's sister. Photo courtesy of the Library of Congress.

While hardly anyone heard about Santiago McKinn's capture, Americans for generations would learn about him thanks to his reappearance seven months after his abduction in a photograph among Geronimo's band of Apaches. Geronimo met with General George R. Crook and surrendered. Brazen photographer Camillus Sidney (C.S.) Fly, based in Tombstone, Ariz., accompanied General Crook and his men, including Capt. John Gregory Bourke, and Tucson mayor Charles Strauss to discuss peace with Geronimo in a series of meetings which lasted several days.

Seizing an opportunity during a lull in the peace talks, Fly made history by taking images of the only known Native Americans in the midst of a war with the U.S. military. One morning, Fly and an interpreter ventured into Geronimo's camp, which contained 30 warriors, and nearly 50 women and children, according to news about the peace talks in the *Arizona Weekly* newspaper on April 3, 1886.

"Fly kept busy with his camera, posing his Apache models with a nerve that would have

After taking the photo of the peace talks, C.S. Fly ventured into the Apache camp where he noticed Santiago McKinn. The photographer took this historic image, which led to Santiago's identification and return to his family. Photo courtesy of the Library of Congress.

reflected undying glory on a Chicago drummer. He coolly asked Geronimo and the warriors with him to change positions, and turn their heads or faces, to improve the negative. None of them seemed to mind him in the least except Chihuahua, who kept dodging behind a tree, but at last caught by the dropping of the slide," recalled Capt. Bourke in his memoirs.

Among the Apache children playing together in Geronimo's camp, Capt. Bourke and Mayor Strauss noticed one boy who looked different from the others. "He was about 10 years old, slim, straight, and sinewy, blue-gray eyes, badly freckled, light eyebrows and lashes, much tanned and blistered by the sun, and wore an old and once-white handkerchief on his head, which covered it so tightly that the hair could not be seen," Bourke stated. During questioning in both Spanish and English, Santiago identified himself and revealed he was captured along the

Closeup of Santiago McKinn among Apache children in Geronimo's band before the 11-year-old was rescued by General Crook in 1886.

Mimbres River in New Mexico. "He seemed to be kindly treated by his young companions, and there was no interference with our talk, but he was disinclined to say much and was no doubt thoroughly scared," Bourke added.

Although Geronimo escaped after surrendering, Santiago stayed with General Crook, who first mistakenly thought Charley McComas had been found. Newspapers picked up the story of Santiago's return to Fort Bowie, Ariz. At first the boy wanted to remain with the Apaches and objected to going home to his family. Santiago was given a new suit and placed on a train to be reunited with his father in Deming, N.M., where locals gathered around the station to view him with curiosity. Hudson recalled Santiago's return and how the boy's changed attitude surprised everyone. Santiago had become "well acquainted with the customs and life of his captors. He could sing Geronimo's war songs and had lived with them long enough that he had learned their society, and told his people he would like to return" to the Apaches, Hudson recalled.

Silver City resident Rawlee remarked: "The boy did not talk much about the life he led with the Apaches. At first, the youngster could not understand what the Indians desired him to do, and they would knock him down with a stick or anything else that was around for a club. He soon learned the language of the tribe and began to get along with the tribe as if he was a member of the tribe instead of a white person...It took the boy some time to become adjusted at all. He was always very quiet and was queer in many of his actions, more like an Indian than he was a white person. He never would talk of his experience with the Indians, only that he enjoyed himself after he could speak their language. He never seemed to be satisfied and was heard to remark that he preferred his life with the Indians than the one he led with his people after he returned."

Santiago led a quiet life. He became a blacksmith in Silver City, married, had children, and moved to Arizona, where he apparently died in the 1950s. Had it not been for his haunting image in the photo of Geronimo's band, it is likely Santiago's tale would never have been known.

Chapter 5: The Comanches

The windswept prairie homelands of the Comanches experienced enormous change during the 1800s. Since the 16th century, the tribe lived in an area claimed and loosely ruled by Spain until 1821, when Mexico declared both its independence and control over the Spanish crown's former land holdings in the Southwest. Within a few years, Americans flocked to Texas, located at the southern portion of Comanche territory containing the best hunting land. Like other plains Indians, the territorial range for nomadic Comanches could extend from 500 to 800 miles.

The homelands of the Comanche, a nomadic tribe of Plains Indians, before 1860 was called Comancheria, which is circled in red. Loosely governed from Spain and later Mexico, Comancheria came under pressure by settlers, traders, and ranchers who began invading previous Comanche territory. The U.S. government claimed land throughout Comancheria by forming states and territories until the homeland was made defunct by U.S. efforts to relocate Comanches to reservations.

Cultivating few crops, the Comanches were buffalo hunters constantly on the move, according to an 1896 report by The Smithsonian Institution. "They were long noted as the finest horsemen of the plains, and bore a reputation for dash and courage," it concluded. "They have a high sense of honor, and hold themselves superior to other tribes with which they are associated." When the United States annexed Texas in 1845 it set off a chain reaction with America claiming one territory after another (including New Mexico) that would box in Comanche homelands with the new boundaries of Colorado and Kansas in the northern prairies, with Oklahoma on their eastern lands, New Mexico to the west, and Texas in the south.

The entry of Texas into the fold of the United States of America provided a significant obstacle to the Comanche. Before the annexation, Comanches had retaliated against incursions in Texas by murdering settlers there and absconding with numerous captive women and children. The Comanches previously raided Texas settlements under Mexican jurisdiction and fled into American lands for safety. However, hostilities continued with Comanches despite the new U.S. jurisdiction, and "once more the entire border swam in blood, and was illuminated by the flames of burning homes," noted an 1895 book on the Texas and Southwest cattle industry.

With the imposition this new U.S. government made on the Comanches, also came greater numbers of settlers into their lands. Accompanying the settlers was the mighty American military with its troops, forts, advanced technologies, and never-ending supply of soldiers, who could provide reinforcements to replace their casualties faster than Comanches could repopulate.

Nevertheless, Comanches were formidable opponents.

My Hispanic ancestors lived in New Mexico since arriving with the Conquistadors in the late 1500s and early 1600s. The Pereas were leaders among the Hispanic families who founded the Santa Fe Trail. Not only did they move freight along the trail, but they traveled down the Mississippi River through the Gulf of Mexico and around the Atlantic coast to trade in Pittsburgh and New York. Perea children also traveled to Catholic boarding schools in the East. Unlike the

A Comanche named Horse Back's Son poses with a bow and arrow (circa 1867–75). Photo by William S. Soule, courtesy of The Smithsonian Institution.

The wagon train of Don A. Perea of Bernalillo, passed through Santa Fe on the 5th, en route for the States. — *Independence Messenger.*

This St. Louis newspaper in May 1858 describes one Perea caravan on the Santa Fe Trail.

Badge from the Albuquerque Police Museum. Photo by Noël Fletcher.

Perea family members who traveled through Comanche homelands along the Santa Fe Trail include: [top left to right] Pedro Jose de los Dolores Perea and Francisco Perea (caravan traders); Filomena Perea (wife of Mariano S. Otero, who joined him as he served in the U.S. Congress); Pedro & Mariano Perea (in St. Louis for boarding school. Pedro served in Congress as a N.M. delegate and Mariano was a rancher who served in local politics. [Lower left] Abram de Jesus Perea (a prominent vintner & rancher), Jose Leandro Jr. (at school. He became a Wild West sheriff and Deputy U.S. Marshal during days of outlaws and train robbers. He also was a county treasurer and active in Perea businesses.

few American women who avoided such travel, the Perea women often rode across the Plains in caravans. Several traveled throughout the 1800s to Washington, D.C. with their husbands and children following the elections of their husbands to Congress. I had heard family stories while I was growing up about encounters between my relatives and Native Americans. My grandmother Desolina Perea was born in 1907. Her relatives moved cattle and sheep from New Mexico during the

1800s along every conceivable direction on a compass—into Mexico, along the Santa Fe Trail to Kansas, as well as to Arizona, California, Colorado, and Texas. The Pereas made dangerous journeys through lands of many Native Americans, including the Navajos and Apaches. But the tribe they feared the most were the Comanches. My grandmother would shake her head from side to side when discussing *"los Comanches."* She said they were unlike any other tribe because they fought without mercy and were brutal killers to their enemies.

This wagon, depicting travel along the Santa Fe Trail, is featured in the New Mexico History Museum. Photo by Noël Fletcher.

Edgar Rye, a pioneer journalist in Southwest during the late 1800s, wrote: "The Comanche came to the attack with shield, bow, and lance, mounted on gaily caparisoned, prancing steeds, and with flaunting feathers and all the gorgeous display incident to…show and pomp. They were probably the most expert equestrians in the world. A Comanche warrior would gaily canter to a point half way between the opposing lines, yell a defiant war whoop, and shake his shield. This was a challenge to single combat."

Captives taken from Comancheria, could become objects of trade. Many passed through New Mexico during their captivity as the tribe wandered. Some captives found freedom by escaping or being ransomed by Hispanic traders from New Mexico, called *Comancheros*. Several of the most infamous cases of women and children kidnapped by Comanches had a New Mexico connection.

Chapter 6: Santa Fe Trader Rescues 3 Captive Women

Santa Fe in the mid-1800s looked like an unassuming high desert metropolis in a largely vacant expanse between the west cost of California and burgeoning Midwestern states in America. Founded in 1610 by Spanish conquistadors who named it "Holy Faith," Santa Fe already claimed title to being the oldest capital city around—beating by 10 years the landing of English pilgrims on Plymouth Rock in what became America. Santa Fe consisted of low-level buildings, made of earthen bricks called adobes, that formed a

Sangre de Cristo Mountains, Santa Fe. Photo by Zita Fletcher.

muted chocolate-brown backdrop against gray sagebrush and green piñon (pine) and juniper trees at the base of the rugged Sangre de Cristo (Blood of Christ) Mountains, which jutted 6,000 feet above the city. The few European and American visitors to Santa Fe in the early-to-mid-1800s often wrote derisive descriptions about the city for being unattractive, while ridiculing its Hispanic inhabitants with derogatory attributes.

Commerce in the 1820s caused some to set their prejudices aside to venture from Missouri into New Mexico on what would become the Santa Fe Trail. The first wagons to roll into Santa Fe along the trail occurred in 1824, when 80 traders formed a caravan with pack mules to transport cargo from Missouri. Among the early fur trappers and Rocky mountain traders came William Donoho, a Kentuckian of Irish descent, who not only conducted trade from Missouri, but also opened a hotel in Santa Fe while the area was governed by Mexico. His most notable achievements were ransoming and securing passage to safety for three women captured in two Comanche attacks: Sarah Horn, Mrs. Harris, and Rachel Plummer. Even 50 years after his death in Texas in 1845, Donoho continued to receive accolades for rescuing the captives and was referred to as: "One of those great hearted, sympathetic men who honor humanity."

Chapter 7: Sarah Horn & Mrs. Harris

The youngest of 10 children raised by her widowed mother in England, Sarah Newton was 18 years old in 1827 when she married John Horn, who worked in London's mercantile trade. A few years later after the death of her mother, the Horns and two sons, John Jr. and Joseph, boarded a three-masted, square-rigged "packet" line ship, called the Samuel Robertson, in July for a month's voyage to America to improve their lives.

"At this period, the public mind was considerably agitated, with the idea of emigrating to America, and among others my husband determined to try his fortune in the land of promise, the Eldorado of the world, as it was then represented," Sarah recalled, in her memoirs.

The family numbered among the 303 people from England who arrived in New York during 1834. Despite finding employment as a clerk, John Horn grew restless.

"About this time the newspapers teemed with accounts concerning

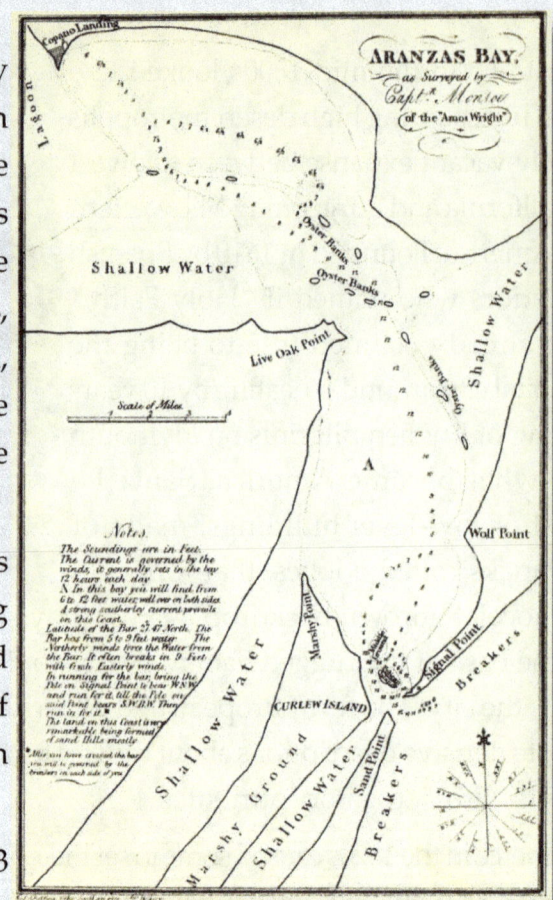

A copy of the nautical map used to guide Sarah Horn's ship to Aransas (Aranzas) Bay, Texas, in 1835. This map was an important part of the expedition led by Englishman Dr. John Charles Beales. It is of interest that this map was given to Londoner William Kennedy in his promotional book on Texas published in 1841. Both Beales and Kennedy must have known each other. Even after the deadly failure of his colony, Dr. Beales continued with land speculation while Kennedy encouraged immigration to Texas.

the new Republic of Texas, and great inducements were held out to obtain settlers in that country," Sara recalled. Swindlers, speculators, and adventurers set their gaze on the wilds of faraway Texas, still under Mexican control. Americans and Englishmen traveled there and wrote glowing accounts about opportunities for settlers, while downplaying risks of Comanche attacks.

One such Texas "expert" was Londoner William Kennedy, who traveled to Texas after his employment ended with the Earl of Durham in Canada. Kennedy wrote a guidebook. "The country frequented by the Comanches is of extraordinary beauty and fertility. The mountains are not high nor continued chains, but are composed of insulated peaks, which shoot suddenly up out of the plains," Kennedy wrote, in *Texas: The Rise, Progress, and Prospects of the Republic of Texas.* He theorized that European farmers could produce "easy and ample returns" from crops in plains and valleys while coastal planters "will be prodigally rewarded by the vegetable treasures" from the tropical climate.

Ashbel Smith (1805–1886), a Yale graduate, surgeon general, Confederate, and diplomat. After Texas declared itself an independent country from 1836 to 1846, it sent ambassadors to Washington, D.C. and foreign capitals overseas. For 2 years, Smith served as a Texas *chargé d'affaires* in London and Paris.

Kennedy held a dismissive attitude toward Comanches, whom he contended were unable to unite as a large group in battle because they depended on their surroundings to meet daily needs rather than preparing an expedition against an enemy. "Nor are they a people enamored of war, when there is any prospect of opposition; their depredations are always committed upon the defenseless. Even a single American armed with the rifle has been known to keep large parties of them at bay, their principle being, that it is better to suffer a dozen enemies to escape, than to run the risk of losing a single Comanche. They hold it to be much more honorable to murder a man in his sleep, than to take him in open combat; and bravery they regard as an inferior quality to deceptive cunning," declared Kennedy, adding, however, that Comanches "seldom destroy the lives of women or children…but they capture and enslave them, incorporating them within the nation, and guarding them so closely that they rarely have an opportunity to escape."

Kennedy's 1841 guidebook contains a nautical chart used by another fellow Englishmen, Dr. John Charles Beales, who would guide Sarah's family and others to disaster on the *Amos Wright* schooner into the Aransas bay in Texas, some 170 miles south of San Antonio. Dr. Beales had formed the Rio Grande and Texas Land Co. in New York to encourage immigrants from England, Ireland, France, and Germany to populate wilderness in Texas.

The Horn family traveled from New York to Texas on a schooner. This painting depicts the "Ajax" Schooner leaving Delaware (1838–1839). By William Meyers, courtesy of The New York Public Library.

Sarah's husband decided to cast his family's fortunes among those of 55 others who were all swayed by a scheme of Dr. Beales, a physician from Norfolk and Texas land speculator, to establish a colony named Dolores (after his Mexican wife) along the Rio Grande wilderness beyond the perimeter of the U.S. boundary. Each settler would receive 137 acres and a lot in town to build a dwelling on.

Three months after arriving in New York, the Horns joined a group including European immigrants from England, Scotland, and Germany as well as a family named Harris, about

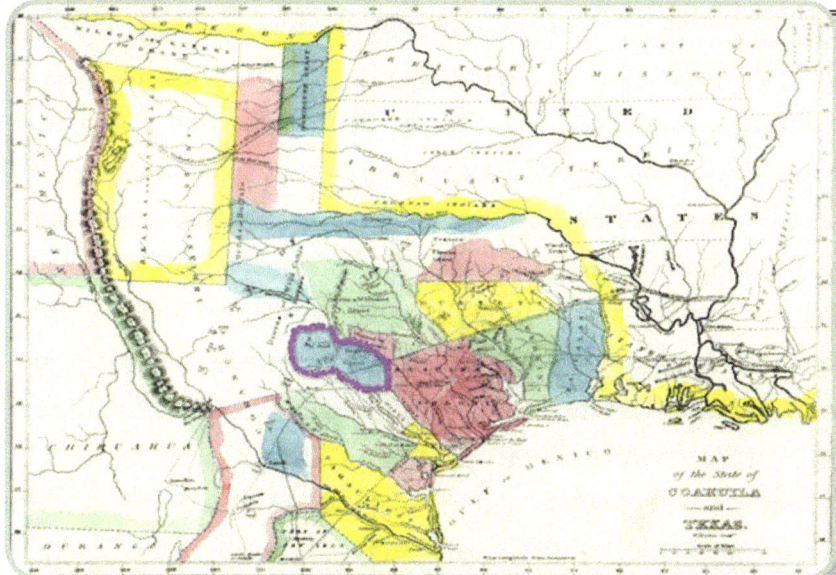

Sarah Horn's family was among the colonists taken to Beales Colony, contained in an oval purple shape. Comanche territory is shown left of Beales Colony. This 1833 map depicts other proposed settlement colonies that land speculators worked out with the Mexican government before Texas joined the United States in 1845. European immigrants were often business targets for these settlements. Map in *"Texas: The Rise, Progress, and Prospects of the Republic of Texas."*

whom little is known except for the fate that would befall them at the hands of Comanches. Together, they sailed through shark-infested waters of the Gulf of Mexico to Texas. In the first of a series of broken promises, the colonists arrived in January 1835 after nearly two months at sea—double the amount of travel time they were told.

The group, led by 29-year-old Dr. Beales, continued inland towards their destination despite repeated warnings by Hispanic residents about Indians. Proceeding onward past San Antonio, the settlers came upon an American named Mr. Smith, who "lay by the roadside weltering in his blood" after he and three Spanish guides waged a losing battle for three hours against Indians, according to Sarah. "Poor Mr. Smith, though much exhausted by the dreadful struggle and the loss of blood, was still able to converse, and gave us an account of the whole affair," she noted. "The Doctor [Beales] extracted a number of balls and slugs from the body of the sufferer, and, having dressed his wounds, sent him to San Antonio, where, I afterward learned, he died."

The settlers traveled onwards for 30 more miles to their expected destination—previously described as the limits of safety. As the group neared what they thought would be their final

Replica of cargo transported on mule carts in the Southwest during the 1800s. Photo by Noël Fletcher.

destination, they cheered and decorated their wagons with English and Mexican flags. A member of the party named Mr. Little even carved a remembrance on a tree to mark their entrance. However, they learned they had to move 30 miles farther into the wilderness before they could set up stake. So fearful of Indian attacks, their Spanish guides refused to accompany the group or provide use of their mule teams. Yet, the settlers ventured forward until arriving on March 16, 1835 at the site for the town of Dolores. It had taken them three months to reach that spot since first setting foot on Texas. Four days later, the group celebrated the 30th birthday of Dr. Beales and elected him town mayor. Nine days later, Dr. Beales left the group on business never to return.

The men in the group, numbering 40, decided the place offering the most protection from Indians was a thicket. They cleared an area for the settlement in the middle and made a high wall of piled branches to form a barrier against Indian attacks. Next to their dwellings, each family planted crops. The settlers were unprepared for the surprises they found. Water had to be carried in from a half-mile away. Crops refused to grow without irrigation in the salty ground. Flies and mosquitoes abounded. Summer temperatures there, which can soar above 90 degrees Fahrenheit, forced people to stay inside from noon to 3 p.m. each day from April through September. With "cruel disappointment," Sarah said the settlers discovered that the reason for their relocation 30 miles beyond their original destination was to populate the hinterland faster—thereby increasing land prices for Dr. Beales and others.

"We had been told that the soil would repay the husbandman with two rich crops in the year, but after all our toil we could not get even one that deserved the name. We had also been told that the Rio Grande was navigable so as to answer the ends of commerce; but this was equally unfounded," she noted, adding that the soil was so terrible that her husband didn't even bother to pay survey costs to find his 137 acres, which they never located.

When the first anniversary of the settlement came, nearly everyone had left due to the poor conditions and danger. Only 11 remained, including Sarah, her husband, and their two young sons, aged six and four, as well as Mr. and Mrs. Harris and their three-month old daughter. Two events drove them to flee the settlement and Texas.

The Alamo (1858). Photo courtesy of The Smithsonian Institution.

Firstly, Mexican relations with Americans in Texas had become grievous—the Alamo fell four days before the settlers decided to leave. The second and final blow was a Comanche attack on a farm 40 miles away from the settlement, which killed four men and a boy. The lone survivor was another farmer, who had been scalped. "His sufferings must have been indescribable, having remained upon his face, his bare skull exposed by day to the heat of the burning sun, and otherwise dreadfully wounded…with the loss of an arm. He said that the savage who took his scalp, after he made the incision round his head, stood upon his shoulders and tore it from him as he would the skin from a slaughtered sheep," Sarah recounted.

After hearing this news, Sarah said the last 11 settlers decided flee to the coast of the Gulf of Mexico and sail for England. Seeking to avoid Mexican troops and Comanche movements between the Rio Grande and the Nueces River, the settlers avoided roads and ventured for nearly three weeks into the wilds until they reached a lake near the Nueces River. They set up camp there at noon. None of the settlers kept guard. For the next several hours, they engaged in individual

An alligator in the southern United States. Photo by Zita Fletcher.

pursuits. The men shot a deer for food, while Sarah's husband killed an alligator in the lake.

"We had turned out the [livestock] teams to feed—some of the men were cooking dinner (from a fine deer), some were fishing, and others were fixing their guns, and reading. Mrs. Harris was a short distance off, gathering some wild fruit, and my husband was sitting on the ground near me, with our little sons. He had got some teeth of the alligator, and was making holes through them with a gimlet, in order to suspend them about the necks of the children to please them," Sarah remembered. Cradling the Harris baby, she went to a wagon when she saw "a large company of strange-looking men mounted on mules, armed, and nearly naked."

Since the Comanches considered their territorial range to spread for hundreds of miles, they may have been seeking a water source for their horses at the same lake where they discovered Sarah's group. The Native Americans likely may have heard the sound of the settlers' rifle blasts aimed at the deer and alligator. It is probable that the Comanches pinpointed the group's location from the scent of roasting meat and rising campfire smoke.

Running in fear back to the camp, Sarah told her husband she thought she had seen Indians. "He looked up in my face, and, smiling, said he thought there could be no danger, but while he was speaking, the Indians came in sight, and the work of death commenced. The first thing I perceived, an arrow had found its way into the breast of one of our men standing by my side. He drew it out with his own hands, when the blood flowed in a stream, and he fell on his face and expired."

Chaos ensued. Mrs. Harris hid in the bushes, but was captured. A Comanche raised a double-barreled rifle toward Sarah's husband, who was struck, fell face down, and died. She estimated the Comanche band to number between 40 and 50 warriors. The Comanches tore her children from her. "Having thrown everything out of the wagon, they selected such things as they were disposed to take away at this time. Then they placed myself and Mrs. Harris behind two of the party on horseback, she having her babe in her arms, and two of the men took charge of my children….we left the spot, where in one short moment, we had buried our fondest earthly hopes."

Three Comanches on horseback (1891). Photo by Hutchins & Lanney, courtesy of The Smithsonian Institution.

The next morning, one Comanche warrior killed the Harris infant by throwing her high into the air three times and dropping the baby to the ground in front of both women. Later that day, as the Comanches traveled to rejoin their band, some warriors rode up with two settlers—Mr. Harris and a German man—who had survived the massacre at the lake. Both men were brought before the two captive women, who were forced to watch the murders. "Mr. Harris had a handkerchief bound about his head. As we rode up, he cast an agonizing look at his dear wife and myself, but he uttered not a word. As soon as the company came to a halt, they were very particular that we should look on while they shot them both dead upon the spot."

An 1839 illustration of Sarah Horn in *"A Narrative of the Captivity of Mrs. Horn, and Her Two Children, with Mrs. Harris, by the Camanche Indians."* This drawing likely was created after her release; she died three years after being freed from injuries sustained while a prisoner.

Infrequently in contact with each other, the captives were split up among different Comanche bands as they roamed the plains in and around New Mexico. One day, Texas traders affiliated with a merchant named Holland Coffee, who were known to ransom captives, tried to buy Sarah from the Comanches but met with refusal.

"There were three branches of the family in which I lived, residing in separate tents. One branch consisted of an old widow woman and her two daughters, one of whom was also a widow. The next was a son of the old woman, who claimed me as his property, and the third was a son-in-law of the old woman," Sarah explained. "It was my task to dress the buffalo skins, to make them up into garments and moccasins, to cut up and dry the buffalo meat, and then pound it for use, and to do all the cooking for the family. I spent a considerable part of my time with the old woman. She was an exception to the general character of these merciless beings, and greatly did she contribute, by acts of kindness and soothing manners, to reconcile me to my fate."

At various times, Sarah said all the captives were beaten, starved, threatened with death, and traded among different masters. Mrs. Harris suffered the harshest treatment. Nearly starving to death, she seized any opportunity to obtain meat from Sarah and devour it raw. After a short while, Sarah heard nothing about her youngest son, Joseph. Occasionally, she saw her eldest child John, who was eventually adopted by a kind family. "I learned that his mistress [owner] was a Spanish woman, who, with her brother, had been captured by these Indians in childhood, and she had remained with them ever since, having married among them; and it was no small consolation to me that she appeared of an amiable disposition, and seemed much interested in the care of my child."

While living a nomadic life for months with the Indians and witnessing murderous attacks on settlers, a year passed until the fate of Sarah and Mrs. Harris came to the attention of businessman Donoho in Santa Fe. He sent Hispanic Comanchero traders from New Mexico to negotiate for the women. The Comancheros failed to gain the release of Sarah, but successfully purchased Mrs. Harris, who was escorted to Santa Fe after a year and a half of captivity.

Three months later, Sarah's fate took a turn towards freedom. The kind old Comanche woman assisted in selling Sarah to a Comanchero agent of Donoho. Sarah recalled that before her departure to the village of San Miguel, N.M., where the exchange would take place, "the old woman shed tears at the thought of parting with me. She painted my face, neck, and arms, with a sort of red paint, which they use upon the persons of their friends, as one of the highest tokens of friendship." Once in San Miguel, Sarah was ransomed for a horse, four bridles, two blankets, a pair of mirrors, two knives, tobacco, gunpowder, and musket balls.

She passed through various hands, including a welcoming family of merchants in Taos, N.M., before she made her way to Santa Fe to rendezvous with Donoho. Her friends tried to ransom her five-year-old son, Joseph, but his captors refused. She received word that her eldest, John, had died long before.

On Aug. 22, 1837, more than two years after her abduction, Sarah left New Mexico for Missouri using the Santa Fe Trail, a dangerous journey that few women dared to take. Sarah met Donoho after she arrived in Missouri. He was unable to meet her in New Mexico because he was busy making arrangements to escort Mrs. Harris and another freed captive, Rachel Plummer, from Santa Fe to Missouri.

Never returning to England, Sarah at age 30 penned her story in 1839 shortly before her death as *"A Narrative of the Captivity of Mrs. Horn, and Her Two Children, with Mrs. Harris, by the Camanche Indians."* Both Sarah and Mrs. Harris died prematurely within a few years of their release due to injuries they sustained while in captivity.

Chapter 8: Scalping Survivors: Robert McGee & Josiah Wilbarger

Sarah Horn's tale recounts a neighbor who survived an attack and scalping in 1836. This photo shows scalping survivor, Robert McGee in 1890. Photo by E.E. Henry, courtesy of the Library of Congress.

In 1864, 15-year-old orphan Robert McGee joined a government caravan bound for Fort Union, New Mexico with supplies from Leavenworth, Kansas. In need of money, McGee tried to volunteer for frontier duty in the Army, but was refused due to his age and small stature. McGee found employment as a teamster for an unscrupulous wagon master, who needed men for the dangerous journey to Fort Union. The caravan, under military escort, had traveled 18 days and was 300 miles into the 1,100-mile journey when it stopped on the outskirts of Fort Larned. It was 3 p.m. on a hot day when both the mules and men were tired. Deciding it was safe, the soldiers stacked their weapons a half mile from the wagon train and went to camp to eat dinner. The caravan and the teamsters were left alone. No military lookout was left to guard them. An hour later, Sioux Indians under chief Little Turtle attacked the caravan. All the teamsters were killed. Only the young McGee survived. He was shot in the back with his own revolver and pierced with knives and lances. Then he was pinned to the ground by two arrows, while the chief cut off a 64-square-inch section of his scalp.

The soldiers returned and found the carnage. They buried the dead and took McGee to Fort Larned for treatment. "How he survived is unaccountable. When he reached the hospital he was unconscious from shock, loss of blood, and want of food. It was several days before he could whisper so as to be understood. He was handled by raising him in a sheet, his many wounds, some 14 in numbers, about chest, arms, and abdomen, prevented us lifting him in the ordinary manner," said Dr. Hulbert H. Clark, a surgeon at Fort Larned, who treated McGee for three months until his release. After his recovery, McGee became an "Indian hunter" desiring revenge on the tribe who scalped him. He lived until at least 47 years of age, when his head injuries rendered him almost incapacitated.

Another scalping survivor was a Texas settler named Josiah Wilbarger, who moved in 1832 to Austin's Colony. Wilbarger was surveying land near the present city of Austin in August 1833 with four other men. The group saw a lone Native American and chased him, but the warrior escaped. The warrior could have been a Comanche. The Plains Indians relied on hunting parties to provide sustenance for their families. As nomads, the men hunted by day for food while the woman remained in camps. No doubt, the warrior was angered after being driven away and told his comrades about it.

Illustration of the scalping of Josiah Pugh Wilbarger in a book written in 1888 by his brother John Wesley Wilbarger, called *"Indian Depredations in Texas."*

Soon afterwards, Wilbarger and his friends stopped at a spring to rest. The men ate while three of their horses were unsaddled while grazing. Then bullets rang out from guns wielded by a band of unidentified Indians. Two surveyors managed to escape, but one died and another was wounded as an arrow entered Wilbarger's calf; his hip sustained a flesh wound. Despite his injuries, Wilbarger ran after his departing friends and tried to jump on the back of one of their horses, he was hit by a musket ball that passed through his neck. The Native Americans killed the other survivor and left Wilbarger for dead after stripping him naked and taking part of his scalp.

Alive but delirious, Wilbarger dreamt of his sister, who lived in Missouri and had died without his knowledge the day before. "Brother Josiah, you are too weak to go by yourself. Remain here, and friends will come to take care of you before the setting sun," noted John Wilbarger, who wrote about his brother Josiah's attack.

Meanwhile, an elderly woman who lived in nearby colony awoke that same night and told fellow settlers she dreamt that Wilbarger had survived with injuries and was sitting under a tree. She convinced a group of men to search for Wilbarger, who found him under a tree as she described. Wilbarger lived for 11 years after the attack, until he accidentally bumped the top of his head against a low door frame in his house and died.

Chapter 9: Rachel Plummer & Cynthia Parker

Before Rachel Plummer found freedom in Santa Fe thanks to Irish trader Donoho, her family would experience depredations from a Comanche attack remembered today for the kidnappings of five captives—including herself and nine-year-old cousin, Cynthia Ann, whose eventual marriage to a Comanche chieftain produced influential Native American chief Quanah Parker.

A burro (left) watches two men ride by an adobe house in Santa Fe (circa 1890). In the background, wall posters advertise "The Rose" opera and Seligman Bros. General Merchandise. Photo by George P. Thresher, courtesy of The Huntington Library, San Marino, CA, photCL 449 (111).

Rachel arrived in Texas as a pretty redheaded 16-year-old bride of Luther Plummer. She hailed from the Parker family, a close-knit group of devout Christians. The family was led by Elder John Parker. He was a noted pioneer frontiersman who fought in the Revolutionary War, became a frontier ranger against the Cherokees, and was on such good terms with famed woodsman Daniel Boone that he named his eldest, Daniel, in honor of their friendship. Seeking opportunities, the Parkers turned their attention from Illinois, where the clan lived, to Texas.

The first of over 30 Parkers to relocate there was Daniel Parker, a frontier preacher for the Primitive Baptist Church. He moved to an area that he named Palestine, Texas. In that area, settlers built Fort Houston—a 150-foot by 80-foot blockade around log houses, located 130 southeast of Dallas.

A buffalo herd grazes on the plains (1880). Photo by L.A. Huffman, courtesy of the California Historical Society and the University of Southern California, Libraries.

Rather than live near his son Daniel, the Elder John Parker, a few years shy of 80 years old, decided to establish a homestead 70 miles southwest at the edge of Comancheria hunting grounds in an area considered by settlers as the "advanced guard of civilization." The large Parker clan (including the Elder Parker's three other sons Benjamin, Silas and James) as well as a few families in their church group made the long journey from Illinois to a wilderness area in the present city of Groesbeck, Texas.

Texas was important not only to immigrants, but also to the Comanches since it formed an integral part of their homeland. Their area in Texas extended from the northern Panhandle through the central region. The tribe had migrated there a century before the arrival of Texas settlers and lived scattered in groups throughout the area. The Comanches kept large herds of horses that required grazing land—the famed Texan feed grass was just as important for Comanche horses as it would be for American cattle.

The Parker settlers rolled up their sleeves to build Parker's Fort in August 1835. The Elder's experience of frontier life was put to good use. Located next to a steady supply of fresh water, Parker's Fort was a square blockhouse constructed from split cedar logs, whose strong timbers

A replica of Parker's Fort, placed in the original location, was rebuilt in 1936 with government funds during the Depression within Fort Parker State Park. The replica, now called Old Parker's Fort, is a tourist and wedding destination in Texas. Photo courtesy of Old Fort Parker in Groesbeck, Texas.

were planted deep for stability and rose 15 feet high. Portholes in the walls provided visibility to shoot intruders. The inside grounds spanned an acre, providing ample space and living quarters for families. The group consisted of almost 40 men, women, and children.

"Here the struggling colonists remained, engaged in the avocation of rural life, tilling the soil, hunting buffaloes, bear, deer, turkey and smaller game, which served abundantly to supply their larder at all times with fresh meat," according to an April 1909 newspaper account from Palestine, Texas.

The area in which the Parkers settled was likely important for Comanche hunting parties, whose diet primarily consisted of meat, especially buffalo.

Within Parker Fort, the settler families lived a very isolated existence. They slept inside the fort at night, but over time the men felt safe enough during the day to venture outside to establish their own farms with cabins and work in their fields.

Acquainted with some East Coast Native American tribes, the Elder John Parker couldn't have built a better blockade for protection. However his lack of experience with the nomadic Southwestern Comanches would prove fatal.

Illustration of a meeting of U.S. Army dragoons and Comanches (1850). By George Catlin, courtesy of The New York Public Library.

Nine months after the creation of Parker's Fort came the fateful day of May 19, 1836. That morning, a party of four men—Rachel's father, her husband, brother, and brother-in-law—left the fort at 9 a.m. for distant fields to finish laying their corn crops. Inside the fort, only six men remained who could handle a rifle, including Rachel's elderly grandfather and her uncles Silas and Benjamin. Rachel was among 11 women and 18 children inside the fort.

After an hour, hundreds of Comanches approached the fort while waving a white flag of truce. Confusion ensued among the settlers. Rachel's sister fled to warn the men in the fields. Her grandfather, the Elder Parker, his wife and others ran away from the fort to hide in the woods. She heard her uncle Silas confront a man trying to escape with his family. "Uncle Silas said, 'Good Lord, Dwight, you are not going to run?...Stand and fight like a man, and if we have to die we will sell our lives as dearly as we can.'"

Two warriors appeared at the gate and announced they wished to make a treaty. Benjamin met them and returned inside the fort to tell the others he thought it was a war party and everyone should get prepared. Despite objections, Benjamin ventured out to speak with the warriors because he sought to avert trouble. "When Uncle Benjamin reached the body [group] of Indians,

Parker's Fort massacre survivors Abram Anglin (left) was 19 years old and had just joined the Texas Rangers, while his father Elisha (right) was 47. They were at Elisha's farm, one mile from the fort, near the men who had gone to the corn field. They rushed to the fort upon hearing of the attack and helped rescue survivors in the final stages of the battle. They were among a smaller group of survivors who saved Granny Parker. When they returned to the fort hours later to get horses, money, and food, Elisha pulled arrows out of the body of his friend, the Elder Parker. Photos by Joseph E. Taulman (circa 1850–1890), courtesy of the DeGolyer Library, Southern Methodist University.

they turned to the right and left and surrounded him. I was now satisfied they intended killing him," Rachel remembered. "I ran out of the fort, passing the corner I saw the Indians drive their spears into Benjamin. The work of death had already commenced. I shall not attempt to describe their terrific yells, their united voices that seemed to reach the very skies, whilst they were dealing death to the inmates of the fort."

As Rachel ran with her 18-month-old son James Pratt, she was knocked down to the ground by a hoe, dragged by her hair, and separated from her child. She found herself taken to the area where her uncle Benjamin had been mutilated; arrows had been stuck in his body, and passing warriors thrust spears into it.

After the attack, the death toll at the fort numbered 5 settlers, including the Elder Parker, who had been shot with an arrow and scalped. Rachel recognized his gray hair on a scalp that had been taken.

The five captives were 17-year-old Rachel and her son; her cousins Cynthia Ann (9 years old) and John Parker (6), both siblings; and her aunt Mrs. Elizabeth Kellogg.

Mrs. John Parker was lanced with a spear, stripped, and left for dead. Mrs. Duty also was wounded. Stabbed, stripped down to her underwear and left for dead, Granny Parker crawled away to safety where she was discovered that night. Two settlers returned briefly to the fort the next day to retrieve food and money, but left without burying the dead because they feared the warriors' return.

Survivors of the Fort Parker massacre prepare to eat a skunk, in *"Indian Depredations in Texas."*

"On arriving at the fort we could not see a single human being alive, or hear a human sound. But the dogs were barking, the cattle lowing, horses neighing and the hogs squealing, making a hideous and strange melody of sounds," survivor Abram Anglin, told a newspaper in 1909.

A group of 18 survivors—mostly women and children ranging from one to 12 years old—journeyed for several days over 90 miles through the wilderness to safety at Fort Houston, near Palestine, Texas, the location named by relative and frontier preacher Daniel Parker.

"We were truly a forlorn set, many of us bareheaded and barefooted, a relentless foe on the one hand and on the other a trackless and uninhabited wilderness infested with reptiles and wild beasts, entirely destitute of food and no means of procuring it. Add to this the agonizing grief of the party over the death and capture of dear relatives," recalled Rachel's father, James Parker. The group went days without food, catching and eating two skunks and two turtles. After traveling five days, the women and children could no longer travel. Parker volunteered to seek help alone for the remaining distance to the Fort Houston while another man guarded the group. "I have often looked back and wondered how I was able to accomplish this extraordinary feat. I had not eaten a mouthful for six days, having always given my share of the animals mentioned to the children, and yet I walked 35 miles in about 8 hours. God in his bountiful mercy upheld me in this trying hour and enabled me to perform my task."

When abducted, Rachel was a few months pregnant. In the months that followed, Rachel accompanied the tribe as it left Texas and traveled for hundreds of miles through northern prairies and into snow-covered mountains. "I had to mind the horses every night, and had a certain number of buffalo skins to dress every moon. This kept me employed all the time in daylight; and often would I have to take my buffalo skin with me, to finish it whilst I was minding the horses." Her second son was born in October but only lived a few weeks before the baby was killed in front of her.

Three Comanches lean against a tipi in their camp (circa 1867). Photo by William S. Soule, courtesy of The Smithsonian Institution.

During her time among the Comanches, Rachel witnessed an extraordinary assembly one spring when many tribes gathered to discuss their grievances about American intruders. By that time, Rachel had learned to speak Comanche and listened from a distance to council meetings among different groups of Native Americans. She recalled their camps at the gathering extended as far as the eye could see.

"They said that the white men had now driven the Indian bands from the East to the West," she recounted, adding that the Indians planned further attacks against settlers to protect their native lands and rights.

Rachel eventually became prisoner of an old man, his wife, and daughter.

"Having lived as long, and indeed longer than life was desirable, I determined to aggravate them to kill me." She refused an order to retrieve a device for digging roots. The daughter of the household attacked Rachel, who held the daughter down and beat her on the head with a buffalo bone.

"I was determined if they killed me, to make a cripple of her." The Comanches yelled and all gathered around to watch as the daughter, in defeat, cried out for mercy. "No one touched me…I let go my hold of her, and could but be amazed that not one of them attempted to arrest or kill me, or do the least thing for her. She was bleeding freely, for I had cut her head in several places to the skull. I raised her up and carried her to the camp."

To her amazement, the tribe acted as if nothing happened, as Rachel washed the daughter's face and gave her water to drink. The daughter, despite her wounds, became friendlier. Shortly afterwards, one of the chiefs approached Rachel and spoke: " 'You are brave to fight—good to a fallen enemy—you are directed by the Great Spirit. Indians do not have pity on a fallen enemy. By our law you are clear. It is contrary to our law to show foul play. She began with you, and you had a right to kill her. Your noble spirit forbid you. When Indians fight, the conqueror gives or takes the life of his antagonist—and they seldom spare them.' "

However, the mother of the injured girl decided to burn Rachel to death. She ordered Rachel to get a large bundle of straw. Then she told Rachel to cross her hands to be bound. Rachel refused. "She caught up a small bundle of the straw, and setting it on fire, threw it on me. I soon found I could not stand fire. I told her that I should fight if she burnt me any more (she had already burnt me to blisters in many places." When the mother tossed another burning bundle of straw at her, Rachel pushed the woman into the fire and held her there until the woman became just as burned.

"She got hold of a club and hit me a time or two. I took it from her, and knocked her down with it," Rachel recalled. "During the fight, we had broken down one side of the house, and had got fully out into the street. After I had fully overcome her, I discovered the same diffidence on the part of the Indians as in the other fight. The whole of them were around us, screaming as before, and no one touched us."

Rachel took the mother into the house to address the old woman's injuries. Then Rachel fixed the broken side of the house. The next morning, a dozen Comanche elders assembled with both women. The older one told the truth about the incident "without the least embellishment." Rachel said she agreed with the version of events. When asked if she wanted to comment, Rachel answered: "I told the court that they had mistreated me—they had not taken me honorably; that they had used the white flag to deceive us, by which they had killed my friends—that I had been faithful, and had served them for fear of death, and that I would now rather die than be treated as I had been." The elders decided Rachel should replace the broken pole in the house "and all was peace again."

Rachel's travels with the tribe took her hundreds of miles, even into many parts of New Mexico. The group never stayed longer than three days in one place. One evening while encamped near the Rocky Mountains, a Hispanic trader asked for her master and successfully

> **THE MADISONIAN.**
> VOL. I. WASHINGTON CITY, THURSDAY, DECEMBER 28, 1837. NO. 48.
>
> *From the "Far West," printed at Liberty, Mo.*
> **WHITE WOMEN REDEEMED FROM THE INDIANS.**
> Since our last, we learn from one of the Santa Fe traders, that they have in company, two American women, whom they purchased in Santa Fe, of the Camanche Indians, for the sum of four hundred dollars.
>
> The circumstances, as far as collected by our informant, are as follows: Some time in the spring of 1835, Harris and Plummer, (such were their names,) were emigrating

Due to the isolation of New Mexico and reliance on word-of-mouth communications, news reached Washington, D.C. several months later in 1837 about the rescue of Rachel Plummer and Mrs. Harris by Santa Fe trader William Donoho. This article appeared at the bottom of the front page of The Madisonan newspaper on Dec. 28, 1837. By the time the article appeared, Rachel was traveling to Texas to be reunited with her family.

negotiated her purchase in June 1837. After a difficult 17-day trip from the mountains in northern New Mexico, Rachel reached Santa Fe. Santa Fe trader Donoho and his wife took her into their home. People in Santa Fe raised $150 in donations to meet her needs. The Donohos took her and former captive Mrs. Harris to Missouri, where Rachel's brother-in-law L.D. Nixon met her. She trekked another 1,000 miles with Donoho and Nixon through the cold winter to reach her father's house on Feb. 19, 1838 in Montgomery County, Texas.

"She presented a most pitiable appearance; her emaciated body was covered with scars, the evidences of the savage barbarity to which she had been subject during her captivity," her father wrote. "She was in very bad health, and although everything was done to restore her, she lived but a short time to enjoy the company of her kind husband and affectionate relatives…from the time she returned to her paternal home, she calmly breathed out her spirit to him who gave it, and her friends committed her body to the silent grave."

An arroyo in Santa Fe amid mountain ranges. Photo by Noël Fletcher.

Throughout her freedom unto her deathbed, Rachel prayed continuously for the preservation and deliverance of her son James Pratt. She lived with her husband and tried to settle into married life. Rachel died at age 20, three months after having her third child, Wilson, who died two days after his mother in March 1839.

She wrote about her experiences in a short narrative published in 1838. Six years later, after Rachel had passed away, her father, James Parker, wrote about his efforts to find her and republished her story as an appendix to his work. In 1927, his granddaughters republished both accounts as *The Rachel Plummer Narrative.*

A group of Delaware (Lenape) Indians pose, some with weapons (1868). Displaced from their homelands near New Jersey and New York by European immigrants, the Lenape were continuously forced to live further west. In 1829, the U.S. government relocated some Lenape to what is now Kansas. Others migrated to Texas, including the band who bought and sold Rachel's aunt Elizabeth Kellogg. Photo by Antonio Zeno Shindler, courtesy of The Smithsonian Institution.

"Oh, Lord be pleased to see," her father recalled. "She often said that this life had no charms for her and that her only wish was that she might live to see her son restored to his friends. Although she was denied this happiness, I rejoice to feel that her prayers were heard and answered in the deliverance of her child."

During Rachel's captivity, her father had searched for her relentlessly. He traveled alone through the wilderness to meet with traders, Native Americans, Texas Rangers, and anyone who could possibly provide information about Rachel's whereabouts.

"Sometimes I would not see a human being, except Indians, and they at a distance off, for two months. My only food was wild meat, without salt or bread, and that often uncooked. My only resting place, the cold ground, and my only covering, the arched dome of heaven," recalled James Parker. "On many other occasions when I was afraid to shoot game [for fear of his gunfire being heard by Natives he was tracking], I have carried water in my hat a considerable distance to drown out the prairie dogs from their burrows, and in this way procured the food that kept me from starving."

Although he was unable to personally locate his daughter, James Parker's unrelenting quest helped return other captives taken at the same time as Rachel. Soon after being abducted from Parker's Fort, Mrs. Elizabeth Kellogg was sold to a southern group of Native Americans called the Kichai tribe. Four months later, she was ransomed from the Delaware Indians, who purchased her for $150 from the Kichai. Texas politician Sam Houston paid the same amount $150 to win her freedom. James Parker rode to Nacogdoches, Texas, where Elizabeth was taken. Along with a group of men, he escorted her for 140 miles to the family home. Elizabeth became the first of the four captives to find freedom six months after her abduction. According to Texas newspapers from the 1800s, Elizabeth only lived for a few years after her release and died before 1861.

Sam Houston (top) in 1851. Fort Gibson (below) in Oklahoma. Photos courtesy of Wikimedia Commons.

Rachel's missing son, James Pratt, and his cousin John Parker were rescued in 1842 after having spent six years with the Comanches. By this time, Rachel had already passed away and did not see her son's safe return. The boys were taken to Fort Gibson, Okla. Rachel's father traveled there to bring his grandson and nephew home.

Acknowledging that the boys spoke little English, James Parker wrote: "As I could not well understand them, nor they me, I was relieved from the pain of listening to their recital of the sufferings they had endured whilst among the Indians. The evidences, [of injury]…were visible upon the backs of these unfortunate children; for there was scarcely a place where the finger could be laid, without it covering a scar made by the lash."

Upon being repatriated to his grandfather in Texas, Rachel's son James Pratt reintegrated

Texas Ranger Lawrence Sullivan (Sul) Ross captured Cynthia Ann Parker as she fled with her baby girl during a surprise attack on a Comanche village by his men. Ross went on to become a Confederate Army general and governor of Texas. Photo (circa 1860) courtesy of Wikimedia Commons.

well. He later married, had several children, and died at age 27 while fighting for the Confederates during the Civil War.

His cousin John Parker was returned to the care of his mother, who had escaped the raid on Parker's Fort. The boy's father, Silas, had been killed during the raid. His sister, Cynthia Ann, had been taken captive and separated from her brother as they traveled with different Comanche bands. At the time of young John Parker's return, Cynthia Ann remained a captive.

In contrast with the happy domestic life of his cousin, John had trouble readjusting to life with his family. He returned to the Comanches and chose to live with them for many years until he became an adult. As a young man, he joined them in raids. He fell in love with a captive Mexican girl who lived with the same tribe. John returned her to her family in Mexico, and the couple married. Afterwards he never returned to the Comanches. Instead, he fought for the Confederates during the Civil War, but refused to leave Texas. He and his wife became ranchers and lived happily together.

His sister, Cynthia Ann Parker, seized at age 9, was the last captive found from the Parker's Fort massacre. She was recovered by Lawrence Sullivan (Sul) Ross in 1860. She had been seen at age 14 among a group of Comanches, who refused to sell her to rescuers. During the years that followed, Cynthia Ann married a Comanche chief in what has been described as a mutual love match. The couple had three children together, two boys (one of whom became the celebrated

Cynthia Ann Parker and her daughter Prairie Flower, shortly after she was seized from the Comanches. Photo (circa 1860) courtesy of the Hardin-Simmons University Library, Texas.

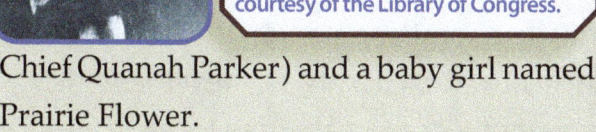
Uncle Isaac Parker (left) took Cynthia and her daughter to live in his cabin, built around 1848 and preserved in the Log Cabin Village in Fort Worth, Texas. Apparently she used to run outside this cabin into nearby woods to slash herself and mourn the loss of her Comanche loved ones. Isaac sent her away to live with other relatives. Photo by C.M. Highsmith, courtesy of the Library of Congress.

Chief Quanah Parker) and a baby girl named Prairie Flower.

In December 1860, some 40 Texas Rangers, including Sul Ross, along with a 70-man posse attacked a Comanche village in retaliation for a raid on settlers. Ross was chasing fleeing Comanches and shooting after them.

As he closed in on one rider, whom he mistook for a Native American man, the rider raised a child in the air to surrender. Upon closer examination, Ross saw the prisoner was a woman and had blue eyes—indicating to him she was a white captive. The woman turned out to be 34-year-old Cynthia Ann Parker with her infant daughter. Cynthia Ann's uncle Isaac Parker escorted her back to her waiting family. After more than 20 years with the Comanches, Cynthia Ann became a curiosity and Prairie Flower was dubbed by some newspapers as a "little barbarian."

Called an "alien among her own," Cynthia Ann yearned for her Comanche family. She desired to return to her husband and sons and made several escape attempts. However, the American Civil War broke out in 1861 within months after her return to Texas. Cynthia's difficulties readjusting to life away from the Comanches should have come as no surprise to the Parker family, which witnessed her brother John have so much trouble assimilating that he ran away to rejoin the tribe.

For the next decade, Cynthia Ann and Prairie Flower were moved at least a half dozen times

This photo of Cynthia Ann was taken in 1861 in Austin when her family took her there to ask for public financial assistance. Photo by W.W. Bridgers, courtesy of the DeGolyer Library, Southern Methodist University.

to live among various relatives. Her family even took her to Texas lawmakers to seek a public pension for her as compensation for being a Comanche captive. Prairie Flower died of pneumonia within a few years. After that, Cynthia Ann was described as having lost the will to live. She died in 1870.

After her death, her son Quanah Parker, became a Comanche chief upon the death of his father. He was known for his bravery as a warrior, keen intellect, and diplomacy in working with Americans. He counted President Teddy Roosevelt among his friends. Quanah took his mother's last name as a token of his love for her. He was her only child to survive. Cynthia's eldest child, Quanah was about 10 years old the last time he saw his mother.

A strong advocate for Comanche rights, he was proud of his heritage, had seven Comanche wives and refused Western conventions to cut his long hair, which he wore in braids.

His love for his mother was so great that he placed an ad in the *Fort Worth Gazette* seeking a photograph of her, according to the Smithsonian. Sul Ross sent him a copy of her photo, from which he had an artist paint a portrait to hang in his home near Fort Sill, Okla. Quanah also had the bodies of his mother and sister relocated from a Texas cemetery to be near him.

Comanche Chief Quanah Parker sits next to a painting he commissioned of his dead mother and sister in his home. Photo by Hutchins & Lanney, (1892) courtesy of The Smithsonian Institution.

Of interest is that Quanah Parker adopted a captive German teen named Herman Lehmann, whose parents were immigrants that settled in Texas. The Apaches snatched 10-year-old Herman as he scared away birds in 1870 from the family's wheat field. Herman left the Apaches 6 years later after killing a tribal member and sought refuge with Comanches. He lived with Quanah Parker's family for two years and even moved to a reservation in Oklahoma with them. However, Herman's appearance and blue eyes made him recognizable as a captive. The U.S. Army took Herman to his relatives, but he had trouble assimilating. Herman rejoined Quanah Parker's family and received U.S. government recognition as a member of the Comanche Nation after Quanah provided legal documents as evidence of his adoption of Herman.

When Quanah died in 1911, his funeral was attended by a crowd of 2,000 people, including Natives and whites. His body was dressed as a Comanche warrior and each of his fingers wore a gold band. Silver dollars were placed over every eye. Natives kept a vigil over his grave for a week to protect his remains.

One Sunday four years later, one of his wives came to visit his grave and discovered it desecrated by grave robbers. The casket had been broken and bones were scattered around. The Comanches gathered all his bones they could find, cleaned the remains, and reburied their dead chief. He became the last Comanche chief. The U.S. government refused to allow the Comanches to have another chief. Instead, the government forced the Comanches to be governed by a three-member tribal committee.

Former captive Herman Lehmann, wearing Native dress, in the *Frontier Times*, June 1926.

Chapter 10: Comanches Slaughtered at Texas Peace Council

March 1840 marked a turning point in Comanche relations with Americans. Insincere peace talks with Native tribes, a familiar pattern in treachery used by some Americans, was about to take place in San Antonio, Texas. This would lead to decades of hatred and bloodshed.

As with the Apaches and Navajos, the Comanches were divided into different bands governed by chieftains rather than a single unifying leader. When American politicians and military officers entered into a treaty with a particular band of Natives, they held the entire tribe responsible

An early view of the military plaza of San Antonio a few years after the Republic of Texas joined the United States. Illustration by Arthur Schott (circa 1848–1855) in *"Report on the United States and Mexican Boundary Survey,"* W.H. Emory, Washington, D.C., 1857.

for abiding by that treaty. In reality, the treaty often had been made by one chieftain—who only represented his group's individual interests rather than those of the entire tribe. One chief couldn't negotiate terms for his peers because that was beyond his scope of authority. However, Americans in the 1800s held all members of a tribe personally accountable for broken treaties, stolen livestock, raids, or kidnappings. They punished the Natives regardless of individual innocence or guilt. Some scholars attribute this lack of distinction to Anglo ignorance about Native customs. However, in examining original source documents from that time, this injustice appears to have been due to racism. Discrimination against Natives, Hispanics, and other people of color was rampant among most Anglos, who operated under a double standard of justice.

The attack carried out March 19, 1840 by the leading Anglo citizens of San Antonio against 65 Comanches—invited there to make peace—was a savage encounter. It ended in the murder of every able-bodied Comanche man in attendance except for two elders and a group of 30 women and children.

The Comanches rode into San Antonio at the request of Col. Henry Karnes. Three chiefs had approached Col. Karnes in January 1840 to discuss an end to hostilities. Col. Karnes informed them peace was possible only if they returned all Texan captives in their possession. The chiefs agreed to the terms and to meet again several weeks later in a fateful encounter that would live on as "The Council House Fight."

Matilda Lockhart's feet are burned to prevent her escape, in *"Indian Depredations in Texas."*

In a sign of good faith, the chiefs brought their elders, wives, and children as well as the only captive they had—a 15-year-old Matilda Lockhart, captured two years earlier. What the Comanches didn't know was that Texas leaders had devised a military trap. The Comanche warriors were ushered into the government Council House located within the Court House, while their women and children waited nearby. Some Americans held up coins for the young Native boys to shoot at with their bows and arrows to keep them distracted while two companies of infantry soldiers secretly surrounded the Council Hall.

"The chiefs were then called together, and asked: 'Where are the prisoners you promised to bring in to this talk?' Muguara, the chief who held the last talk with us, and made the promise, replied: 'We have brought in the only one we had; the others are with the other tribes.' A pause ensued, because, as this answer was a palpable lie, and a direct violation of their pledge, solemnly given scarcely a month since, we had the only alternative left us," wrote Col. Hugh McLeod, Adjutant-General, in his report of incident. Col. McLeod had been appointed a commissioner for the talks by Texas President Mirabeau Lamar.

Noticing the ensuing silence from the Texans, Chief Muguara quickly replied: "How do you like the answer?"

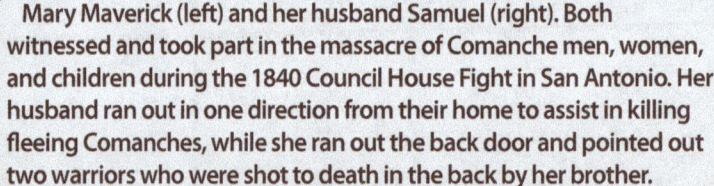

Mary Maverick (left) and her husband Samuel (right). Both witnessed and took part in the massacre of Comanche men, women, and children during the 1840 Council House Fight in San Antonio. Her husband ran out in one direction from their home to assist in killing fleeing Comanches, while she ran out the back door and pointed out two warriors who were shot to death in the back by her brother.

The warriors were informed they would be held as hostages until all Comanche captives were returned. Then the Comanches were told they were surrounded by military troops and that the warriors could send a few of their boys to convey the ultimatum to the tribe.

"A rush was made to the door," Col. McLeod wrote. "They now all drew their knives and bows, and evidently resolved to fight to the last."

Peering at the Court House through a neighbor's picket fence was 22-year-old Mary Maverick, a young mother from Alabama and relative of James Madison, the 4th U.S. president. Her husband Samuel was inside their home with her brother Andrew Adams, oblivious to the situation as they looked over land tracts. Sam was a lawyer, trying to amass large land holdings in Texas and among those who signed the Texas Declaration of Independence. Both Mary and Sam came from affluent plantation families. They brought 10 Black slaves with them in the family move to Texas. Mary described the scene in her memoirs. "When the deafening war-whoop sounded in the Court Room, it was so loud and shrill, so sudden and inexpressible horrible, that we women, looking through the fence cracks, for a moment could not comprehend its purport. The Indian boys [outside], however, instantly recognized its meaning, and turning their arrows upon Judge Robinson and other gentlemen standing near by, slew the judge on the spot."

The 12 chiefs in the Council Hall were immediately shot to death, noted Col. McLeod, adding that warriors outside "fought with desperation." Since the Comanche delegation arrived at the meeting to negotiate, it is unlikely they were well armed to fight a battle with the Texans. In fact, they brought along valuable buffalo robes and horses typically used in bartering transactions.

Col. McLeod continued: "They were repulsed, driven into the stone houses, from which

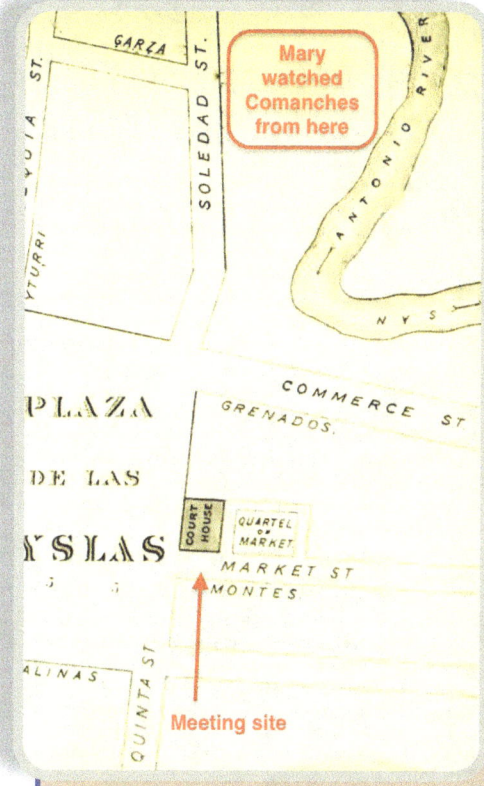

Part of an early map of San Antonio that shows where the Comanches met for the peace talks and the area from which Mary Maverick witnessed the events. Her home was also in the same area. She describes Comanches trying to flee to safety by the river (upper right). The map is from *"San Antonio de Bexar, A Guide and History,"* compiled & edited by William Corner, 1890.

they kept up a galling fire with their bows and a few rifles. Their arrows, when they struck, were driven to the feather… In a melee action, and so unexpected, it was impossible to discriminate between the sexes, so similar in dress; and several [Comanche] women were shot… The regular troops did their duty, and the citizens rallied to our aid as soon as the firing was heard."

Mary said the first volley of American gunfire killed Texans as well as several Comanches. "Soon, all rushed out into the public square, the civilians to procure arms, the Indians to escape and the solders in close pursuit…The Indians generally struck out for the river. Some fled southeast towards Bowdens Bend, some ran east on Commerce Street and some north on Soledad. Soldiers and citizens pursued and overtook them at all points. Some were shot in the river and some in the streets. Several hand-to-hand encounters took place, and some Indians took refuge in stone houses and closed the doors. Not one of the 65 Indians escaped; 33 were killed and 32 taken prisoner." Mary ran out to her backyard where she screamed out the locations of two fleeing Natives for her brother Andrew to take aim. He shot to death both warriors in the back.

Capt. Matthew "Old Paint" Caldwell received praise for his actions both by Mary and in a newspaper account of the massacre. Caldwell wrestled a gun away from an escaping warrior and killed him with it. Then he broke the gun by beating another Comanche to death with the butt of the gun. Caldwell further "distinguished himself by the great good judgment and efficacy with which he fought with stones after being shot through the leg, and losing his knife between the ribs of a Comanche," according to an April 21, 1840 article in the

Southern Argus. The Mississippi newspaper obtained details of this event from Mary's husband, Sam, during a business trip.

"The Indians dealt blows with some great skill on all they passed, so that some seven or eight of our citizens are now lying under severe wounds," the article commented. "The Indians acted with great courage and desperation, but they were all easily dispatched [killed]."

A special article (left) in the *Southern Argus* newspaper on April 21, 1840 detailed the Anglo version of events of the slaughter of Comanches to readers in Mississippi. The article based much of the information on an interview with Samuel Maverick, who traveled there on business from San Antonio. The tone of the article and the description of a wounded Native elder being hacked to death with a garden hoe (above) indicate a contempt for Comanches.

At the conclusion of his March 20, 1840 report to President Lamar, Col. McLeod noted the seizure of the Comanche group's 100 horses and large quantities of buffalo robes and animal pelts.

The injustice to the Comanches didn't end there. According to Mary, the town doctor, named Weideman, severed the heads of a deceased Comanche man and woman, to keep as "magnificent specimens" and took "the entire bodies" of another man and woman to preserve their skeletons. However, town residents discovered the doctor had cooked away the flesh from his macabre trophies in a soap boiler in his backyard and dumped the fluid into the ditch that provided San Antonio's drinking water.

"There arose a great hue and cry and all the people crowded to the mayor's office—the men talked in loud and excited tones, the women shrieked and cried—they rolled up their eyes in horror, they vomited, and many thought they were poisoned and must die," Mary recalled. The doctor, heaped with abuse, was arrested and stood trial. "He took it quite calmly, told the poor they would not be hurt—that the Indian poison had all run off with the water long before the day—paid his fine and went off laughing…The Mexicans, when they saw the

Captives of the Southwest

The Comanches at the San Antonio peace talks brought valuable buffalo robes such as the one above worn by a Pawnee warrior. Instead of taking quantities of arms to defend themselves, they brought large supplies of robes and animal pelts, confiscated by the Texans who massacred more than half the Comanche group. Pawnees, also Plains Indians, traded with Comanches. Photo of Luh-Sa-Coo-Re-Culla-Ha (Esteemed Sun) in a buffalo robe (1868). Photo by William Henry Jackson, courtesy of The Smithsonian Institution.

A ceremonial buffalo robe, thought to originate from Comanches in Texas (circa 1800s), painted in a prayer motif to the buffalo. Plains Indians painted and embroidered the soft interiors of buffalo hides, wearing the decorative designs outside with the soft fur as an inner lining. Native Americans bartered with Anglo and Hispanic traders for brightly colored dyed leather, in such hues as red. Native women would peel off the dyed surface leather to embroider buffalo hides. Comanches and other Natives often traded buffalo robes, which were considered an important commodity for bartering. Photo courtesy of The Smithsonian Institution.

doctor on the streets, would cross themselves, and avoid him…He set his skeleton Indians up in his garden, in his summerhouse, and dared anybody to steal on his premises." Three years later, Dr. Weideman died while crossing a river, remarked Mary, in the *"Memoirs of Mary A. Maverick,"* published in 1921.

Nine days after the massacre, young Comanche chief Isamani and another warrior rode boldly into San Antonio, while their band of 300 waited near the town. The Chief, adorned in war paint, circled the public square repeatedly as he shouted and challenged the people to fight. However, a military officer refused to engage in battle since a 12-day truce remained. The Texans had ordered all Comanches to return captives during that time period. Chief Isamani finally left after calling the officer a liar and coward. The Comanches returned no prisoners. Instead they tortured to death everyone in their possession except those adopted by Comanche families, who were considered members of the tribe.

The captive Comanches who survived eventually returned to their tribe after escaping or being exchanged. Although some Comanches previously had peaceful intentions towards settlers, the massacre unified Comanches in a strong hatred of Americans. There would be no more peace overtures for several decades as the Comanches united in an unrelenting campaign to wage war on Texans.

Chapter 11: Taos Fur Trapper Rescues Texas Boy

A Native youth stands among rooftops in Taos Pueblo, the northernmost of 19 Indian pueblos (villages) in New Mexico (circa 1898). Its multi-story, terraced buildings were made to defend against attacks, with thick walls and access to the inside via rooftop ladders. Taos Pueblo is the only living Native American community designated both a UNESCO World Heritage site and a U.S. National Historic Landmark. Photo by the Detroit Photographic Co. courtesy of the Library of Congress.

Unlike the politically conservative capital city of Santa Fe, the frontier community of Taos reveled in its isolated wilderness location and its mountain men, who mingled boisterously with Hispanic locals during the early 1800s. The town of Taos, located in north-central New Mexico about 45 miles below the Colorado border, was populated by Native Americans long before Hispanic and Anglo settlers arrived.

In fact, the town took its name from the Native village of Taos Pueblo, inhabited around 1,000 A.D. The Pueblo is nestled between two mountain ranges on either side of a flat plateau split by a volcanic field above a rift in the earth's surface. At the base of the rocky sides of the rift are the cool waters of the Rio Grande, fed by snow melts. The river, which flows in a north-south direction, connects to numerous tributaries that nurture green meadows and abundant wildlife. The area is home to a wide array of wildlife—eagles, antelope, deer, elk, bighorn sheep, mountain lions, wild turkeys, and beavers. Other Indian tribes—such as the Apaches, Comanches, Kiowas,

A beaver trap popular in the early 1800s. This trap would have been set with beaver musk oil bait in the water near a beaver dam. Trappers preferred to kill beavers in the fall and winter when the animals had thicker fur coats. In New Mexico, fall beaver trapping seasons started in mid-September in the mountains. Trappers received from $8 to $16 per beaver hide. Beaver pelts could be used for mainly 3 types of clothing articles: as a luxuriant fur, as leather or suede, and a felt material. Photo courtesy of The Smithsonian Institution.

Remnants of a beaver dam (lower right) in the Sangre de Cristo Mountains outside Taos, N.M. The former dam is located within the grounds of the old U.S. military site Fort Burgwin. A strong spring rainstorm flooded this dam and forced a longtime family of beavers to move elsewhere. Fort Burgwin was reconstructed by Southern Methodist University and has been an educational center since 1973 known as SMU-in-Taos. Photo by Noël Fletcher.

Utes, and those of the other 19 Pueblos in New Mexico—trekked through mountain wilderness to trade with the Taos Pueblo Indians since the 1500s.

Multiple deadly confrontations in Taos occurred between Native Americans and Spanish settlers—the first Conquistadors arrived in 1540, with Spanish settlers following in 1615. While peace was established with Taos Pueblo, the Spanish settlers fought at times in the area with the Utes and Comanches. In the 1700s and 1800s, Taos became an important frontier trading area between traveling merchants from Mexico, visiting Native Americans, and locals. Attracted to Taos due to its beavers and wildlife, French Canadian fur trappers based their operations there in that isolated outpost. Other immigrants seeking adventure and commerce followed. Intermarriages with Hispanic wives provided outsiders with access to trading privileges.

Once such trader was John A. Rowland, an American born in the Mid-Atlantic region. He moved to New Mexico in 1823 (a few years after its independence from Spain). Rowland married a local Hispanic woman from Taos in 1825 and gained Mexican citizenship, which enabled him to build a business empire with Englishman William Workman. By the time of the New Year in 1841, Rowland had expanded his business ventures beyond fur trapping to include a more lucrative whiskey distillery enterprise with Workman. They made a variant of a potent *aguardiente* brew, described in 1898 by William "Buffalo Bill" Cody as a "very bad quality of whiskey made in Taos in the early days, which, on account of its fiery nature, was called 'Taos Lightning.'"

Mountain men consumed large amounts of the Taos Lightning upon their return to civilization in Taos. The famed liquor is mentioned fondly in numerous personal accounts of pioneers, frontiersman, and soldiers from the 1800s throughout the Southwest. Col. Henry Inman, an Army Quartermaster, wrote an 1899 remembrance of time he spent on the Santa Fe Trail. He noted that foreign traders used Taos Lightning in commerce with Native Americans. The potent alcohol was a "profitable article of barter with the Indians, who exchanged their buffalo robes and other valuable furs for a supply of it, at a tremendous sacrifice," Inman stated.

Little did Rowland know in January 1841 that several months later, he would use profits from his dealings to ransom the little son of Texas judge James W. Smith, who was snatched on his ninth birthday during a Comanche attack in Austin.

On Jan. 22, 1841, Judge Smith made the fateful decision to leave his family home in Austin with his young son, identified as Fayette, to ride two miles north of town to feed his hogs.

The Smith family, which included an uncle and grandfather, had moved from Alabama to Texas only a few years earlier. Gaining prominence in Texan politics, the Smiths relocated to Austin along with other rising figures when the capital shifted away from the Houston area.

At the time, Texan immigrants had already revolted against Mexico and created their own Republic of Texas,

Taos fur trapper and liquor distiller John Rowland (circa 1856). This photo was taken 15 years after he ransomed the Smith boy. Rowland and his business partner William Workman moved to California shortly after the boy's return to his family. Photo courtesy of the University of Southern California Libraries and the California Historical Society.

CAPTIVE WOMEN AND CHILDREN OF TAOS COUNTY

In August 1760, around sixty women and children were taken captive in a Comanche raid on Ranchos de Taos. That raid is an example of the danger of living on New Mexico's frontier during the 17th and 18th centuries, for Hispanic and Indigenous communities alike, raided each other and suffered enormous consequences. Thousands of women and children were taken captive. Most were never returned.

Travelers entering Taos from Santa Fe must pass by this historical marker sign by the State of New Mexico. It stands along the highway to remind people about past captives. Photo by Noël Fletcher.

independent from American statehood. Flexing their muscles at Mexico, Texans also were determined to encroach on Native American lands and use lethal means to destroy any resistance. Mirabeau Lamar, the second President of the Republic of Texas, declared that his first priority in office would be to subjugate the Natives. Under his orders, the Shawnees were relocated, the Cherokees driven out, and Comanches chastised severely, noted an 1857 *Texas Almanac*.

Mirabeau Lamar, photo courtesy of Wikimedia Commons.

In addition, Lamar is credited with devising the idea to seat the Texas government in Austin after he rode there during a fruitful buffalo-hunting expedition and liked the area. It was no concern to him that the Austin area, with its abundant buffalo, was an important site for Comanches to obtain their winter meat and leather hides for clothing. It doesn't appear that Lamar had any problem with ordering the killing of any Natives who refused to comply with his mandates. Consequently, Comanche warriors fought hard and with deadly force to retain their homelands in Austin.

It was in these circumstances in 1841 that Judge Smith and his boy would be numbered among the many victims of violence—including both settlers and Natives.

Despite being described as armed and well mounted that day, Judge Smith rode from the safety of Austin on a horse. His son was seated behind him on the horse, holding onto his father's back. They soon encountered about five Comanches, likely a small hunting party, who emerged from some bushes. The warriors shot arrows and a gun at the Smiths. The boy later recalled that one arrow grazed his forehead before piercing and breaking his father's left arm. Their horse spooked, whirled around and bounded for a tree. A branch swept both Smiths off the horse. The Comanches seized Fayette and killed his father.

"Judge Smith's brother, on the same day, and only a few miles from where the judge was killed, was pursued by the same band of Indians, but his good horse saved him. Just 10 days after the killing of Judge Smith, his [paternal grandfather] went alone into the country four miles south of Austin to cut a bee tree, and while out was discovered by the Indians and killed. It seems strange to us at this day that men could become so reckless of danger," wrote Texan historian J.W. Wilbarger in 1890.

Fayette's life as a captive lasted for several months. During that time, he traveled northwest from Texas with a large band of Comanches into New Mexico. His surviving uncle joined a friendly group of Tonkawa Indians, nomads who lived near San Antonio and were allies of the settlers against the Comanches. Together, the uncle and the Tonkawas searched for the boy as far as Santa Fe. They spread word that they sought to ransom Fayette. Having no news of the boy, the uncle took the Santa Fe Trail to Independence, Mo. to continue his campaign to find Fayette.

A section of an 1862 map of the New Mexico Territory showing the distance from Taos to Santa Fe. A portion of the Santa Fe Trail (upper right) is shown as the route wended from Fort Union through Las Vegas and the town of San Miguel before connecting to Santa Fe.

In the meantime, Fayette had been purchased by Hispanic Comancheros acting on behalf of Taos trader and liquor purveyor Rowland. It seems likely that Rowland's brother, who lived in Texas, informed the Taos Lightning distiller about Fayette's capture. Reclaimed by Rowland, Fayette stayed in Taos until arrangements could be made for his travel to the United States. This time lapse prevented Fayette from crossing paths with his uncle. After some time, Rowland sent the boy in an overland wagon train to Independence, but his uncle had taken his search to St. Louis. Eventually, Fayette's maternal grandfather from Alabama took Fayette back to his mother in Texas.

What distinguishes Fayette's account of his captivity from others is that he sympathized with the plight of the Native Americans.

"I had no more experience with the Indians, and I do not want any more, yet I hold no ill-will toward them, as I think that they have been badly treated and robbed of a country, the best for their purpose in the world," he stated in a narrative about his experiences, included in an 1888 book called *Indian Wars and Pioneers of Texas,*" by John Henry Brown.

Chapter 12: Comanchero Traders & Captives

Despite mutual attacks against each other over the centuries, New Mexicans and Comanches enjoyed times of peaceful relations, especially when both sides benefitted economically. Each party offered unique commercial advantages. The Hispanics—living under the dominion by Spain for over 200 years and then nearly 30 years under Mexican rule—controlled access to foreign wares from across the Southwest and California to the Pacific Ocean. The nomadic Comanches had access to areas well beyond New Mexico's eastern borders. Their territory extended into central lands, where they could obtain goods from other Plains Indians, American traders in the Midwest, and French traders in Louisiana. A testament to the Comanche entrepreneurial spirit is the fact that Comanche was the Native American language for conducting commerce in the Southern Plains during the 1800s.

A Hispanic horseman wearing attire typical of Comancheros and ranchers in New Mexico during the mid-1800s. Illustration by Thompson Willing in *"The Old Santa Fe Trail -The Story of a Great Highway,"* by Col. Henry Inman, former U.S. Army assistant quartermaster, (1899).

Trade between the Hispanic Comancheros from New Mexico and the Plains Indians, especially the Comanches, began in earnest in the 1780s. Natives from New Mexico's Pueblo tribes sometimes assisted the Hispanics in business negotiations and in locating the tracks of potential customers who roved across the prairies beyond New Mexico. One of several routes that Comancheros used to locate trading partners extended across the Texas Panhandle through a 30,000-square-mile area "El Llano Estacado" (the Staked Plains). Lacking water for nine months out of the

A view of a summit of the Llano Estacado (Staked Plains). Photo (circa 1899) from the *"Twenty-First Annual Report of the United States Geological Survey,"* published in 1900.

year, this flat, barren country was so treacherous that Comancheros were crediting with staking a path through the area (200 miles wide in some places) so travelers could find their way to safety as they passed in and out of New Mexico. Dying of thirst was a reality. Watering holes could be difficult to find and could be located from 50 to 80 miles apart. Despite the hardships, Hispanic traders ventured along marked paths with wooden carts to conduct business. The Llano Estacado trail became an important byway followed by other traders, settlers, ranchers, and the U.S. military.

Lt. James William Abert encountered Comancheros during an 1845 U.S. military reconnaissance across the plains. "They proved to be a small party of traders, who had come out under the guidance of one of the Pueblo Indians, and told us they had been 20 days in reaching this place from Taos, N.M. They were dressed in conical-crowned sombreros, jackets with the stripes running transversely; large bag breeches extending to the knee; long stockings, and moccasins. They were badly armed, and presented a shabby and poor appearance, though we learned that they were a good specimen of the class to which they belong. They are called 'Comancheros,' and make frequent trading excursions into the country of the Indians, with whom they exchange their stock for horses and mules," Lt. Abert noted. "Their defenseless state gives the Indians little to fear."

As people without farms or factories, the Comanches and other nomadic tribes relied on a bartering system to obtain some daily necessities. Because of the fertile valleys around the Rio Grande, Hispanics could provide non-perishable food items—flour, sugar, salt, pinto beans, dried fruit and vegetables (especially plums, apples, pumpkins, and corn), and baked bread. The nomads also needed weapons: knives, muskets, pistols, ammunition, flint, gunpowder, and steel tips for arrows. The Native women liked beads, blankets, fabric, and vermilion for painting. Popular luxury items included whisky, mirrors, awls (for piercing holes in leather), and tobacco.

Part of an 1875 military map depicting watering holes and trails for U.S. Army expeditions through the Llano Estacado (Staked Plains). The complete map details trails for expeditions by: Col. R.S. Mackenzie of the 4th Cavalry; Col. Nelson Miles of the 5th Infantry; and Lt. Col. J.W. Davidson of the 10th Cavalry. Courtesy of the Hardin-Simmons University Library, Abilene, Texas.

From the Natives, the Comancheros obtained horses, mules, pelts, moccasins, leather, buffalo robes, and cattle. Texans were a common enemy to both New Mexican Hispanics and Apaches, Comanches, Kiowas, and other tribes.

"In Comanche trade, the main trouble consists in fixing the price of the first animal. This being settled by the chiefs, it often happens that mule after mule is led up and the price is received without further [avail]," recounted Josiah Gregg, a Santa Fe trader from 1831 to 1840. He noted that the sales price of a mule also had to include assorted sundry items such as beads, tobacco, and blankets.

He commented about how American traders in caravans along the Santa Fe Trail sought to avoid doing business with Natives "for fear of being treacherously dealt" with during the close encounters that had to transpire over a few days of trading. Typically, trading partners would camp beside one another and hold close discussions. Americans were uncomfortable with having personal contact with Natives. However, based on his experiences, Gregg said he found Indian trading partners "much less hostile to those with whom they trade…They are emphatically fond of traffic, and, being anxious to encourage the Whites to come among them, instead of committing depredations upon those with whom they trade, they are generally ready to defend them against every enemy."

A typical trading camp scene with Comanches that Josiah Gregg, a Santa Fe Trail merchant, included in his 1844 book, *"Commerce of the Prairies: or the Journal of a Santa Fe Trader."*

Comancheros traded with Natives for over a century before Americans became aware that this commerce even existed. Most trade was conducted peaceably. Some Comancheros treated Native peoples with respect and conducted legitimate business. Others exploited tribes and traded in stolen property. It is unknown if trade generally resulted in fair transactions between the Comancheros and Natives. Sometimes Natives sold items that had been stolen during raids. They also sold hides. They were at a disadvantage when trading because they lacked

Comancheros and other Hispanic merchants relied on mules and burros to transport their goods. Mules could travel over sandy deserts and rugged mountain terrain with heavy burdens weighing up to 400 pounds. A mule carrying a heavy load could only walk for no more than 6 hours per day, at a rate of 15 miles. Muleteers, mounted on fast horses, worked teams of about 8 mules to ensure cargo stayed in place during journeys. This drawing of a burro train in New Mexico was created by English artist Peter Moran, who traveled there in the 1860s and 1880s. Illustration (circa 1881), courtesy of The Smithsonian Institution.

knowledge about the market value of the pelts or other property they sold—this made them vulnerable to being cheated by unscrupulous traders.

"It is astonishing how poorly Indians are compensated for their robes and furs. In Colorado, some Indians had been very successful in killing buffaloes, had plenty of meat, and purchased with their robes flour, sugar, coffee, dry goods, and trinkets from the White and Mexican [Comanchero] traders, but they did not realize one-fourth their value," commented Edmund B. Tuttle, a former New York newspaperman who became an Episcopalian Army chaplain. He wrote about activities he witnessed from 1867–1870. Although the wholesale value of a buffalo robe was at least $8, traders paid far less. For a buffalo robe, Indians only received a combination of $2 in groceries, 75 cents in brass wire or trinkets for a robe, and a few cents worth of sundries.

Not only were the Indians cheated from the sales of buffalo hides, but they were exploited further. Encouraging Natives to kill buffalo furthered the destruction of their way of life. The large-scale slaughter of buffalo resulted in their near extermination. In Native cultures, the buffalo is sacred. To the Plains tribes, the animals also area a vital source of food and clothing.

"Six tribes in 1864 furnished at least 15,000 robes, which at $8, would amount to $120,000. The traders literally swindled the poor Indians," Tuttle remarked. In a further exploitation, traders supplied hard liquor to Natives, who often gave the buffalo robes "off their backs for a bottle of whisky on the coldest day."

Some Hispanic traders also used alcohol to obtain goods. This provided the traders with an unfair advantage in business dealings. An American military expedition in 1836 in Colorado area noted Hispanic traders from Taos had brought beans, corn, bread, flour, and whiskey to trade with a group of Plains Indians who were off hunting buffalo. In an account of this meeting, the military noted with outrage that many Natives remained behind the hunting party extremely drunk after having been provided with liquor by traders.

After the 1830s, the Comanchero trade evolved to include high-priced items, such as lucrative plunder (horses, cattle, and captives) stolen by Natives during raids into Texas and contraband weapons used against the U.S. Army.

Hispanic traders stocked items to please all members of tribal families, including Native women, who were interested in beads, blankets, cloth, and other sundry items. This photo is of a Comanche girl, whose name in English was translated as daughter of Gap in the Salt (her father's name). Photo by Alexander Gardner (1872), courtesy of the National Archives.

Comancheros bought some captives to ransom them to grieved relatives for financial gain. They also purchased captive women in order to sell them to others as servants or spouses.

Former Comanchero Vicente Romero, aged 86, shared rare insights into this secretive trading world during a 1937 interview. His uncle, Guadalupe Marquez, passed down the covert art of prohibited trade to his descendants, teaching them ways to sneak around U.S. military forts in New Mexico and, into Comanche territory. Romero, born in 1851, reminisced about his youth spent at home in a mountain hamlet called Cordova, some 35 miles north of Santa Fe.

"Four times I have been on trading trips to the Comanches and three times to the Plains on buffalo hunts. We used bows and arrows and the lance as weapons when hunting at first. Later we were able to trade for guns at Santa Fe. We would take venison and fish and other things to trade in Santa Fe," Vicente reflected.

His uncle was the Comandante (leader) on Vicente's first two trips, until the young man learned to speak Comanche and gained experience about Native customs to take charge himself. Vicente traded with Comanches and Kiowas.

Some crumbling adobe military buildings still stand at Fort Union. Photo by Noël Fletcher.

Vicente fondly recalled his first experience at age 18 as a Comanchero. That journey lasted three months. Barter items included blankets, dried fruit, salt, bread, and iron strips for arrowheads. Their first challenge was to leave eastern New Mexico by traveling past Fort Union at night to avoid detection by Americans. The next step was to find the Indians, who "were always traveling, hunting, or following the buffalo herds, so that we never knew where we would find them. We went here and there over the plains looking for signs of the Indians. When we finally found the trail of a large group, in which there were signs of women and children, we knew we were close."

When the trail became fresh, the Comandante ordered the group to camp and unpack near the closest water source while he climbed to the highest point nearby and made a smoke signal for the Natives to see. Returning, his uncle said, "Now boys, in the morning we should have the Indians here, and we can start to trade. Be very careful how you act with the Indians.' "

The next morning found the traders surrounded by a large group. The Native women set up an adjacent camp. "The children and the dogs made lots of noise. At first the children were afraid of us, but after a few days became very friendly, always begging for something," Vicente said. "The Comanches are a very fine-looking Indian, light complexioned and well built."

Before business started, the Natives held a feast for the traders, who lived among them as they moved from place to place—following buffalo, relaxing together, and holding trade discussions over many days.

"Sometimes an Indian and one of us would fix up a horse race. They liked to bet and that way we won many articles from them," Vicente remembered. The younger Hispanic traders also engaged in foot races with Native warriors, helped break wild horses, held shooting matches with bows and arrows, and wrestled together. "I enjoyed this life very much. It was very new to me. We were always watchful and on our guard for some act of treachery on the part of the Indians. But they had need of the goods we had to trade so they treated a trading party with a certain regard and usually avoided any act which might cause trouble."

> The attention of all persons, whom this may concern, is called to the following articles of war, which will be enforced against all offenders:
>
> "ARTICLE 56. Whoever shall relieve the enemy with money, victuals, or ammunition, or shall knowingly harbor or protect an enemy, shall suffer death, or such other punishment as shall be ordered by the sentence of a court martial.
>
> "ARTICLE 57. Whoever shall be convicted of holding correspondence with, or giving intelligence to the enemy, either directly or indirectly, shall suffer death, or such other punishment as shall be ordered by the sentence of a court martial.
>
> "Approved April 10, 1806."

A notice of war (above) against the Apaches published in 1854 in a Santa Fe newspaper that declared the death penalty for giving them food or other assistance. Comancheros were charged with these federal crimes for dealing with Comanches.

One time, a 16-year-old member of Vicente's group risked his safety trying to save a captive Texas girl, who had been seized by Comanches while taking clothes to wash at a stream near her house. "One of them took her on his horse and rode off, followed by the other two. A short distance from her father's ranch they were joined by others in charge of stolen stock, also belonging to her father. She was shown the mutilated bodies of two of her father's herders and by sign showed her what to expect if she did not go quietly."

The girl, who became the wife of one of her captors, begged the Comancheros to rescue her and promised that her father would reward them with gold and cattle.

"Her pleas were very pitiful and some of us younger fellows felt like risking a rescue." Rather than returning her home, some wanted to take her home as a their bride. However, the Comandante refused. "Any effort to free her or take her away might destroy our whole party—as far away as we are from home and as few as we were for the number of Indians against us. Even if we were so lucky as to get her away with little or no loss, none of us could ever return to trade with these Indians."

Ignoring the objections, the 16-year-old trader planned to save her at all costs, but was seized and bound until he agreed to follow orders.

"This seemed very cruel, but it was very necessary for the good of our whole party," Vicente noted, adding that the poor girl may have spent the rest of her life as a captive. "Those were very hard times."

After trading ended, the normal practice was for the Natives to safely

> Charge 2. Aiding & Abetting the Enemy
> Specification. In this, that Jose Esquipula Lucero a Citizen of N. Mx. did, in direct violation of lawful orders received from the Comdg. Off. at Fort Bascom N.Mx. proceed to the Comanche Country, (sneaking at night through the Pickets) and did furnish the Kiowa & Comanche Indians, who were, as he was duly advised, in open War with the U. S. of America, with Victuals, Ammunition &c.

The U.S. Army arrested in December 1864 two Comancheros named Jesus Anaya and Jose Esquipula Lucero from a small agricultural village called Anton Chico, known for its fruit orchards and grapes. The town, located on the eastern side of New Mexico towards the Llano Estacado, had been a provisioning stop for Comanchero traders since the early 1800s. Anaya and Lucero learned that trade with the Comanches and Kiowas was no longer business as usual. They set out Oct. 29, 1864 to trade with the Natives before winter set in. A week before, Brig. General James Henry Carleton issued General Order No. 32 on Oct. 22, 1864 authorizing the U.S. Army in New Mexico to engage in an expedition to wage war in the Plains against the Comanches and Kiowas. A month later, both Hispanic traders were arrested by officers from Fort Bascom, N.M. and accused with three of the most serious offenses listed in U.S. law books.

Charge 1: *Violation of the Laws of War—for trading with the Natives after the Fort Bascom commander supposedly informed the men that war had been declared by the U.S. against the Kiowas and Comanches.*

Charge 2: *Aiding & Abetting the Enemy—for sneaking through the pickets at night and providing both tribes with ammunition and "victuals" (food).*

Charge 3: *Giving Intelligence to the Enemy—informing members of the two tribes that a U.S. military expedition against them was about to leave Fort Bascom.*

These charges were signed by 9 witnesses. The fate of Anaya and Lucero is unknown. However, the number of witnesses against them makes it likely they were incarcerated in a military jail and faced trial before a military tribunal, which would have rendered judgments and pronounced sentences under such grave charges. If found guilty of these crimes, the penalty was death.

This U.S. Army shako insignia (circa 1850s) was worn on the front of a dragoon hat. It is on display in Santa Fe at the Palace of the Governors, built in 1610. It is oldest continuously used public building in the United States. The insignia was found along a wall outside the Palace. Photo by Noël Fletcher.

escort the Comancheros out of the Plains for several days by offering protection against attacks by other tribes. "After again slipping by Fort Union, we were very happy to be on our way home. We were still in some danger from Apaches or Navajos, who liked to come through that part of the country to raid the Pueblos and even [go] on horse-stealing trips among the Comanches." As Vicente's party approached home, they raised their firearms to shoot salvos of thanksgiving to St. Anthony, while their friends and families climbed rooftops to count the number of returning traders to determine if anyone was missing. Vicente was among those who participated in the Comanchero trade during its height from the mid-1800s though the 1870s. When the United States took over New Mexico as a territory in 1850, military authorities tried to regulate Hispanic traders and stop transactions with any Native tribe that Americans had declared war against.

A turning point in Comanchero trade occurred after Brigadier General James Henry Carleton, from Maine, became commander of the U.S. military Department of New Mexico from 1862–1867. During this time, Carleton reimposed martial law on everyone in New Mexico. He ruthlessly pursued violent suppression of nomadic Native tribes—even using them to fight each other as a tactic of war that he waged against Navajos, Apaches, and Comanches. Having defeated the Confederates in their bid to take New Mexico at the onset of the Civil War, Brig. Gen. Carleton so disliked the peaceful trade between Hispanic traders and the Comanches that he took measures to wage war on Comanches and prevent the flow of goods to tribes in the Plains. He successfully quashed any American who stood in his way.

Carleton complained in a letter to Indian Agent Michael Steck in October 1864 about the trade. He claimed that Comanches unfairly discriminated against whites in favor of Hispanics. "The Mexicans, finding themselves thus favored, of course, feel inclined to favor the Indians in return, and the Mexicans would doubtless…desire to continue the trade which is carried on with these Indians." In addition, Carleton informed Steck that a military expedition had been just begun and was headed out to the plains "for the purpose of making war upon the Comanches and Kiowas."

Dr. Steck (a Pennsylvania physician) had been an Indian Agent for the Apaches in New Mexico before he was appointed Superintendent of Indian Affairs for the Territory of N.M. Indian Agents were U.S. presidential appointees charged with overseeing tribal matters, enforcing government policies, and promoting peaceful relations. Dr. Steck's authority enabled him to issue permits for Hispanic traders to conduct business with natives. He answered to political rather than military authorities.

Carleton took issue with Steck's advocacy on behalf of Natives and embarked on a campaign with military leaders on Capitol Hill that eventually forced Steck out of his job. Soon after Carleton's letter, the military situation further deteriorated with the Comanches. This fact is evidenced in a December 1864 letter to Dr. Steck from Levi J. Keithly, an Indian Agent appointed by President Lincoln to oversee dealings with the Utes and Apaches in northwestern New Mexico.

Brig. Gen. James Henry Carleton (left) and Indian Agent Dr. Michael Steck. Both men were at odds over the treatment of Natives in New Mexico. Carleton favored deadly force and removal of nomadic tribes from their traditional homelands to be held as virtual prisoners of war in reservations. In contrast, Dr. Steck opposed reservations and sought to achieve peaceful solutions with the tribes through negotiation.

"The Southern Comanches have for many years been on most friendly terms with New Mexico, and from accounts never were more friendly disposed than they were previous to the recent attack on them by the [military] forces…When I was living near Hatch's Ranch, I frequently saw parties of Comanches who came into the settlements to trade, and when in the settlements I know to be fired upon three different times by our troops. They didn't at that time resent the injury. They came with friendly intentions and it was my opinion at the time that they were badly treated," Keithly noted.

Although Keithly was born in St. Louis, he had lived in New Mexico for decades. He had even briefly earned the title of Speaker of the House of Representatives in a local political effort to oppose

> **No. 47.**
>
> **OFFICE OF SUPERINTENDENT INDIAN AFFAIRS,**
> *Santa Fé, New Mexico, July 31, 1866.*
>
> SIR: Upon investigation I find that the Comanches have been attracted to this Territory by the number of Mexican traders constantly visiting them with donkeys loaded with merchandise, and in many instances with whiskey and ammunition.
>
> These traders exchange goods for cattle and horses, thereby giving a market and encouraging the Comanches to steal from the inhabitants of Texas and Arkansas, which I consider very unjust to the people of those States; and I have no doubt that these Mexican traders, being generally opposed to the Bosque, have incited the Comanches to make these late raids upon the herds of the Navajoes, in order, not only to get their horses to sell and use, but also to make the Navajoes still more dissatisfied with their situation; and, worse than all, these traders doubtless have supplied the Comanches with ammunition and whiskey.
>
> On my way back from the Bosque I met not less than sixty or seventy of these donkeys, loaded with goods, and about half that number of traders, and all claim to have permits to trade with the Comanches from General Carleton, and in one instance from General Pope. But when I would ask for the permits, some other man ahead had it. In conferring with General Carleton, I find that he has, in some instances, granted such permits, and when a Mexican gets one, fifty will trade on the same license, claiming they are doing business for the man that has the permit. This trade has been really immense of late. I know of one man here in Santa Fé who took about one hundred and fifty dollars' worth of goods there, and came back with about one hundred head of Texas cattle for his goods.
>
> I consider that General Carleton really had no right to grant such permits. I believe he thinks so himself now, and agrees to co-operate with me in putting a stop to it altogether. I have therefore caused to be published an order revoking all permits heretofore issued and not duly approved by the Commissioner of Indian Affairs at Washington, D. C., and stating that all persons found violating this order should be punished to the full extent of the law.
>
> Hoping that my action in this matter will meet with your approval, I am, very respectfully, your obedient servant,
>
> **A. B. NORTON,**
> *Superintendent of Indian Affairs.*

N.M. Indian Agent Abraham Baldwin (A.B.) Norton of Ohio was appointed by President Andrew Jackson in 1866. Norton was critical of the incarceration of 9,000 Navajos and 500 Apaches in the reservation at Fort Sumner, N.M. called Bosque Redondo. This reservation, the brainchild of General Carleton, was a place of death and enormous suffering for thousands of Natives taken away from their lands before the U.S. government abandoned it. In the letter above to D.N. Cooley, Commissioner of Indian Affairs, Norton discusses a visit to Bosque Redondo and his disapproval of Comancheros trading in stolen property.

slavery. Keithly stated that the Utes and Apaches under his jurisdiction had returned from an expedition under Carleton's military designate to the plains, where a battle occurred with Comanches. He feared this action would "have disastrous consequences" on frontier settlers and communications from the Territory to the United States.

He called the battle "a great error" and undeserved since the Comanches had been such good friends to the people of New Mexico. "The people of this frontier dread the consequences that may follow…particularly when the country [in the midst of the Civil War] is unprepared to meet so powerful an enemy."

The military prevailed over the Indian Agents. Some Comancheros were caught and prosecuted by the Army, which was authorized to fine and imprison New Mexicans in military prisons. Americans defined Comanchero dealings as trading with the enemy during wartime. Yet, military prohibitions against Comanchero trade failed due to Hispanic resistance, porous land borders, and corrupt U.S. government authorities who profited from sales of contraband and stolen property. Even the building of Fort Bascom in 1863 near the New Mexico/Texas border failed to deter trade with Comanches, Kiowas, and Apaches. "The spoils often found their way to the possession of people ranking high in wealth, respectability and official station. This traffic had gradually become a settled business," according to a February 1897 article in the *Indianapolis Journal*.

Chapter 13: Propaganda & Jane Adeline Wilson

On a cold Christmas Eve in 1853 as Santa Fe's 6,000 residents likely were bundled inside adobe homes kept warm by burning aromatic cedar and piñon logs, a newspaper there broke a story about a rescued captive woman that would spread like wildfire across American newspapers.

Little snow had fallen over Santa Fe, where temperatures at that time of year average a high of 40 degrees Fahrenheit. Hispanic women would have been preparing traditional foods such as *posole* (corn, pork, and chili soup) and *biscochitos* (cinnamon sugar cookies). The men would be busy preparing *luminarias* (lanterns) around the entrances of their residences to light the way for baby Jesus to find and enter their homes. A Christmas Ball with a fancy supper beckoned the Anglo community to the Exchange Hotel, a popular venue for Americans at the corner of Santa Fe's plaza (town square).

Among those celebrating Christmas was a 16-year-old widow and orphan Mrs. Jane Adeline Wilson, pregnant with a child who would be stillborn. She had escaped from a band of Comanches and endured three weeks surviving alone in the wilderness before being rescued by Comancheros. Among the Hispanic traders was a 13-year-old Pueblo Indian who risked his life to

Groups of Hispanics in traditional New Mexican garb are depicted around a Catholic church in Santa Fe. The American flag waves from Fort Marcy, built by the Americans on a hilltop to dominate the capital city. Illustration by Curtis B. Graham (circa 1846), in "Notes of a Military Reconnaissance from Fort Leavenworth in Missouri to San Diego in California," by Lieut. Col. W.H. Emory, 1848.

The same Dec. 24, 1853 issue of the *Santa Fe Weekly Gazette* published both the sensational story about Jane Adeline Wilson and this ad for the Christmas Ball at the Exchange Hotel, a popular American establishment in Santa Fe.

David Meriwether served as governor of New Mexico from 1853--1857. He was only four months into his term when he met Jane Wilson in December 1853. Image courtesy of the University of New Mexico.

save Jane. She wore men's clothes provided to her by the Comancheros to replace the rags they found her wearing. Together, Jane and the traders trekked for 38 days until the end of November before she reached safety in Pecos, N.M. The wife of an American officer, who was passing through, gave some of her dresses to Jane. The Comancheros invited Jane to come with them to their homes elsewhere in New Mexico, but she decided to rest in Pecos. An Anglo man named Richard Northrup, who worked for the Quartermaster at Fort Union, had a home there and offered help. Jane, in an advanced stage of pregnancy, stayed temporarily at Northrup's home.

Shortly after her arrival in Pecos, military authorities in New Mexico got word of the rescue and sought to punish her rescuers —the Comanchero were accused of trading with the enemy. The Army mistook Northrup for a Comanchero, but the actual traders had already departed. Army officials made other errors in reports during the confusing early days of Jane's rescue. They thought Northrup took Jane to Fort Union, which he had not. Major W.A. Nichols, assistant adjutant general in Albuquerque, issued the following order Nov. 10, 1853 to Fort Union commander Lt. Col. Philip St. George Cooke: "If the man above [Northrup] is a soldier he will be confined, and charges preferred against him. If a citizen in the employment of the government, he will be immediately discharged—and turned over to the civil authorities for trial."

Furthermore, the order called for Jane to be delivered forthwith to N.M. Governor David Meriwether at the Palace of the Governors in Santa Fe.

The Palace of the Governors (right) is an adobe structure built in 1610 by the Spaniards. It faces the north end of the Plaza. Photo by G.E. Moore (circa 1885), courtesy of the California Historical Society and the University of Southern California Libraries.

Although this 1866 view (left) of the east side of the Plaza (town square) was taken a decade after Jane Wilson was there, life in Santa Fe changed little during that time. The Plaza always has been the focal point for the community, businesses, and government in Santa Fe. Photo courtesy of the National Archives.

After being escorted to Governor Meriwether, Jane would go on to tell the story of her captivity. Meriwether, of Kentucky, was no stranger to New Mexico. At 18 years old, he became a trapper for the American Fur Co. A year later, he joined a group of Pawnee Indians on a mission to trade furs and start business ventures there while it was in a foreign country outside of the United States. New Mexico troops attacked the party, killing most of the Natives and seizing Meriwether and a Black slave, Alfred. Accused of being U.S. spies, the pair was imprisoned for a month in Santa Fe. Upon their release, they were ordered to leave New Mexico immediately. They were forced to travel during the onset of winter over 1,000 miles to the nearest U.S. settlement. Meriwether appealed to the governor of New Mexico for assistance since they had no horses, provisions, or arms, but only possessed the clothes on their backs. His plea gained them each a mule, a gun, and a small amount of ammunition. After trekking in dangerous conditions for many months, Meriwether reached safety. Apparently so grateful for the assistance of his companion, Meriwether freed the slave Alfred, who saved him from an Indian attack during their travels.

In August 1853, Meriwether entered New Mexico 34 years later as governor of the territory. Thousands of people watched the solemn procession of carriages, military personnel on horses,

A sign in Santa Fe recalls the site of the 1st Catholic chapel, demolished in 1714, and likely the location where Don Diego de Vargas was buried beneath the chapel floor in 1704. This sign outside the Palace of the Governors provides a glimpse into the colorful history of the building. It was first built for Spain's royal governor of New Mexico, Don Pedro de Peralta. For 400 years, it was the headquarters and home to New Mexico's governors under Spain (1610–1680, 1693–1821), Mexico (1821–1846), and the United States (since 1846). The Palace was the territorial capitol until 1886 and governor's home until 1909. Photo by Noël Fletcher.

and dignitaries in buggies ride past arroyos through Santa Fe. Arriving at the plaza, Meriwether stepped out to be introduced. A newspaper described residents greeting him with shouts and huzzas. Meriwether took residence at the Palace of the Governors, where he had once been imprisoned in a room in the west section.

While traveling to Santa Fe to become governor, Meriwether's party was joined by a wagon train also headed west. One of the wagons contained two young Mexican girls rescued from a group of Kiowas. The Kiowas chased the caravan the previous day seeking the return of the captives. The girls, both from Chihuahua, were aged 15 and 16. While herding livestock, they saw the wagon train and ran to it. The wagon master hid the girls and denied having them when confronted by the Kiowas. One girl had been stolen a year earlier, while the other couldn't recall how long she had been held prisoner.

By the time Meriwether arrived in Santa Fe, he had been informed in detail about their hardships as captives. He asked for the girls to be sent to Santa Fe where he would make arrangements for them to travel to El Paso, Texas to be given to the Mexican Consulate. When Meriwether heard about Jane's plight, he demonstrated great sympathy towards her.

Army officials investigated the circumstances surrounding Jane's rescue and found Northrup blameless. Instead he was described as having "humane and charitable motives" in caring for her and even offering to send her back to the United States. Lt. Col. Cooke conveyed this information to Gov. Meriwether along with his thoughts. "This affair revives the recollection that New Mexicans were long used to traffic with Apaches…and suggests a suspicion of such friendly intercourse with these aggressive savages." Cooke suggested that military action be taken against the Natives rather than a friendly approach. Cooke would later go on to be known as the "Father of the Cavalry" for his expertise in warfare. Major James Henry Carleton, who would later become Brig. General and command all military operations in New Mexico, conducted the investigation into Northrup. Carleton was to provide a military escort to bring Jane to Santa Fe. In the meantime, Meriwether sent his 20-year-old son Raymond with two horses to fetch her. Arriving in Santa Fe some 10 days before Christmas, Jane was taken into the home of Rev. Lewis Smith and his wife, both American Baptist missionaries.

From there, the story of her capture and survival went into the hands of the following three ambitious young men—all in the early stages of their careers and seeking to advance themselves.

Rev. Lewis Smith.
Photo courtesy of the Hightstown-East Windsor Historical Society in New Jersey.

Rev. Lewis Smith (33)—born in Chester County, Pa. to a Baptist pastor. Smith converted at the age of 20 and embarked on a career similar to his father. He arrived in Santa Fe as a missionary in 1851 to convert the Hispanics from Catholicism. A lack of students in a school run by his wife prompted Smith to become a military chaplain at Fort Marcy. Undeterred by disinterest among the Hispanic population, Smith turned his attention to American residents and soldiers from military garrisons. His plans included building the first Baptist Church in Santa Fe, able to seat 200 congregants. He was one month away from completing construction of that church, designed to combine Gothic and modern Grecian architecture, when he and his wife took Jane Wilson into their home to assist with her recovery.

Major James Carleton (39)—the son of a ship captain from Lubec, Maine. Carleton served under distinguished career officer Gen. John Garland and married his niece in 1848. Favoring the strong arm of the military over peaceful dialogue with the Natives, Carleton was no friend to Indians. In December 1853, Carleton commanded Company K of the 1st Dragoons and was involved in Indian campaigns. He had been in New Mexico for three years during his first tour there when he met Jane Wilson.

James H. Carleton.

William Watts Hart (W.W.H.) Davis (33)—a native of Bucks County, Pa. and only son of a powerful politician with Washington, D.C. connections.

William Watts Hart (W.W.H.) Davis poses in his Civil War uniform. Photo courtesy of the Bucks County Civil War Library and Museum in Doylestown, Pa.

An attorney, Davis served in the Mexican-American War with Franklin Pierce. In March 1853, his friend Pierce became a U.S. President and appointed Davis six months later as U.S. District Attorney in N.M. After arriving only a few weeks to start his federal job, Davis associated himself with the *Santa Fe Gazette,* one of only two city newspapers, and assumed editorial control. After he got the story of Jane Wilson, Davis led the biggest news media propaganda campaign ever seen from New Mexico.

Prominently displayed at the top of page 3 under "W.W.H. Davis, Editor" was a headline intended to ignite passions rather than objectively inform *Santa Fe Gazette* readers on Dec. 24, 1853. The headline declared in bold letters: *"The capture and sufferings of Mrs. Wilson—Shall the Comanches be punished for their savage cruelty?"*

Davis wrote a preamble about Jane and the article about her experiences. He described meeting Jane, who appeared youthful, intelligent, and modest. Davis referred to what happened to her as "one of the most remarkable accounts of personal sufferings on record." His derogatory views about Natives filled nearly half the page. "And shall such an outrage go unpunished? Shall these Ishmaelites of the prairies receive no chastisement for their inhuman cruelty to a woman? Shall these inhuman fiends be allowed to steal our women and children, and worse than murder them, and suffered to escape punishment? It remains for the government at Washington to answer."

Davis said he hoped everyone in the United States would read the article to "understand the true character of the wild Indians of the plains." The language in his introduction also sought to rally people to take political action. "There will be many captives among the Indians so long as they are paid to give them up—let blood be the only ransom paid, and there will soon cease to be captives," Davis stated. "But we intend this state of things shall be so no longer, because we will force the government and the people to take notice of these depredations; they must afford us protection, even if it should be necessary, in doing so, in the language of Kit Carson, to 'wipe out' the Indians."

Rev. Lewis issued a statement for publication alongside Jane's narrative. He said he hoped publication of her story would lead the government to adopt a more vigilant oversight and stringent policy against Plains Indians.

These men seemed to ignore the fact that the person most responsible for saving Jane's life was a Native American.

Next followed both a headline and article that would be repeated almost word for word in newspapers in Texas and across the eastern United States:

Certificate of appointment on Sept. 19, 1853 by President Franklin Pierce to William W.H. Davis as U.S. District Attorney for the Territory of New Mexico, courtesy of the Beinecke Rare Book and Manuscript Library, Yale University.

The Santa Fe Gazette greeted William Watts Hart Davis on Nov. 26, 1853.

"*A good appointment.*—The President appointed Capt. W. W. H. Davis (son of that veteran Democrat, Hon. John Davis) of Bucks county in this State, District Attorney of New Mexico. Capt. Davis served his country gallantly in the Mexican war, and is a young man of more than ordinary powers in his profession. He is withall a radical Democrat, and a genleman of unblemished reputation.'

"A Narrative of the Sufferings of Mrs. Jane Adeline Wilson, During Her Recent Captivity Among the Comanche Indians"

Jane's account began with a description of her family background. She was born in 1837 in Illinois. When she was nine years old, her family moved to Mississippi where her father William Smith kept a ferry. She had five brothers (only three survived) and four sisters, one of whom was a dwarf. Unsatisfied with their life there, the Smith family sought to improve their situation by moving to Paris, Texas. However, this relocation resulted in tragedy and the destruction of their family. "Her father and mother, reduced to want [poverty] and suffering by continued bad health and the exactions of a heartless landlord, were both taken from her on one day, by death, and the large household of children, many of them small and helpless, without a relative in the country, were parceled out among the neighbors," noted a Texas newspaper in 1854.

Jane, at age 15, found refuge in marrying 19-year-old James Wilson, a young farmer with land, horses, and cattle. Instead of building a life in Texas together, they succumbed to the call of the Gold Rush. "We had heard that people became rich very fast in California, so we concluded to move and commence life in that distant country," Jane recalled. The Wilson family—consisting of the married couple, her father-in-law and his three youngest sons Hugh, George, and Meredith, decided to all leave Texas. They gathered their property and joined a group of emigrants—52 men, 12 women and several children—in a convoy of 22 wagons that left in April 1853 for El Paso. Along the way, Apaches stole a dozen cows from the group.

Illustration of emigrants crossing the plains to California, in "*Ballou's Pictorial Drawing-Room Companion,*" January 1859.

When they reached El Paso, Jane's husband was unable to continue. Instead of returning to Texas, the Wilsons decided to wait until another passing group arrived so they could join them on their way to California. Several weeks passed. During that time, Mexicans stole most of Wilson's remaining livestock and property, leaving them without sufficient resources to continue onward. The only option was to return home.

"About the last of July, we started on our return with the fragments of our property which the thieves had spared. On the first day of August, my husband and his father left us and fell into the hands of the Indians. I saw them no more after this. I was told that they had been murdered," Jane recalled. She returned to El Paso with her three brothers-in-law. A month passed before the Wilsons joined a small group (five American men and one Mexican) headed back towards her home in Eastern Texas. The group was led by Simeon Hart, a local judge who ran a profitable flour mill in El Paso.

She hoped to arrive home in a few days. "As we had seen only one Indian on the route we flattered ourselves that we should not be molested by any of the tribes which infest this route." Along the way, the group began to suffer due to thirst, which caused some mules to run away

One of the few remaining buildings in Fort Phantom Hill near Abilene, Texas. Photo by C.M. Highsmith, courtesy of the Library of Congress.

in search of water. Hart and the eldest Wilson Boy, 14-year-old Hugh, left the group and returned several hours later with the mules. In their absence, the remaining men in the group except for a Mexican driver became impatient. They took three of Hart's horses and left to seek water.

Despite having great wealth from lucrative contracts providing the military in Texas and southern New Mexico with flour to feed the troops, Hart became enraged over the theft of his three horses. Anxious to overtake the men, he rode off with Hugh Wilson to chase after them. Left to fend for themselves with little water were Jane, George, Meredith, and the Mexican wagon driver. The Wilson boys were about 12 and 10 years old.

The next day, the wagon lumbered along the rolling prairie towards Fort Phantom Hill. The desolate military post, north of Abilene, was built to protect travelers taking a westward route along the Texas frontier.

Four Comanches charged at the wagon. Two warriors attacked from the front and two attacked from the back. "We were all very much frightened and the Mexican jumped out of the wagon and went towards the Indians in order, if possible, to gain their friendship. The mules in our wagon, four in number, becoming frightened by the war whoop of the savages, turned out of the road and commenced running as fast as they could. One of them fell down before we had gone far, and the others were then obliged to stop," Jane remembered. "The Indians now came upon us, and ordered the Mexican to take the mules out of the harness. While

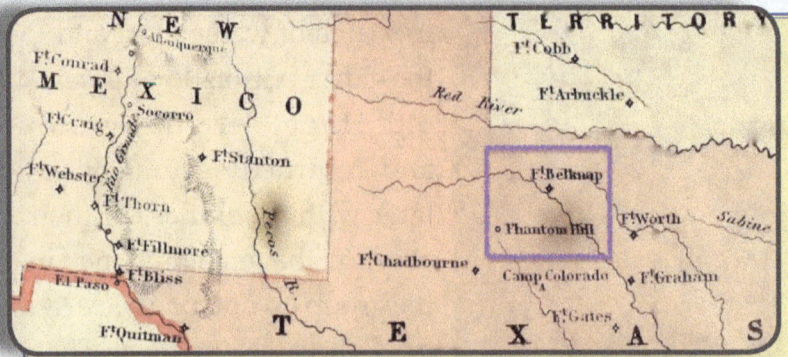

After being wounded and scalped, the Mexican driver walked to Fort Phantom Hill, while the German man who tried to save him wandered 100 miles away to Fort Belknap. Both forts are located within the purple box in a selection from an 1861 U.S. military map.

this was going on, I got out of the wagon, and looked on in breathless suspense."

Stripped of his clothing, the Mexican had his hands tied behind his back and was ordered to sit on the ground. He was shot in the back and stabbed several times with a large butcher knife. "His scalp was cut off before he was dead, and put into his own hat; the hat was then worn by one of his murderers. I was stupefied with horror as I gazed on this spectacle and supposed that my turn would come next. But the Indians mounted us on mules and ordered us to go with them. As I left, I looked back and saw the poor Mexican weltering in his blood, and still breathing."

Jane thought no one would know about their fate, but others soon found out about the attack. A German man from their group lagged a mile behind due to a lame horse. The man knew nothing of the attack until he came upon the injured Mexican and burnt remnants of the smoldering wagon. The German tried to place the Mexican on the horse, but the animal was unable to carry a load. So the German left on foot to find help. The injured Mexican gathered enough strength to walk for days until he reached Fort Phantom Hill. While recovering there he told an officer about the German man. Wandering through the plains for several days, the German man ate mesquite beans to survive. A group of dragoons from Fort Belknap left to find him. They located the German man, who was in poor condition, living in a hole 50 miles from their outpost. Fort Phantom Hill and Fort Belknap are 100 miles apart.

In the meantime, Hart became concerned when the wagon failed to arrive at the Fort. So, he started back with Hugh to look for Jane's group, and encountered the German and injured Mexican. Hart raised an alarm at the fort. Soldiers left to find the captives but were unable to follow the Comanches' trail.

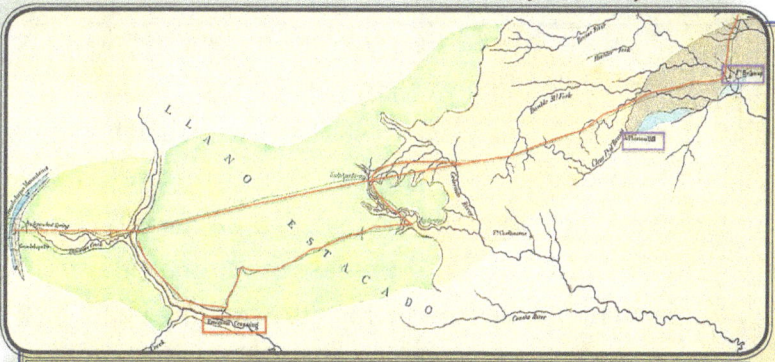

Part of a U.S. War Dept. map from 1854 showing emigrant wagon train routes (in red, left to right) across Texas to New Mexico and California. Forts Phantom Hill and Belknap (in purple) are on the upper right. The Llano Estacado (Staked Plains) area in traditional Comanche territory is in the center (green). Jane and the Wilson party would have traveled this route to El Paso and back near Fort Phantom Hill when her group was attacked by a small band of northern Comanches.

At nightfall, the Comanches camped with the captives. "Here the plunder, consisting of blankets, bedding, clothing, bridles and some money which I had in my pocket, was divided among the Indians. Some articles considered useless were thrown into the fire. My clothing was taken away except barely enough to cover my person. In the distribution of captives, the eldest boy [George], about 12 years of age, was claimed by the chief. I became the property of one of the others…one of our captors was a Mexican who had been stolen from the state of Chihuahua when an infant. He was now as savage as the Indians and claimed the youngest boy [Meredith] for his prize."

Placed on good horses, the two Wilson boys were given bows and arrows and their faces were painted like Comanches. "They appeared to enjoy this new mode of life, and were never treated with excessive cruelty," Jane said. The captives then began to live a nomadic existence typical of Comanches.

"We traveled every day—we usually started about 10 o'clock in the morning, and halted about 4 in the evening. The Indians were accustomed to go to the tops of the highest hills and stand there gazing in every direction. We always spent the night on a hill and were thus exposed to the cold autumn wind; we slept on the ground, generally without covering. When it rained the Indians made a tent out the blankets and wagon sheets they had stolen from us, but I was not allowed to take shelter in it; I preferred sleeping outside in the storm," Jane remembered.

Despite being visibly pregnant, Jane was beaten, subjected to having her long hair cut off and worn by her captors, jabbed with a spear, made to ride an unbroken mule that repeatedly bucked, taunted with the scalp of the Mexican, hit with rocks, and struck with riding whips.

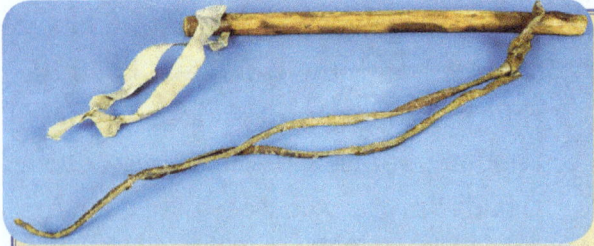

A Comanche woman's whip, obtained in 1868 by U.S. Army surgeon Dr. Edward Palmer. He was hired by the U.S. Department of Agriculture (with the Army Medical Museum and The Smithsonian Institution) to obtain botanical specimens in a collecting expedition in New Mexico and Arizona. Palmer arrived at Fort Wingate in N.M. in May 1869 and ended his journey in January 1870 in San Francisco. Photo courtesy of The Smithsonian Institution.

"I was obliged to work like a slave while in camp; while there was any service to perform I was not allowed a moment's rest. I was compelled to carry large loads of wood on my back, which being destitute of sufficient clothing was mangled till the blood ran down to my feet. I had to chase the animals through briars and bushes until what little clothing I had was torn into ribbons," she recalled. "I have gone two days at a time without food. The Indians depended on hunting for their subsistence, and sometimes had nothing to eat themselves—unless there was there was an abundance of food, I received little or nothing."

Jane suffered greatly from thirst but only was allowed to drink while at camp rather than stop at passing streams for refreshment. While traveling during the day, she was beaten if she lagged behind the others and had to keep pace with the group despite her injuries and swollen feet. After several weeks with the group, she had to travel on foot instead of riding the mule.

"After the party was ready to start in the morning, the direction of the route was pointed out to me, and I was required to go before the others, in order not to hinder them. They usually overtook me before I traveled far. I had always intended to make my escape as soon as I found an opportunity," Jane noted. "On the morning of the 25 day after my capture, I was sent on in advance as usual. I had eaten no breakfast, and was very weak, but the hope of escape now supported me. I hastened on as fast as I could, and finding a suitable hiding place I turned aside and concealed myself in the bushes. After this I saw nothing more of my captors; I found afterwards by the tracks of the animals that they had searched for me; they probably thought I would die, and therefore took less trouble to find me."

When Jane realized she was alone, she reflected on all that had happened to her within a few months: her husband's death, losing their property, and being held captive for three weeks by Comanches. Then she found herself wandering alone without any resources in the desolate plains of the Llano Estacado.

"My situation was now distressing beyond all description; I was alone in an Indian country, some hundreds of miles from the nearest friendly settlements. I was without food, without shelter, and almost without clothing. My body was full of wounds and bruises, and my feet were so swollen that I could hardly stand. Wild beasts were around me," she stated. "Winter was coming on, and death in its most terrible forms stared me in the face—I sat down and thought of my lonely and exposed situation."

Mexican gray wolf. Photo by Zita Fletcher.

Afraid her captors would return, Jane hid for three days until she felt safe enough to walk a short distance away to a grove with vegetation, where she built a hut of grass and brush. She stayed there for nine days.

"My only food was the hackberries which grew on the bushes around. I quenched my thirst at a spring nearby. My wounds pained me exceedingly, and I was wasted to a mere skeleton for want of proper nourishment. It rained upon me seven nights in succession, and my little house was unable to protect me from the cold storms. More than once I spent a sleepless night, perfectly drenched in rain; while the wolves, sometimes coming within five steps of me, would make the woods ring with their frightful howlings. They would also follow close behind me when I went to the spring during the day; I expected some time to be devoured by them, but they are great cowards and I could easily frighten them away."

Trying to avoid starvation, she foraged near the stream for something to eat. She found a couple of frogs, turtles, and a snake, which she killed and ate raw.

Alone in the wilderness, Jane likely thought she had been forgotten. However, efforts were being taken in Texas to find her and the Wilson boys. An Indian Agent named

Major Robert S. Neighbors, a strong advocate for the Comanches, had engaged one of their chiefs called Shanaco to locate the captives. Shanaco was a leader from a southern tribe who sought peace. He sent several bands of Comanches to search for the Wilson prisoners, but they returned empty-handed with information that the captives had been taken by northern Comanches. Using sympathetic Natives to assist in the search was a tactic tried by Major Neighbors and other Indian Agents in Texas. "The agents have adopted that plan as offering better prospects of succeeding than a pursuit by the military, which would alarm and anger the Indians without effecting anything," according to the *Tri-Weekly State Times* of Austin on Nov. 14, 1853.

Hispanic traders with a caravan of pack mules, from "Scenes and Incidents in the Western Prairies during Eight Expeditions," by Josiah Gregg, 1856.

Nearly two weeks after Jane's escape, she climbed to the top of a small hill to survey the area. In the distance, she noticed Comancheros from New Mexico making their way across the plains in search of Comanche villages. She continued watching the caravan to ensure they were not Indians. Five traders seeking firewood for the party approached the spring near Jane's hideout. She startled one when she called out to him. Thinking he heard something supernatural, he fled to the others. With their rifles extended, the men cautiously returned to the area and found Jane. She was in such a bad condition that she had to be carried in their arms to the caravan.

"They kindly offered to take me with them, and I gladly bade farewell to my house in the woods. The Mexicans put me upon a burro and gave me a blanket and some men's clothing in which I dressed myself very comfortable. Two or three days after this we suddenly came in sight of a band of Comanches, and as it was not safe for me to be seen by them, I was left behind in a ravine, with the promise that the Mexicans would return for me at night. As they didn't fulfill their promise, I started towards their camp about midnight; while wandering among the bushes a Comanche Indian passed within 20 steps. I thought I was a captive once more, but he didn't see me. I threw myself on the ground and waited for day."

San Ildefonso Pueblo. Photo (by John K. Hillers, circa 1879), courtesy of The Huntington Library, San Marino, CA, photCL 190 (7).

Jane set out for the Comanchero camp after daylight broke. On her way there, she met 13-year-old Juan Jose Gabaldon, a Native youth and member of the trading group. He was herding animals at a distance from the camp when he saw Jane.

"To him more than any other man in the party do I owe my present freedom," she recalled.

Juan Jose was far from his home in San Ildefonso Pueblo, located at the base of a volcanic hill called Black Mesa some 25 miles north of Santa Fe. The traditional name for the Pueblo means "where the water cuts through" because the village is located opposite the Rio Grande.

"He told me the camp was full of Comanches, and if they saw me it would be impossible for the party to save me. He made me lie down on the ground while he covered me with dried grass. I lay here all day, and at night crept forth to quench my almost intolerable thirst. Juan came and brought me some bread and told me not by any means to leave my hiding place."

The hours passed slowly for Jane, who heard Comanches continuously pass her and converse among each other. That night, Juan Jose crept back to her. He brought a blanket, a gourd for water, and several loaves of bread. Jane learned that she had to stay there alone for at least a week because the traders had to continue the bargaining while accompanying the Comanches as the nomads moved onward. There was no possibility of taking Jane because she would be discovered and enslaved again.

As Jane watched the group depart the following day, she resolved to wait rather than give into despair.

"In a ravine nearby I found a large log which had been left burning. This fire I kept alive day and night until the Mexicans retuned, and without it I should probably have frozen to death as the weather had become very cold. I covered a hollow cottonwood stump with bark and leaves to keep out the cold wind. This stump was my house during my stay here. When I could endure the cold no longer I would leave my house and run to the fire, but was afraid to stay there long lest the Indians should see me. The wolves soon found out my place of retreat, and frequently while I was in the stump they would come and scratch around and on its top. The hackberries were very scarce here. Had it not been for the bread Juan Jose gave me I do not see how I could have been kept from starving to death," she said.

A sentinel at San Ildefonso Pueblo. Photo by Edward S. Curtis, courtesy of the Library of Congress.

The days passed slowly until she heard men calling out to each other on the 9th day of her solitude. At first Jane thought the voices belonged to Indians. However, the traders forgot her exact location so they shouted to each other in the hopes that she would hear them and come out of hiding. The Comancheros were trying to find her as they traveled back to New Mexico.

"I was so overjoyed that I rushed towards them unmindful of briars and sore feet. Juan gave me a fine horse to ride, and the whole party treated me with the utmost civility and kindness," Jane remembered.

Her condition was so delicate that the Comancheros had to stay there with her for a few days before they could move her. They constructed a travois with two poles attached to a horse for her travel. Barefoot and with her body covered by bruises and wounds, Jane lay on buffalo robes that lined the travois as it made a bumpy journey dragging across the plains for 38 days until the group reached safety in Pecos, N.M. The Comancheros invited her to accompany them to their villages, but Jane opted to stay in the care of a German, who spoke both English and Spanish. She remained in Pecos for a week.

A detachment of Army Dragoons learned about her while passing through Pecos. They sent an Indian runner to Santa Fe with the news. A wife of one of the officers supplied her clothing to Jane. From there, Jane met Major Carleton, who formed an escort with Raymond Meriwether to take her to Santa Fe.

"To Governor Meriwether and also to the American ladies of this place, I cannot be too thankful for their friendly sympathies and uniform kindness," Jane concluded. "The past seems like a horrid dream. I have related nothing but facts and no language that I can use can fully express the suffering of mind and body, which I have endured. My two brothers-in-law are still captives and unless reclaimed will be as savage as the Indians. The Mexicans saw them with the Comanches, but were unable to procure their freedom. One is 12 years old, the other 10."

Under the care of Rev. Smith's wife, Jane convalesced in Santa Fe where she had a baby boy, who was stillborn. Newspaper accounts describe her as a young and pretty teen, whose misfortunes aroused much sympathy from the American community there. "Gov. Meriwether speaks of her as a lady of fine personal appearance, of modest deportment, and only 17 years of age," commented the *Texas State Gazette* newspaper in January 1854.

Gov. Meriwether sent a former Army officer to discuss Jane's situation with Texas Gov. Elisha Pease. Soon the Texas Legislature became familiar with her ordeal and the kidnapping of the two Wilson boys.

Clothing worn by Hispanic *vaqueros* (cowboys) in New Mexico during the 1800s. The bandolier belt (*correa*) is from 1840, the hat (*sombrero*) is from 1850, and the *charro* jacket, vest, and pants are from 1890. These items are on permanent display at the Albuquerque Museum. Photo by Noël Fletcher.

> **AUSTIN AND DALLAS UNITED STATES MAIL LINE.**
> **Four Horse Coaches.**
> VIA
> WACO, BELTON and GEORGETOWN.
> LEAVES Dallas on Mondays, Wednesdays and Fridays
> Through in three days.
> Travellers by this line will find good teams, comfortable coaches, and safe drivers, and can rely upon being carried through punctually.
> It connects at Dallas with the Clarkesville Stages, and at Austin with the Houston line.
> T. F. CRUTCHFIELD, Agent.
> Dallas, July 1st, 1854—20:tf

It is likely Jane took this stagecoach as she traveled across Texas to reach her family and friends. Passengers usually traveled on stagecoaches under contract to deliver U.S. mail since this mode of travel was more reliable due to regularly scheduled stops. It was also safer because the drivers were armed to protect contents in the mail.

In the summer of 1854, Gov. Meriwether provided her with a horse and an escort of dragoons to accompany her across New Mexico and over the Texas border into El Paso. From there, two Army officers traveled with Jane on "Smith's train"—a wagon train operated by William T. Smith. It made regular runs carrying passengers and freight between El Paso and San Antonio. The number of wagons in one convoy could vary from over 25 to a dozen. The 500-mile trip between both cities took 35 days to complete. Once Jane arrived in San Antonio, she boarded stagecoaches to Dallas and the northeastern Texas town of Bonham. She reached her friends in August 1854.

By the time Jane reached her family and friends in Texas, the Wilson boys had been retrieved. The government had offered a reward to assist in their recovery. Newspaper articles state that the Comanchero traders who rescued Jane tried to buy the boys. Governor Meriwether was described as sending out emissaries to purchase them. At the same time, Texas authorities worked to obtain their release.

In October 1853, Indian agent Major R.J. Humphreys sent a group of 17 men from Fort Washita in present-day Oklahoma to the headwaters of Red River near the Wichita Mountains. The objectives were to trade mules with Comanches and purchase any white captive children they encountered. Among the traders were: Aaron Brown (a Chickasaw trader), Charles Cohea (a mulatto agent for Humphreys), a Kickapoo trader named Johnson, and a Kickapoo guide known as Possum. Other Natives in the party included Black Bear (a famed Delaware Indian interpreter, whose correct name likely was Black Beaver) as well as seven other Kickapoos and several Chickasaws.

In December, the group met the Comanches who held George Wilson after talking with other bands they had encountered. According to Cohea, the chief who held George "was very" much opposed to the giving the boy up on any conditions as he said he was old and he wanted the boy to catch his horse for him. The traders informed the chief that unless he returned the boy, the whites would pursue him and give him no peace until George was released. The chief again refused.

Finally, Possum convinced the chief to sell the boy in return for a horse and enough goods to procure another horse. Cohea and Brown immediately agreed. All the traders took George Wilson with them and left Possum behind to complete the transaction. They stayed at a friendly Kiowa camp 25 miles away. When Possum rejoined the group, he informed them that a Comanche warrior demanded to be paid for the return of George. The warrior claimed the mule from the Mexican wagon, which George was forced to ride when he was captured. "He required that we should purchase the mule at his own price or he would kill the boy—we had no alternative. We paid a very extravagant price for the mule after which he had no trouble," Cohea stated, adding that the price for George was around $140.

The traders learned that George's brother, Meredith, was being held by a separate group of Comanches traveling nearby. The traders tried to catch up with the band, but were unable to overtake them. "George wanted very much to be placed in his brother's stead as he said he was afraid they would kill him as he was too small to do much for the Comanches."

The group split up. Johnson, the Kickapoo trader, was instructed to find Meredith, while the others returned in February 1854 with George.

> Charles Cohea, a mulatto agent for the U.S. government, only received $150 in reward for his efforts rescuing both Wilson boys. The money, $50 less than recommended, was paid five years after the boys were ransomed.

A Kickapoo named Babeshikit holding a fan (circa 1875). Photo by Charles Milton Bell, courtesy of The Smithsonian Institution.

A Chickasaw named Shonion (Sho-ni-on) in 1869. Photo courtesy of The Smithsonian Institution.

A Delaware named Black Beaver, a famed trapper, guide, interpreter, and scout (1872). He was fluent in Spanish, French, English, and 8 Native languages in addition to his own Lenape tongue. Photo courtesy of the National Archives.

"Johnson kept his word and brought Meredith to Fort Arbuckle [Oklahoma] three weeks after we got home," Cohea noted.

Both the Texas Legislature and Congress each allocated $1,000 to fund the return of the boys. The money could be used to reimburse actual costs and pay rewards.

Brown received most of the Texas funds. The remaining money was divided among another Native trader and Major Humphreys (to defray his costs in housing George for several months). It also was used for travel costs to transport the boys to Texas.

The mulatto, Cohea, and the other Native Americans involved in the rescue of the boys were cheated from their rewards. They received nothing until Cohea approached Indian agents to set the record straight and get recognition for Natives who played key roles in the successful rescues of the Wilson boys. Questions arose and continued through 1856 about the distribution of the $1,000 in unallocated Congressional reward money. A Chickasaw delegation brought up the matter to an Indian agent in Fort Smith, Arkansas. U.S. officials stated that people who had no role in the rescue wanted a share of the reward. Eventually, it was recommended that $200 each would be paid to Cohea and Johnson; and $50 each would go to Possum and another Native. The other members of the trading party were to receive medals for their efforts.

In mid-1854, the Wilson boys returned to their former home in Hunt County in northeastern Texas, located 50 miles north of Dallas.

Although Jane emphasized how much she owed her survival to the Native youth Juan Jose Gabaldon from San Ildefonso Pueblo in New Mexico (who was among the Comancheros), Carleton, Smith, and Davis downplayed this fact in their media campaign. Instead, the sensational article was devised and distributed to newspapers in Texas and throughout the United States to increase American hostilities against Indians.

> Juan Jose Gabaldon (the Native youth from San Ildefonso Pueblo who was instrumental in saving Jane) is listed in the 1860 census for the Territory of New Mexico. While Jane's story has been retold throughout the years into the present time, no one has shown interest in finding out about Juan Jose, or even his surname since Jane never mentioned it. His pueblo has a small population compared to others. This census was taken seven years after he saved Jane. In 1860, he still lived with his parents, had just married, and was a farm worker on his family's tract of land. He appeared to be living an ordinary life on the pueblo. Gov. Meriwether apparently gave rewards to Jane's rescuers. Since Juan Jose and the Comancheros left Jane in Pecos where U.S. authorities claimed her, it would seem unlikely that the Comancheros or Juan received any reward, especially since the military wanted to prosecute the traders. It is more likely that the money went to the two Anglo men in Pecos who took Jane in and cared for her there.

Santa Fe Gazette publisher W.W.H Davis made his editorial debut in the Dec. 24, 1853 issue that carried Jane's detailed story of her capture and escape. She had arrived in town only a week after Davis set foot in Santa Fe on Nov. 26 to become the U.S. District Attorney. Four weeks later, he sent the article to other newspapers that reprinted it word for word.

In those days, it usually took three months for word from Santa Fe to reach Washington, D.C. However, articles rapidly appeared in quick succession across the Midwest to the

East Coast. Among the newspapers to publish the Davis article were: the *Plymouth Banner* (Ind.), the *Gallipolis Journal* (Ohio), *The Spirit of Democracy* (Ohio), the *Perrysburg Journal* (Ohio), the *Sunbury American* (Pa.), *Cooper's Clarksburg Register* (W. Va.), the *Monongalia Mirror* (Morgantown, W. Va.), and the *Wheeling Daily Intelligencer* (W. Va.). The *Daily Evening Star* newspaper in Washington, D.C. ran the article in two front-page installments on Feb. 7 and 8, 1854.

The article created a snowball effect in the media. Not only did newspapers print copies of the articles received from the *Santa Fe Gazette*, but smaller papers began copying the article from other newspapers. For example, *The Jeffersonian* from Stroudsburg, Pa. on March 2, 1854 reprinted the Davis article on Jane—called *"A Thrilling Narrative"*—from the *St. Louis Daily Missouri Republican*.

The *Gallipolis Journal* on Feb. 23, 1854 printed the Davis article about Jane along with this notice (above).

The *Gallipolis Journal* noted on its Feb. 23, 1854 front page that Davis provided their editors with a copy of the article, which it published. In addition, next to the article on Jane was a lengthy editorial from the *St. Louis Republican* about Jane and kidnappings in New Mexico. "It is the duty of the government promptly and efficiently to furnish the means of putting an end to this cruelty, and of punishing the Indians. In the early history of our country, the Indians paid some respect to the virtue of the female; in the progress of his connection with civilization, he has lost even this attribute. He is now as beastly as he is savage, and the government should provide the means to punish them whenever they violate the laws of humanity," the editorial concluded.

Facts of the case also became distorted. Mescalero Apaches were erroneously blamed for kidnapping Jane and the boys in a March 1855 article in the *Texas Ranger*, which quoted the *San Antonio Ledger*. "Indians should be flogged into respect for the lives and property of our citizens, if they will not regard treaty stipulations," the *Texas Ranger* declared on its front page.

The massive publicity generated by the Davis article on Jane also resulted in some newspapers publishing short articles about the recovery of the Wilson boys. Some articles on the Wilsons boys mentioned the role of Chickasaw trader Aaron Brown in the rescue. However, the various positive roles that many diverse Natives—including friendly Comanches—played in this saga went unnoticed.

Jane remarried in July 1856. She and her husband William Roberts settled in northeastern Lamar County, Texas where they had several children. In 1863, Jane died at age 25. She lived longer than most former captive women, who usually died within two years of their rescue.

The March 8, 1854 issue of the *Cooper's Clarksburg Register* from W. Va. published the Davis article on Jane. Editorial comments concluded with the statement above calling for the extermination of the Comanches. Ironically, the newspaper's motto (top) about equality failed to apply to Natives.

As for the three ambitious men in Santa Fe who capitalized on her story, they saw their careers improve.

🖋 **Rev. Smith**—In August 1854, the Smiths left Santa Fe for New Jersey. Instead of being placed in another frontier post, Smith obtained a preaching position as a pastor in Trenton, the capital of N.J. and an important commercial and industrial center on the Eastern Seaboard. As a pastor, he also tended to the spiritual needs of Baptists 14 miles away in Hightstown. In poor health, he died at age 44. After his death in 1864, his wife published a collection of his sermons. After two years, the Santa Fe church that Smith built was abandoned and sold in 1867 to Presbyterians.

 Major Carleton—He would attain the rank of Brigadier General and Commander the U.S. military Department of New Mexico from 1862–1867. Carleton gained infamy for issuing numerous inhumane orders to troops in New Mexico. For instance the following orders were typical: "to promptly attack and destroy any and all grown male Indians whom you may meet" while sparing women and children, to devote attention "to hunting and killing Indians," and "to kill every male Navajo and Apache Indian who is large enough to bear arms." Given his determination to eradicate nomadic tribes in New Mexico, it is a wonder that Native tribes, particularly the Navajos and Apaches, survived his brutal military reign. Carleton died in 1873 at age 58 in San Antonio.

 W.W.H. Davis—rose steadily up the ladder of political success during his four years in New Mexico. His positions included Territorial Secretary; Acting Governor for 11 months; and Superintendent of both Indian Affairs and Public Buildings. The Santa Fe press opposed him in July 1857 when he took it upon himself as Secretary of the Territory to charge people 50 cents for every impression of the seal of his office or official certificate despite already receiving an annual salary of $2,000 for his government post. Davis was described as setting "himself up here in New Mexico for making money out of the pockets of the people, and that he has never been scrupulous as to how he should accomplish his object." He published a book in 1857 based on his experiences in New Mexico called *"El Gringo: or, New Mexico and Her People."* The book earned the ire of New Mexicans for saying that people in the territory were unable to

---

W. W. H. DAVIS,
(DISTRICT ATTORNEY OF THE UNITED STATES FOR NEW MEXICO,)
ATTORNEY AND COUNSELLOR AT LAW,
SANTA FE, NEW MEXICO,

WILL practice in all the courts of the Territory.

Office in the same room occupied by the Secretary of the Territory.

REFERENCES.

Hon. C. Cushing, Att. Gen. U. S.
Hon. Geo. M. Dallas, Philada.
Hon. R. Brodhead, U. S. Senate.
Hon. Simon Cameron, Penna.
Gen. R. Patterson, Philada.
Col. Thomas J. Whipple, New York.
Haddock, Reed & Co., Philada.
James, Kent & Santee, "
Wood, Bacon & Co., "

Less than six months after Davis arrived in New Mexico as its U.S. District Attorney, he was seeking private clients as a lawyer, while also editing and publishing the *Santa Fe Gazette*. Davis continually ran this ad for clients on the front page of the newspaper. It is unclear how he maintained legal objectivity and impartiality in cases since represented private clients at the same time he represented the government. Conflicts of interest issues could have arisen easily given limited numbers of lawyers and prosecutors then. His actions show his ambition.

govern themselves. After his departure from New Mexico, staff of the *Santa Fe Gazette* accused Davis of plagiarizing newspaper information provided by others to use as his own in his book. While working in his official capacity in New Mexico, Davis admitted later he "collected" historical materials and "saved" a valuable manuscript in Santa Fe dating back from the Conquistador era, which he used as a basis for a book about the Spanish Conquest of New Mexico. During the Civil War, Davis distinguished himself in battle and rose to the rank of General. An author of other historical books, Davis died in 1910 at age 90 in Doylestown, Pa.

Gov. Meriwether was 53 years old when he met Jane. Despite having a two-decade-long career in Kentucky politics after leaving Santa Fe in 1855, he never forgot about her. He wrote about Jane's story in 1889, four years before his death at age 92. Meriwether is credited with paying a reward for her rescue as well as financing her care in Santa Fe.

Indian Agent Major Robert Neighbors, who had sent friendly Comanches to seek Jane and the Wilson boys, was assassinated in September 1859 by Texans angered by his good relations with Indians. He was criticized for protecting Natives who had been wronged by whites. At 11 a.m. three men waited in the street as Neighbors walked from this hotel to Fort Belknap. They stopped him to ask a question. As he attempted to answer, one of the men, Englishman Edward Cornett, shot Neighbors in the back. No arrests were made for the murder.

While detailed newspaper articles and books were written about captive whites, little attention was paid to New Mexico's captive Hispanics seized by Indians.

> **Plagiarism of "El Gringo."**
>
> In looking the other day over some old numbers of the Santa Fe Gazette, we came across an editorial article which we immediately recognized as having seen almost *verbatim* in Mr. Davis' book, "El Gringo." We compared the two, and detected the plagiarism. We found that the author had actually been drawing upon the columns of this paper for his *very witty* account of an incident of the rainy season of 1854. This discovery forcibly reminded us of the statement of our correspondent C. P. C., published on the 27th of June last, that a large proportion of the book was taken, without the proper acknowledgement, from a volume in the posession of a gentleman at Fort Defiance, and the plagiary in this instance goes far towards establishing the correctness of our correspondent's statement.

After Davis published his book on New Mexico called *"El Gringo,"* his former newspaper the *Santa Fe Gazette* published several articles discussing his plagiarism. This Aug. 8, 1857 article compared passages in the Davis book with articles from the newspaper. The issue of plagiarism is interesting because historians often have discussed *"El Gringo"* as a significant and authentic early account of New Mexico's territorial days without any mention of plagiarism.

Chapter 14: Hispanic Captives

While the American media, politicians, and military officials generally took notice and action when Indians kidnapped whites in New Mexico, they adopted a different view towards the abduction of Hispanics. In the first place, Americans made no distinction between the Hispanics of New Mexico (most of whom were of Spanish lineage) and those who lived across the U.S. border in Mexico. The term "Mexican" applied to all. Newspapers and books written by white Americans in the 1800s and early 1900s mostly described Hispanics in New Mexico in derogatory terms. Hispanics and Natives became targets of widespread racism in the Territory. U.S. legislators refused for over 60 years to grant New Mexico statehood until 1912.

Hispanics in New Mexico sought protection from the U.S. government after the area was ceded by Mexico to the United States in 1848 and was organized as a Territory in 1850. They wanted the Army to intervene with raiding nomadic tribes. Before New Mexico came under American control, Hispanic communities would retaliate against raiding Natives by gathering up a force of men to chase after a warring group or take revenge against innocent members of the same tribe that they held responsible for an attack. This "eye-for-an-eye" mentality of revenge existed for centuries before American troops assumed command of New Mexico. The revenge mentality changed little afterwards. The Army in the Territory protected U.S. interests and demonstrated more concern for white Americans than anyone else. Anglo settlers mostly behaved the same way, only looking out for one another.

The vast majority of Hispanics snatched in New Mexico by Apaches, Navajos, Comanches, Utes, Kiowas, and other nomadic tribes never made headlines, never had rewards offered for their safe

The flag was designed to incorporate the state's Native American and Spanish heritage. In the center is the sun symbol (for the circle of life) from Zia Pueblo. The red and yellow are colors from Spain in tribute to the Cross of Burgundy flag brought to the New World by the Conquistadors. Photo by Noël Fletcher.

return, and never experienced U.S. military rescue missions.

If the Hispanic captives found freedom, it was accomplished either through single-handedly escaping from captors or being discovered in the aftermath of a victorious military battle against Indians.

An unusual case concerning a Hispanic captive involved Dr. Felipe Padilla. His encounter with a band of Apaches took place in a ranching community called Rito Quemado in high-desert plains. For centuries, Natives tribes such as the Apaches, Navajos, and Zunis had lived in that region of western New Mexico near today's border with Arizona. It was largely unpopulated and ideal for nomadic tribes. Hispanic settlers eventually established the village of Quemado (as it is now known) near the northern base of the Gila National Forest, a traditional Apache homeland. A decade after the Hispanics set up ranches, an Apache raid occurred. Like other settlers, the Padilla family was grazing sheep across the open range. Wool was big business in New Mexico at that time.

"In 1880, sometime in May, some Apache Indians under Chief Victorio captured me when I was about 14 years of age while I was herding sheep on the hills," Padilla told an interviewer in 1936. "When the Indians surrounded and captured me, they took me on horseback around the mountains [toward the Gila forest]…they saw a large herd of wild horses and were so anxious to capture some of the horses that they left me in the care of a [woman]."

Wild Mustangs roam freely in New Mexico. These hardy horses are descended from the horses of early Spanish explorers.

> **CHILD FOUND.**
>
> The following letter appeared in the *New Mexican* of the 26th of October:
>
> FORT STANTON, N. M, Oct. 16, 1875.
> Editors *New Mexican*.
>
> On the 14th instant I found with an Indian recently arrived at this agency a girl of Mexican parentage about twelve years of age, who had evidently been sometime with the Indians. I have the child now with me and desire to give such publicity regarding her as may lead to the discovery of her parentage. She had nearly forgotten her native language, but remembered sufficiently to say that her name is Tuncinta. She speaks of a man named Jose; of a woman Dolores; of children named Petra and Santiago, and avers that she had a relative named Jesus. Beyond this, she can give no information regarding herself or relatives; cannot tell how long she has been a captive or where she was captured. Please give publicity to this matter through the columns of your journal and by doing so you may be the means of restoring the child to its friends and relatives.
>
> W. D. CROTHERS.
> U. S. Ind. Agent.

William D. Crothers, who worked with Apaches at Fort Stanton, placed this ad about a found Hispanic captive in the *Las Vegas Gazette* on Nov. 6, 1875. When recovered, many children taken at early ages remembered little about their former lives.

After being driven from his homeland and relocated to three reservations within a decade, Apache Chief Victorio went to war with settlers. He was killed at age 55 in battle in Mexico in 1880.

"When the Indians returned from running the horses, they told me to go in front of them. After traveling 200 or 300 yards, one of the braves struck me across the face with a quirt [a rawhide whip often made with horsehair and a wooden handle]."

Although the Apaches seized Padilla, they decided against taking a captive. They now had a group of wild horses, which needed to be broken before being ridden. Having to assimilate Padilla into their tribe would have been an extra burden.

"Then the Indians, thinking perhaps they had killed me, ran their horses at full speed westward," Padilla recalled. Recovering from the injury, he walked home to his family.

What makes Padilla's story unusual is that he survived after being rejected as a captive by the Apaches. Most other unwanted captives did not.

Three months later, a group of Apaches rode through Rito Quemado, where they killed three men and stole two 10-year-old boys (Milton Madrid and Teófilo Sanchez) who were held captive for three years.

Capt. John Bourke, who served with the 3rd Cavalry in New Mexico, wrote about Apache captives based on his experiences. "Where the captive was of tender years, unable to get along without a mother's care, it was promptly put out of its misery by having its brains dashed against a convenient rock or tree. But where it happened that the raiders had secured boys or girls sufficiently old to withstand the hardships of the new life, they were accepted into the band and treated as kindly as if Apache born," Bourke stated.

Many Hispanic captives who remained among the Apaches "amassed property and gained influence among the people who led them into slavery," he added, providing as examples the names of a few women—Concepcion, Francesca, and Maria—and some men—Antonio, Jesus Maria, Severiano, and Victor.

"It was often a matter of interest to me to note the great amount of real, earnest, affectionate goodwill that had grown up between the Mexican captives and the other members of the tribe; there were not a few of these captives who, upon finding a chance, made their escape back to their own people. But in nearly all cases, they have admitted to me that their life among the [Apaches] was one of great kindness, after they had learned enough of the language to understand and be understood," Bourke remarked.

His assessment about the good treatment of some Hispanics was echoed by a woman named Mrs. Tafoya. Her brother, Jose, was kidnapped by Indians in northeastern Mora County. She was nearly 100 years old when she provided an oral history of the account in 1936. Although Mrs. Tafoya failed to name the tribe, Natives who traveled in that area included Apaches, Navajos, and Utes.

A captive Hispanic (left) sits next to a Coyotero Apache warrior (1880). The captive, described as a great drunkard, was with the Apaches when this photo was taken. He likely was from New Mexico and remained with the tribe after his abduction. Photo by Carlo Gentile, courtesy of the Library of Congress.

Jose was taken captive one day while he went to the river in the village. A band of Natives surrounded him. As he was taken away, Jose noted his surroundings and the areas he passed so he could find his way home.

"The Indians were good to my brother, treated him kindly. They kept him for a year and a half to take care of their horses," Mrs. Tafoya said.

Her brother decided to flee one day after he saw the Natives tie a different captive to two poles and light a fire underneath him. She provided no specifics about that hostage. Others in the 1800s have described this kind of torture as way that some Natives exacted revenge, made an example of an individual, or tried to gain intelligence about military activities. It was done only to adult male captives, usually U.S. soldiers, who were unintended for assimilation into the tribe. After being tortured, these hostages were executed or left to die.

"Jose was so frightened that he wanted to escape right away. He had been so long with the Indians that they did not watch him any more. He knew their habits so well that when he saw they were starting out to hunt, he knew they would be gone several days; and as all the horses were away, he would be left to help the [women] in the fields," Mrs. Tafoya said.

As soon as the men left the camp, Jose took his wooden hoe as if he were going to the fields, while the women remained in the camp.

Jose Tafoya was captured near the river in Mora County, in northeastern New Mexico. The town of Mora (named mulberry in Spanish) is located 100 miles east of Santa Fe, as shown above on a portion of an 1886 map.

"Back at the camp, his escape was discovered, and an Indian runner sped to the hunters, who came back in prompt pursuit. A long stretch of plains lay before Juan. He could hear the whoops of the Indians in the forest behind," she stated.

Being out in the open, with no shelter anywhere except for a large rock 100 yards away, Jose cried out a prayer to St. Anthony to help him. The youth ran to the rock and crept underneath it.

"The fleet of horses of the Indians was soon heard approaching. Around and around they rode. Then they went away a little distance, returned, and rode around again, but they did not see Jose. At last they rode away. Jose waited until dusk, then calling on his St. Anthony again, he ran towards home."

The next morning, Jose reached his family's home but his mother had gone to a neighbor's house. "My sister and I were very much frightened to see an Indian standing at our door. He had long bone earrings and was very dirty. Then Jose spoke and asked us if we did not know him. We were so happy. I ran for my mother, but did not tell her why I wanted her. She did not know my brother either. When he spoke, she knew his voice and cried for joy. When he had cleaned himself, she took the old bone earrings and gave him a pair of silver ones, which he wore the rest of his life."

When Jose was captured, there probably was no public mention. American men managed the majority of newspapers that sprang up in New Mexico in the 1800s. Hispanic captives were not seen as newsworthy and were barely mentioned. Below are a few examples.

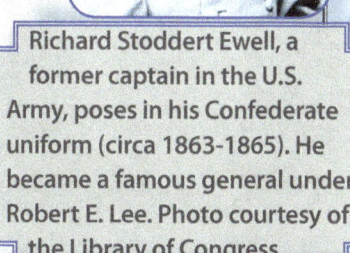

Richard Stoddert Ewell, a former captain in the U.S. Army, poses in his Confederate uniform (circa 1863-1865). He became a famous general under Robert E. Lee. Photo courtesy of the Library of Congress.

🖋 Under the headline *"Navajo Expedition,"* an article discussed the return of Col. Edward W. Newby and his detachment from the Illinois Regiment of Infantry to Santa Fe. "We believe this to be one of the best expeditions, and to the best effect, that has ever been made against this savage tribe. The Colonel, it seems, after having whipped them in a small skirmish, made peace with them, which, if not a permanent one, is deserving of much credit, for he did not return with merely their good promises, but he returned with some eight or nine captives, among whom was a young Mexican girl, who has been a captive for two years, and was taken some 10 days after she was married. She was the daughter of Jesus Pino, one of the most respectable families in Rio Abajo [N.M.]. The balance was all young boys. He also brought in 50 head of horses and mules." —*The Republican*, June 17, 1848.

🖋 A news report described military actions in western New Mexico near the Gila River. It concerned an encounter between

Colonel Dixon S. Miles sits on his horse at Harpers Ferry, W. Va. (1862), before he died there from a leg wound. Photo courtesy of the Library of Congress.

Coyotero Apaches and Colonel Dixon Stansbury Miles of the 3rd Infantry as well as Captain Richard Stoddert Ewell of the 2nd Dragoons. "The Indians were immediately attacked, and a sanguinary battle ensued. In this fight, 41 Indian warriors were killed and 45 were taken prisoners. Numerous cornfields of the enemy were destroyed, 125 horses were taken, and a Mexican captive recovered." — *Santa Fe Weekly Gazette*, June 25, 1857.

This captive from Mexico, named Pablino Diaz, never returned to his family. He remained with the Kiowas under the name "Pai-lo," became a distinguished warrior, and married a Kiowa woman. Photo (1898) courtesy of the [Fort Sill Collection] U.S. Army Heritage and Education Center, Carlisle, Pa.

🖋 "On the 4th of this month, three Navajos attacked a sheep ranch belonging to Juan Martin; wounded three men and carried off a captive boy named Francisco Martin aged 12 or 14 years. They also stole three horses. On June 12, a party of 59 Navajos stole from the Cañones, 12 miles from Abiquiu, about 50 head of cattle, 300 head of sheep, and three boys. One of the boys named Andres Valdez, aged 13 years, was killed; one named Caspio Garcia, aged 15 years, made his escape and returned home; and the other named Jose Miguel Garcia, aged 12 years, was carried into captivity." — *Santa Fe Gazette*, June 27, 1863.

🖋 A raid by Jicarilla Apaches was reported on the Pecos River 30 miles from Santa Fe. "About 30 of the above-mentioned Indians attacked the ranch of Jose Maria Valencia between the Rio de la Baca and the settlement on the Pecos, about 3 miles from Pecos, and succeeded in getting possession of about 800 sheep and carried off two boys captive. One, the son of Jose Maria Valencia, and the other the son of Marcos Rodriquez, aged respectively 9 and 12. The citizens as soon as possible mounted themselves and made pursuit of the Indians and overtook them at the Valle de la Piedra and had a fight with them in which the Indians were whipped, and, in making their escape, abandoned all the booty they had with them, but retained possession of the captives. One boy was wounded in the fight." — *Santa Fe Weekly Gazette*, June 13, 1868.

As shown in the above accounts, newspaper editors frequently mentioned Hispanic captives next to tallies of stolen or recovered livestock. There were few personal details about the captives.

When Hispanics were abducted by Natives, Hispanic volunteers in communities and local militias primarily pursued their return. The U.S. Army was rarely involved. This occurred before, during, and after the Civil War.

The rescue of the captive children stolen from the vicinity of Belen by the Apaches, brings to mind the fact that Luna our present candidate for Congress, was the man who organized and armed at his own expense a militia company which at the time of that raid took the field against the marauders and drove them from that part of the country.

This news brief reminds people in New Mexico that Tranquilino Luna (right), from a prominent Hispanic family in Los Lunas, organized a militia in response to an Apache raid and capture of local children. The unnamed children were recovered, according to the *Santa Fe Daily New Mexican* on Oct. 31, 1880. That same year, Luna was elected to U.S. House of Representatives. Photo courtesy Wikimedia Commons.

The following news report shows a typical response of a local militia leader and villagers to raids. "Apaches attacked the herds of Mariano Yisario near the town of Anton Chico, wounded the herder, carried captive a boy, and ran off 4,000 sheep. Upon the reception of the news, Brig. Gen. Gallegos, with commendable zeal, started in immediate pursuit of the Indians, but we have not heard what success he has met with. On the 8th [of July], a party of the same tribe ran off five animals from Pecos, the property of Vicente Quintana. The people of the town pursued them as far as the hills of Ojo Caliente, but on account of the recent heavy rains they were unable to follow the trail," noted the *Santa Fe Weekly Gazette* on July 15, 1854.

Local Hispanics also frequently led efforts to have their captive loved ones repatriated from Mexico after the captives escaped or were found after military actions with Natives. Rarely did the various governors of New Mexico (as agents of the U.S. government) provide diplomatic efforts with Mexican authorities to help the Hispanic captives from the Territory come home. For example, a Mexican military raid on Apaches in the state of Chihuahua brought in 65 women and children, including two boys from New Mexico, in November 1880. The Apaches had seized the unnamed boys six months earlier from a herding camp in the Rio Grande valley. A Belen rancher named Felipe Chavez, who employed the herders, was "in correspondence with the Mexican government to get the boys back," according to the *Las Vegas Morning Gazette*.

A year later, a Las Cruces newspaper called the *Rio Grande Republican* in southern New Mexico published a Sept. 30, 1881 letter from the Mexican Consulate to N.M. governor Lionel Allen Sheldon. Two Hispanics from New Mexico were recovered in Mexico. The letter provided information about where their families could send correspondence for their repatriation. The captives were found in Mexico after Apaches attacked a ranch near La Casa del Lano and stole several horses in the Mexican frontier. A group of 60 well-armed men, led by Mexican authorities, sped on horseback in pursuit.

"Two hours after their departure, they overtook the Indians in Cañon del Cristo in the Sierra Madres, where they where they were unable to recover the stock on account of the ruggedness of the mountains and the advantageous position of the Indians. Our people kept skirmishing with them for 9 hours, and then determined to make an open attack. This was done and resulted in a loss of 8 horses and the wounding of one man. A retreat was then made, without being able to ascertain the loss of the enemy. One of the best results of the encounter, however, was that near the place of the fight, two captives held by the Indians made good their escape and came to

---

The Rescued New Mexican Captives.

Sometime ago we gave an account of the escape of two captives from the Apaches in Mexico. They were a boy and a woman and were captured near the Atlantic and Pacific railroad in New Mexico. The Mexican consul at this place wrote to Gen. McKenzie asking what should be done with them. Gen. McKenzie has, in reply, ordered the commanding officer at Ft. Bliss to give them transportation to their homes.—*Lone Star*.

This article (left) from a Texas newspaper demonstrates a lack of consistent U.S. policy for returning captive Hispanics from New Mexico back to U.S. territory. Unsure what to do with the former prisoners, the Mexican Consul contacted General Ranald Slidell Mackenzie, who had been made Army commander of the District of New Mexico. Gen. Slidell apparently sent orders to Fort Bliss in Texas to assist in returning them home to New Mexico, according to the *Santa Fe Daily New Mexican* on Nov. 16, 1881. These former captives were treated differently from two N.M. captives called Placida Romero and Procopio Garcia who were in the news at about the same time.

our camp," according to the *Rio Grande Republican* on Oct. 22, 1881.

The pair, taken from Cubero, consisted of a 30-year-old woman named Placida Romero and her adopted son Procopio Garcia. They were captured after Apaches raided their ranch Aug. 10, 1881 and killed her husband Domingo. They were held prisoner for a month.

After their release, both remained in Mexico for some time. At the end of January 1882, the Territorial Legislature authorized Gov. Sheldon to request their return to New Mexico, reimburse Mexico for their living expenses, and fund their safe return. Shortly after their escape, Placida and Procopio informed Mexican authorities that the band of Apaches had four captive children primarily believed to be from New Mexico—Telesforo Romero (16 years old), Meliton (12), Concepcion (9), and Silvestre (7).

Apache views on captives were illustrated by Major John Cremony in *"Life Among the Apaches,"* published in 1869. He described being in camp one day near Apaches when two boys from Mexico crept into his tent, described their abduction, and asked to be freed. Cremony assisted in their return to Mexico despite objections by several Apache leaders.

A few days later, five prominent Apache chiefs [including Mangas Coloradas and Cuchillo Negro (Spanish for Black Knife)] came with 200 warriors to talk about the captives. Cremony, who spoke their language fluently, translated as the warriors sat in a semicircle.

"You came to our country," said Mangas. "You were well received. Your lives, your property, your animals were safe. You passed by ones, by twos, by threes through our county. You went and came in peace. Your strayed animals were always brought home to you again. Our wives, our women, and children came here and visited your house. We were friends—we were brothers! Believing this, we came among you and brought our captives, relying on it that we were brothers and that you would feel as we feel. We came not secretly nor in the night. We came in open day,

A career Army officer, General Ranald Slidell Mackenzie, commanded the military District of New Mexico before he was promoted to Brigadier General and transferred to Texas in 1883. His promising military career ended due to mental instability related to a head injury he suffered in falling from a wagon. He retired in 1884 and went into an insane asylum.

and before your faces, and showed our captives to you. We believed your assurances of friendship, and we trusted them. Why did you take our captives from us?"

Cremony explained that there was peace with Mexico and a duty to protect Mexicans so the captives were being returned.

The Apaches explained that the captives were taken prisoner under their view of lawful warfare and became their legitimate property. "The owner of these captives is poor. He cannot lose his prisoners, who were obtained at the risk of his life, and purchased by the blood of his relatives. He justly demands his captives," a leader named Delgadito explained. "It is just, and as justice we demand it."

The Apaches reiterated that the owner wanted the boys returned.

"The brave who owns these captives does not want to sell. He has had one of these boys six years. He grew up under him. His heartstrings are bound around him. He is as a son to his old age. He speaks our language, and he cannot sell him. Money cannot buy affection. His heart cannot be sold. He taught him to string the bow and wield the lance. He loves the boy and cannot sell him."

> These photos are of a Kiowa warrior named Tsendon (or Tsatoke), whose mother was a Hispanic captive likely from New Mexico. Her Kiowa name was Sal-bil. It appears that she never returned to her family home and made a life among the Kiowas. Her son, called Hunting Horse, became an Indian scout for the U.S. Army in 1875. He is seated above with one of his wives, and their youngest son Cecil. Standing next to Hunting Horse is his son Albert. The boy on the left with a peyote pouch is Guy Quoetone, who married Hunting Horse's daughter Nellie. Photos (by James Mooney, 1893) courtesy of the [Fort Sill Collection] U.S. Army Heritage and Education Center, Carlisle, Pa.

The military refused to return the captives. They again offered compensation. Eventually, the dispute was settled with the military providing $250 worth of goods from a Commissary store as payment for the boys.

Accounts of freed Hispanic captives say little about their fate, particularly regarding girls and women. Many Hispanic men freed from captivity used their knowledge from living with Natives to become guides for prospectors and military scouts.

Not all former prisoners made a successful return, however. An interesting example was a man named Thomas Padilla, a former captive rescued from the Comanches. An October 1866 letter from a commanding officer at Fort Marcy in Santa Fe alerted his counterpart at Fort Union about Padilla's escape (wearing light blue officer's pants) from the guardhouse—with seven soldiers.

Hunting Horse with his daughters, who are all part Hispanic. He was born in 1846, served under General George Custer and knew General Philip Sheridan as well as General William Tecumseh Sherman. A famous Indian scout, Hunting Horse lived to age 107. His son Monroe Tsatoke became a famous Kiowa painter (and was the grandson of a Hispanic captive grandmother). Photo by J.V. Dedrick (1908) courtesy of the Library of Congress.

"He has lived for many years with the Comanches and Kiowas, and speaks some English, fluently, and Spanish; and for this [he] is thought a great deal by the Indians."

Padilla was described as a small man, known in southern New Mexico at Fort Bascom by only the name Thomas.

"To record all the crimes and outrages committed by him would fill a volume. He has been constantly employed by the Indian as a decoy and through his cunning has led many white men into the power of the Indians. He took part in the attack upon Forts Larned and Dodge, and was present at the fight at Adobe Walls, where he lost the second finger of his left

Black Knife, an Apache warrior (1846), by John Mix Stanley, courtesy of The Smithsonian American Art Museum.

hand. He was also with the party that stole the animals from Fort Sumner some time in August last. He is a cunning and a dangerous vagabond. Should he make his appearance at your post, please have him secured and report his arrest to these headquarters."

The treatment Hispanic captives received compared to Anglos stands in stark contrast. The military did not conduct campaigns to rescue Hispanics as it did with Charley McComas. American community members raised no funds to clothe or care for returned Hispanic captives like those in Arizona did for Santiago McKinn. Wealthy American businessmen in Santa Fe and Taos expended no money to fund searches for abducted Hispanic women and children as was done for Sarah Horn, Mrs. Harris, and Rachel Plummer. The governors of New Mexico didn't pay from their own pocket to assist with the recuperation of Hispanic captives or provide military escorts to accompany them on long journeys home—as Gov. Meriwether did for Jane Wilson, who wasn't even a resident of his territory.

American journalists and publishers demonstrated no interest in the memoirs of former Hispanic captives from New Mexico—unlike the interest shown in white captives from elsewhere, particularly Texas, who were able to publish numerous first-person books about their experiences. In New Mexico, a few Depression-era oral histories were recorded in the 1930s. The only notable publication about a former Hispanic captive from New Mexico occurred when a Methodist missionary wrote about a Hispanic man he met during his ministry to Natives. The story of Andres Martinez—stolen as a boy by Apaches, sold to Kiowas, and returned as an adult to his family in Las Vegas, N.M.—stands alone because it provides a rare, detailed narrative from the 1800s about the kidnapping and survival of a young Hispanic snatched from his family by Natives.

Chapter 15: From Andres Martinez to "Andelle" the Kiowa

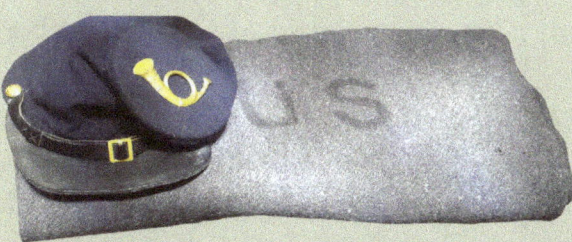

Civil War era Union cap and blanket in the Albuquerque Museum. Photo by Noël Fletcher.

In the fall of 1866, Americans in the United States had entered a period of reconstruction following the end of the Civil War. Lives were being rebuilt, wounds mended, and emancipation rights granted. The federal government enacted the Civil Rights Act of 1866 to grant equality to everyone under the law, including people of color.

The freedom that the Civil War earned for former African slaves did not extend to Natives. The U.S. government viewed Indians as subjects, not citizens. Although Natives were born on American soil, they had no legal standing as American citizens. They had no protection or equality under the law. At best, the U.S. government viewed Natives as wards of the state.

At the same time, U.S. troops in New Mexico were destroying lives based on race rather than criminal guilt. Troops were under orders to imprison all Apache women and children, and kill any Apache male able to bear arms. They were also ordered to arrest and punish any Apache or Navajo who resisted being imprisoned on a faraway corner of the territory near Texas called Bosque Redondo. Due to an inability to farm in an unsuitable area, disease, hunger, and an unfavorable environment for nomads, the Mescaleros escaped under the cover of night in 1865. Some returned to their traditional lands and sought peace, while others favored fighting to the death for their freedom.

Over 100 miles north of Bosque Redondo, where the rugged green, pine-covered Rocky Mountains on the west overshadow the vast beige grassy plains to the east lived the Juan Martinez family. Their homestead was 12 miles west of Las Vegas, N.M. in an isolated mountain town of adobe homes called San Geronimo. As was typical for that time, the family was large. The couple

The family of Andres Martinez would have looked like this typical Hispanic family standing in front of an adobe house in New Mexico in the mid-1800s. Photo courtesy of The Smithsonian Institution.

had seven children, who helped with farming the land and caring for livestock.

For several weeks, Juan, aged 59, and other villagers had heard talk about roving Mescalero Apaches in the vicinity. News of possible sightings of warriors spread via word-of-mouth information that often could be unreliable. Without any fear of impending danger on the morning of Oct. 6, 1866, Juan prepared to thresh wheat in the fields. He sent his youngest son, 8-year-old Andres, out from the homestead into the open range to graze the cattle on wild grass.

A younger relative, named Pedro, failed to listen to his mother and joined Andres. For several hours, the boys played while the cattle foraged. The cattle became restless and tried to return home, but the boys herded them back. Suddenly, voices sounded in the distance. Andres thought it was his father bringing lunch until he saw a band of Apaches heading straight towards him. Some were riding burros stolen from his family.

As the boys hid in some bushes, the Natives focused their attention on a Hispanic villager named Holquin as he walked behind two burros carrying flour on their backs. The boys tried to sneak away when two Mescaleros, who lagged behind the group, discovered them. Each warrior grabbed a boy as they joined the others. Holquin had been surrounded and stripped of his clothing. His sacks of flour were ripped open and white dust blanketed part of the brown earthen road. Holquin and the children were led on foot to a stream near the timberline. A warrior raised a lance to kill the villager, but stopped. He told his fellow Apaches that his father was

Hispanic, so he could not go through with the killing. The boys watched the spear pass to another warrior. Despite being stabbed, Holquin ran towards the forest until he fell after being shot to death by arrows. "With a wild wail of despair, he lifted his hands toward heaven and fell full length at the water's edge," according to Andres, whose story was published by a Methodist preacher. "This was an awful scene to Andres and Pedro, and haunted them in the visions of the night."

Thunderhead clouds gather during the summer over the rolling hills some 30 miles east of Las Vegas, N.M. Photo by Zita Fletcher.

The boys were taken to an area near Las Vegas, where the Natives made camp. Four Apaches watched the boys while the others scattered in different directions to steal horses. As morning of the next day dawned, the warriors returned with horses for everyone. The group journeyed for a few days. Along the way, the boys witnessed the warriors shoot and kill a resting shepherd with a volley of arrows.

Neither boy had eaten since their capture, and Pedro began to cry for his mother. Ropes, that had been used to bind the boys, cut through their flesh. The warriors stopped and held a discussion. Pedro had fainted and continued to cry when he gained consciousness. Andres looked on as a warrior walked up behind Pedro and stabbed the child. Andres slipped off his horse and ran over to catch Pedro as he fell to the ground, but was hit in the forehead by the blunt end of a spear. A warrior lifted Andres up by his hair and tossed Andres over the horse. The band rode away, leaving Pedro's body in the wilderness. Thus Andres began his solitary journey as captive.

When Juan went out to bring the boys lunch, he expected to find them around the base of some shade trees where the cows had gathered. When no responses came to his calls, he rode his horse out in search. He recognized the meaning of moccasin footprints in the dirt. The tracks led

Company headquarters at Fort Sumner (1882). Juan Martinez and the search party from San Geronimo likely visited this location. Apaches and Navajos were imprisoned at the fort. Martinez would have ridden up to company headquarters (above), where soldiers stood outside in Fort Sumner to ask for information about his son's possible whereabouts. Photo courtesy of the N.M. Digital Collections.

to the area where white powder dusted the road. Juan galloped towards San Geronimo to raise a search party. They found Holquin's body the next day. Villagers pursued the tracks until they found no trace of the war party. The search party road more than 100 miles away to Fort Sumner, next to Bosque Redondo where the Apaches had been held. Navajos still remained incarcerated there. Juan stayed there for several days, but could find no news from friendly Indians or anyone about the boys. He returned home. For the next three years, he tried to find Andres and Pedro until he died prematurely. He apparently never recovered from the shock of not knowing the fate of the children.

The Apaches slaughtered a pony on their journey for food. One warrior hit Andres in the head when he refused to eat it raw until the boy acquiesced. After 20 days traveling south, the group reached the band's main camp in a secluded area near the Pecos River. Andres was mistreated by many of the Natives in the camp except for the lame wife of the warrior who had claimed the youth. She treated him with great care and kindness. His life with the Apaches was as a servant whose duties included fetching wood, carrying water, and tending to livestock. Within two months, he had been traded twice among various Apaches.

Trading in New Mexico among various Indians included the Kiowas, who travels took them from Canada to Mexico. A group of Kiowas came upon the Apache camp where Andres lived in misery. One Kiowa was a Hispanic captive. He spoke in Spanish to Andres and related that he had been captured years ago. The Kiowas had watched Andres fight against a group of Apache

Three Kiowa warriors pose for a photo in traditional dress (1898). Their long hair is worn in braids and covered with animal fur. Photo by R.A. Rinehart, courtesy of Wikimedia Commons.

boys and were impressed by his bravery. After a short discussion, Andres agreed that he would like to be taken by a Kiowa chief called Many Bears. The chief wanted to give Andres to his daughter, whose son had died recently. Andres had to slip away from the Apaches at night and hide in the chief's tepee.

Andres arrived safely to the Kiowas, where they fed him and called him "Andelle Ontumbe" (meaning track hunter) because they couldn't pronounce Andres. The next day the chief traded a black mule, a red blanket, and two buffalo robes as payment to the Apaches for the boy. The Kiowas welcomed him and cared for him as one of their own. They dressed his wounds, made him clothes, captured a good mule for him to ride, fashioned a saddle out of cowhide to fit him, and taught him to shoot a bow and arrows. The group rode beyond New Mexico's border across the plains to join other Kiowa chiefs—Stumbling Bear (Set-imkia), Big Bow (Zepko-ete), and Napawat (No Moccasins)—near the Washita River in present-day Oklahoma.

After three years, Many Bears and his warriors (dog soldiers) joined with Arapahos, Cheyennes, and Comanches to fight the Utes. In the ensuing fight, Many Bears died and was scalped by the Utes. Andres then lived with the family of Napawat, who succeeded the dead Kiowa chief.

In 1870, Andres witnessed the aftermath of an Army attack on a group of Cheyennes who were camped near the Kiowas. Soldiers from Fort Reno (in central Oklahoma) discovered the Cheyennes holding a scalp dance with the hair of a white woman they had just killed. Surrounding the Natives, the soldiers began shooting. Andres heard the commotion and helped gather horses for the Kiowas to escape. Instead of fleeing in the opposite direction, he snuck back with another youth the next day to observe what happened.

"Here Cheyenne men, women, and children were slaughtered and lying promiscuously in the snow stained with their own life blood. A woman with her lips burned off, stiff and cold, was propped up against a tree, a horrible, grinning spectacle. Men and women perfectly nude were placed in such positions as would not be proper to describe here. This was done by the civilized soldiers of a Christian land, to mock the barbarous savages of heathen tribes," Andres recounted.

This 1875 ledger drawing recalls a scene from life at a Kiowa camp. Three men and three women are depicted walking under rugs hanging overhead. This picture was drawn by a Kiowa prisoner of war in captivity, who was probably transported from Oklahoma to an old Spanish fort in Florida. Illustration by unknown, courtesy of The Smithsonian Institution.

"This sight enraged the Indians and a yell of revenge went up from them as they looked on. The Kiowas and Comanches from every quarter began to gather to aid their friends, the Cheyennes. They were preparing for the attack the next day, but the soldiers, who were in camp a few miles away, hearing of the proposed attack of the allied tribes, took up the line of march back to Fort Reno. The Indians followed, however, and in the attack cut off a considerable troop of soldiers from their command and killed them nearly all."

For the next few years, the military relentlessly pursued the Plains Indians. By then, Andres had joined in raids and taken Kiowa wives. The Kiowas and Comanches agreed in an 1867 treaty at Medicine Lodge to peace and were assigned to a reservation in what is now Oklahoma. Yet, the Natives still roamed their traditional homelands and some continued to fight for years before taking residence in the designated lands.

In the early 1870s, Napawat and other Kiowas surrendered their nomadic life for the reservation. The tribe camped near Fort Sill, where eight companies of the military could keep them under observation. Capt. R.H. Pratt took a census of the Natives to understand them and found they had 26 captives— 12 Hispanics and 14 whites.

"As each name was called, the Indian had to appear for himself, and answer such questions through the interpreter as were asked. Finally, Andelle was called, and as soon as Capt. Pratt saw him, he, with the other soldiers, gathered around him, for they saw that he was a captive Mexican. Andelle became alarmed, and also very much angered, when they came around him and began to scrutinize him so closely. There were talking very earnestly about him but he could not understand a word they were saying, and if there were any Indians present who did understand, they did not care for Andelle to know, but they rather added to his aversion to the white man by telling him such things as would alarm his fears. As soon as they quit noticing him and left him alone, he threw his buffalo robe up over his head and close around his face so that he might not be seen so easily and afterwards kept as much as possible out of sight of the soldiers."

"Andelle," (left) is seated next to his Kiowa wife, White Sage on the reservation in Oklahoma (1872). When this photo was taken, he was living the life of a Kiowa warrior and had not yet regained his Hispanic identity as Andres Martinez, captured as a boy in New Mexico. Photo by James Mooney, courtesy of The Smithsonian Institution.

Lawrie Tatum, a Quaker Indian agent, took charge in 1869 of Kiowas and Comanches at Fort Sill. Tatum took a special interest in looking for captives among the tribes in his care and returning the prisoners to their families. Tatum learned about Andres and sought out more information about the abduction. The Kiowas had no details since Andres was purchased from Apaches; and Andres would provide no clues.

The Indian agency for the Kiowa, Comanche, and Apache reservation at Fort Sill was moved in 1878 about a day's travel by stagecoach to Anadarko on the Washita River.

Lawrie Tatum (center) sits in 1872 with a group of mixed race and captive children that he rescued after he became an Indian agent to the Kiowas. During his time with the Comanches and Kiowas, Tatum collected Native "souvenirs," such as an official census taken by tribal members, a set of split-sticks, and a lariat made of the long hair from a buffalo's forehead. In a letter, he inquired whether the Smithsonian had any interest in these items which he prized. Photo courtesy of The Smithsonian Institution.

Andres continued his life as a Kiowa until a few incidents changed his life. The first incident was when he saw a railroad train. "It set him to thinking that there must be something better for him than wandering in blanket and wild robe over the prairies like the wild buffalo. The buffalo were fast being killed out by the restless, aggressive white man, and it was probable that the Indian would go likewise, unless there was a change; for the white man seemed as glad to kill an Indian as a buffalo."

The next significant change occurred when Andres decided to learn a skill to earn a living. George Warfield Hunt was a school superintendent and principal teacher. His brother Philemon Burgess (P.B.) Hunt was the Indian Agent employed by the Office of Indian Affairs to manage the Kiowas and Comanches. Andres began to consider working after hearing George Hunt's lecture about reasons why young Natives should learn to live in peace, work, earn money, and have stable homes. Andres asked for a job and went to work for a German blacksmith Fred Schlegel.

Kiowa and Comanche Indian agent Philemon Burgess Hunt (center) is next to his brothers Allie (right) and George Warfield Hunt (left). A motivational speech given by George on the reservation became a turning point for Andres. During the Civil War, the Hunts, from Kentucky, were divided. George and Allie fought with the Confederates. Philemon and another brother took up the Union cause.

The third pivotal moment happened one day while Andres was inside a trading post that housed a Post Office. "He had seen people trading with the merchants, receiving goods over the counter for which they paid money, but he noticed now the merchant seemed to be handing out things for which the people paid nothing. He could not understand it, and his curiosity was so much excited, that he asked the blacksmith, under whom he worked, what it meant. The blacksmith answered that

The Post Office in Fort Sill in *"The West from a Car Window,"* by Richard Harding Davis (1892). Near Fort Sill, the town of Anadarko in the 1890s consisted of six stores, a few homes, Indian Agent facilities, and a hotel. In the West, a collection of seven buildings was enough to designate an area as a city.

A stagecoach owned by L.P. Williamson, who had a stagecoach monopoly and delivered mail to the Kiowa reservation in Anadarko. Williamson provided cheap and uncomfortable travel. A journalist described how much he dreaded traveling on Williamson's stage to Anadarko. "This is not intended as an advertisement for Mr. Williamson's stages. He does not need it, for he is, so his drivers tell me, very rich indeed, and so economical that he makes them buy their own whips. Everyone who has travelled through Indian Territory over Williamson's routes wishes that sad things may happen to him; but no one, I believe, would be so wicked as to hope he may ever have to ride in one of his own stages," noted Richard Harding Davis. Andres and his brothers may have ridden in Williamson's stages to and from New Mexico. Drawing by Frederic Remington (1889), in *"The West from a Car Window."*

the people were getting messages from their friends; that people could talk on paper to one another although they were a long distance apart."

This idea of communicating with people far away triggered something in Andres' mind. Memories of being stolen and his former life began to come back. He recalled his name in Spanish and his older brother's name. He remembered his family surname Martinez, his oldest brother's name (Dionicio), and the location of their home near Las Vegas, N.M. Andres went to see the medical doctor, Hugh L. Tobin, assigned to the Natives. He asked the physician if he could send a communication to his family in New Mexico just as people had done in the Post Office. The doctor agreed to help and wrote to his brother Dionicio in 1883 via the *Las Vegas Daily Gazette* newspaper. A month passed with no response because his brother, who had become a railroad contractor, had moved to Colorado. Undeterred, Andres sent a letter continuously for nearly two years. One day, his brother received the letter on a visit to their elderly mother in Las Vegas. Agent Hunt helped establish the identity

THE CIMARRON NEWS AND PRESS

CIMARRON, NEW MEXICO, THURSDAY, JANUARY 31, 1907

Strange Story of Indian Captivity

Taken Captive by Indians as a Boy Andres Martinez Grows to Manhood as an Indian But is Found and Restored to friends

Dionicio Martinez of Cimarron and his brother Andres Martinez of Verden, Oklahoma, were in the city on Wednesday and returned to Cimarron that day. They had been to [...] virtually became an Indian. He lost his Spanish speech in the nineteen years he lived with the Kiowas.

When the government undertook the civilizing of the Kiowas and other [...]

This newspaper was among several in New Mexico that carried brief articles about the capture of Andres Martinez, his return as an adult to his Hispanic family, and his new life as a teacher and business leader among the Kiowas.

of Andres.

Plans were made for Dionicio and another brother to journey to the reservation to bring Andres to New Mexico. After two decades, they met their long lost younger sibling dressed as a Kiowa. The last time they saw him, Andres was 8 years old. The brothers used a government interpreter since Andres neither understood English nor Spanish. It took four days of dialogue to completely identify Andres, according to *The Cimarron News and Press* on Jan. 31, 1907. "Mr. Martinez is an intelligent man and speaks with feeling of his days of captivity and subsequent Indian life," noted the N.M. newspaper after an interview with Andres. He was in town visiting his brother Dionicio, who lived there with his family.

The Kiowas opposed the notion of Andres leaving them, until Andres promised to return. Before Andres returned to New Mexico it was agreed that he would retain his rights as a member of the Kiowa tribe.

The Martinez brothers left for Las Vegas in March 1885 for a trip lasting over a month until they reached their destination. His sisters and elderly mother still lived there. They were overjoyed to see Andres, who had reached 28 years of age. He was reunited with his mother during the last two years of her life. He spent four years getting reacquainted with his family. During that time, he also attended school as a grown man, completely relearned to speak Spanish, and studied English.

When Andres finally returned in the summer of 1889 to the Kiowas, his Native wife named White Sage had passed away. Other events had occurred in his absence. The Kiowas, Comanches, and Apaches on the reservation had taken up farming with over 4,000 acres under cultivation.

Many traditional tribal ceremonies had been abandoned since the Natives no longer ventured out on annual summer and winter hunts. Traditional Native clothing was beginning to be replaced with American clothes. Young Indian children were targets for cultural replacement in schools where only English was spoken.

Andres became an interpreter and also taught at a preacher's elementary school. A former student, Guy Quetone, of the Methodist school for seven years reminisced in the 1960s about Andres and the school. Guy's father and Andres grew up together as Kiowa brothers and belonged to the same clans. "They were just like full brothers," Guy recalled. "He [Andres] was an adopted Dog Soldier, clan brother." When the Kiowa tribe was placed on a reservation in Oklahoma, Andres became Guy's teacher and inspired the boy to become a Methodist.

Guy remembered his parents taking him to school for the first time and speaking in Kiowa to Andres, who told them to leave the boy there for a month or two before they returned. Andres reassured the parents that Guy would be okay.

Andres Martinez (1894) after his return from New Mexico to the Kiowa reservation in Oklahoma. His forehead still had the scar where the Apache struck him after young Pedro was killed. Photo courtesy of The Smithsonian Institution.

"At that time, my braids were long, wrapped with otter skin fur. And I had a breastplate," Guy recalled. Andres ushered the boy into a room with a white woman and a white barber. "I begin to get excited and they got a chair; this man set me there, and they commenced to hold me. He set me down in that chair, and that lady talked to me and tried to get my attention. While I was talking at her—looking at her—this barber...he came from behind and cut one side of my braid off. I knew what happened." Guy tried to fight, but was held down by two men and

When his parents left him at the Methvin Institute school, Guy Quetone (left) was tricked onto a barber's chair. Guy struggled for an hour as Andres and two others from the school held him down and cut off his braids. Merchants at Fort Sill bribed Kiowas and Comanches to cut off their braids, which were trafficked as curios and sold for wigs.

the white woman. His fierce struggle made it difficult for them to cut his long hair. After almost an hour, Guy's hair was forcibly cut short.

Afterwards, his Native clothing and moccasins were substituted for government-issued clothing—a heavy pair of oversized shoes with a brass buckle and a gray suit.

Native men also had their long hair, worn in braids, taken away, according to journalist Richard Harding Davis, who wrote about his visit to Fort Sill in 1892.

Taking goods from Natives on the reservation in Anadarko for resale was profitable. Records of this trade date back to 1886, showing three traders. The business stationary for C.A. Cleveland (above) was run by Charles Archibald Cleveland. The other trading companies were owned by John Craggs and Dudley Brown. Indians on the reservation also could use their belongings and cash to purchase food items at the trading companies.

"They did hate to loose their long hair, and Lt. Hugh Lenox Scott did not order them to have it cut, but told them it would please him if they did; and so one by one, and in bunches of three and four, they tramped up the hill to the [Fort Sill] post barber, and back again with their locks in their hands, to barter them for tobacco with the post trader."

The trafficking in Native men's hair indicates there must have been a commercial value placed on Indian braids. White men may have sold the braids of Kiowa warriors as souvenirs to trophy hunters and to manufacturers for use in doll hair and wigs.

In their early careers, U.S. Army Maj. Gen. Hugh Lenox Scott (left) and Brig. Gen. James Denver Glennan of the Army Medical Corps (right) were stationed together at Fort Sill. They had leading roles among the Natives on the Kiowa and Comanche reservation, which would later hold Geronimo and other Apache prisoners of war. Glennan was the fort physician. Scott was the main military representative for the Indians. While at Fort Sill, both officers tried to acquire Native valuables. Scott nearly had himself declared a member of a Native tribe to collect 160 free acres of Indian land, but Congress prevented it. Scott's memoirs included an anecdote about trying to buy buckskin pants off a Kiowa chief. Glennan acquired an ancient Kiowa chief's shield. Photos courtesy of the Library of Congress.

The same Lt. Scott who told the Natives to cut their braids rose to become the U.S. Army Chief of Staff and Maj. Gen. Scott. In his memoirs, he wrote about his efforts to collect "Indian curios" during his time at Fort Sill. He tried to buy the buckskin leggings from an old Kiowa chief Big Bow while they rode horses alongside each other on a military expedition. Each outer side of the leggings had 20 parallel markings for Big Bow's accomplishments in battle. In refusing, the Kiowa replied: "I don't want to pick up money for these leggings. I am getting old, and soon my die day will arrive. Then my women will plait my hair, paint my face red, and put these clothes on me, and my spirit will go out of my mouth up to the Wolf's Road. When I get there they will look me all over and will say, 'Big Bow, you are well dressed.' I didn't want to pick up money for these clothes."

Two warriors stand next to Kiowa Chief Big Bow (center), who sits next to a buffalo head. Hugh Lenox Scott, a lieutenant at Fort Sill, noticed a pair of valuable leather leggings worn by Chief Big Bow. Scott tried to convince the chief to sell his Native clothing as the two men rode their horses side by side during a trip from Oklahoma to Texas. Big Bow refused to sell his clothing because he wanted to be buried in it. Photo (circa 1863-1900), courtesy of The Smithsonian Institution.

Scott discussed how his Fort Sill colleague, Army surgeon Capt. James Denver Glennan, also collected Indian curios and wanted a good shield. "I already had the shield in the Southwest, which used to belong to the celebrated Kiowa chief, Satanta, more than a hundred years old," Scott wrote. "When Satanta's son died, he left the shield to me in his will, which was probated by the Indian court while I was in Washington, and the shield was sent to me by the agent. I told Big Bow's son to take the shield to Dr. Glennan and charge him $50 for it, which was cheap enough, for he could probably get $1,000 for it now." Scott noted how easy it was for white men to cheat Natives who were unfamiliar with the values of items "and the white man's way of bargaining."

Fort Sill at that time remained in an area considered Indian Territory by the U.S. government.

According to Scott, the Natives on the reservation lacked representation on Capitol Hill where decisions were made about their welfare. "It had no Congressional delegation to fight for it in Washington; in fact, it had nobody but me, a first lieutenant of the cavalry, who did not count for much in the halls of Congress, where it was not known that I was even alive," wrote Scott.

By the time Andres returned to the Kiowa, another big change had taken place. Two years earlier, an ambitious and impoverished 41-year-old Southern Methodist itinerant preacher named John Jasper (J.J.) Methvin had begun to plant roots on the reservation.

Methvin had seen much failure in his career before he drove his wife and five children in their prairie schooner and camped next to Native tepees. His fight for the Confederacy during the Civil War was on the losing side. After college, he became a lawyer for a short time before turning his back on his profession. At age 24, Methvin obtained a license to preach. Then he decided to become an educator, high school principal, and school administrator in Georgia for a few years before abandoning that career path. His next career path would combine preaching and teaching defeated tribes Native Americans—the disadvantaged who were less likely to challenge someone in his position.

"The policy of many of the whites was to settle the Indian problem by exterminating the Indians and thus coming into possession of their lands. Through the influence of the Christian

Comanche women building tepees (1890). The government issued canvas tepees to the Kiowas and Comanches on the reservation at Fort Sill. Much to the chagrin of government officials and other whites, the Natives preferred to move around the reservation in tepees rather than stay in permanent dwellings. When houses were first built there, Indians still lived in tepees and used the houses to store goods or livestock. It took many years for Natives to abandon integral parts of their nomadic cultural heritage, such as moving around in tepees. Photos courtesy of the Oklahoma Historical Society.

Elements of the Kiowa Sun Dance are shown (above) in an illustration by artist Silver Horn, born in 1860. His family was so opposed to being confined to a reservation that they were among the last Kiowa to surrender. Once the Natives were on the reservation, a squadron of cavalry forced the Kiowas to give up the Sun Dance, which had been an important part of their way of life. Drawing (circa 1885), courtesy of The Smithsonian Institution.

people of the land, the policy of the government towards the Indians changed," Methvin remarked in 1937. "President Ulysses S. Grant and others held the view that our duty towards the Indians was to civilize and Christianize them."

Methvin first went to the Seminoles and then to the Choctaws, but soon left both tribes due to administrative grievances. When Methodist missionaries decided to work with the Kiowas and Comanches soon after they moved onto the reservation, Methvin aggressively lobbied for the opportunity and won it.

First he and his family lived in the wagon that he located next to Kiowa camps. Then he negotiated with a trader to share a shack to accommodate the preacher's family. Methvin took his preaching into tepees and on open fields.

"They were dressed in the wild, fantastic paraphernalia peculiar to their taste; faces painted, the men with hair long, plaited and rolled in the skin of some wild animal. Their ears [were] weighted down with heavy earrings till they nearly touched their shoulders; their bodies, in many instances, half naked and painted in fantastic colors. This was a wild crowd to preach to, but at the signal given they gathered in eager expectancy to hear what I had to say. After announcing that I was not there as a cattleman nor the Indian trader to make money, but to tell them the message of God, to show them the way of salvation, I began reading the Scriptures suited to their condition. They sat around the ground for hours patiently and attentively listened to the readings," he recalled.

The Native religion of the Kiowas also came under attack. The government pressured the Kiowa into abandoning an important religious ceremony, noted Army officer Scott, speaking about his time as a lieutenant at Fort Sill. A squadron of the 7th Cavalry at Fort Sill displayed

Andres and his last wife, fellow Methodist teacher Emma McWhorter. Her father was also a preacher. They both met while working with Native children at the Methvin Institute.

a show of force to make the Kiowas abandon their Sun Dance. "They gave it up very reluctantly, believing that the well being and health of their tribe depended on it, and they held much resentment for a long time," Scott noted. "They were doing no harm to anybody and should have been led away, not forced away, from it."

Methvin encountered difficulty finding an interpreter until he met Andres, who not only could speak Native languages but also was viewed as trustworthy. Two years later, Andres converted and became an industrial teacher at the preacher's new school called the Methvin Institute.

"The history of all nations shows that education always follows Christianity, but not always does Christianity follow education; therefore, our main aim from the very beginning was to Christianize the Indians. To preach the Gospel more effectively, a knowledge of the language of the people with whom we work is very helpful," Methvin said. "The best solution of any heathen mission is that the heathen be converted to Christ and take up the missionary work themselves among their people."

Andres became an important instrument in Methvin's ministry to win students and converts. Eventually, Andres also became a preacher who assisted Methvin. While teaching, Andres met his future wife Emma. As a Kiowa, he had married three times before and was widowed. His last wife was Emma McWhorter, whose father was a preacher. She worked as a matron at Methvin's school. In 1893, Methvin officiated at wedding of Andres and Emma.

After they married, the couple adopted two daughters who were part Indian, according to the *Las Vegas Daily Optic* newspaper in 1957. The girls were Rachel Downing (granddaughter of Cherokee chief Louis Downing) and Hattie McKenzie (whose Kiowa father was named General McKenzie).

Andres reflected on how both he and Kiowas were no longer the same after years of life on the reservation at Anadarko. Andres was with the tribe when it moved onto a reservation in

Oklahoma during the 1870s. During that time, a Quaker teacher named Thomas Battey became a teacher and Indian agent there.

Reflecting back on those years, Andres wrote to Battey's wife in March 1897.

"I was at that time as complete a blanket Indian in habits, customs, superstitions, as any Indian in the Kiowa tribe," he said. "There have been great changes since you were here…Many of the Indians have cast aside the blanket and the breechcloth and are wearing civilized dress; and during the past 4 or 5 years, many houses have been built so that in a few more years, the Indians will quit living in tepees."

Andres said he wished he realized earlier while Thomas worked among the Kiowas that Battey was trying to uplift the tribe. "But I did not know then and could not appreciate his interest in us and his good works. But God has been kind to me and six years ago I was converted and joined the Methodist church, and since then I have been trusting and serving the Lord Jesus. I feel so glad that he has delivered me from the darkness and death of Indian or other superstitions, and that I have been turned from idols to serve the living God."

Still known to the Batteys by his Kiowa name, he closed the letter: "P.S. My real name is Andres Martinez…I found out [about] my people down in N.M. and recovered my Mexican name, stayed with my people a short while, then came back here, and will spend the rest of my days here as I have all the Indian rights. – *Andelle*"

"*Andele: Or, The Mexican-Kiowa Captive — A Story of Real Life Among the Indians*" is the most well known account of the captivity and life of Andres. Methvin wrote the book, published in 1899 by the Pentecostal Herald Press of Kentucky.

Methvin's work contains many minor factual errors. On the first page and throughout the book, it misspells the name of Andres' father as "Jaun" instead of Juan. The identity of the

> Andres Martinez shows the correct spelling of his Kiowa name "Andelle" in a March 1897 letter. Methodist preacher Methvin didn't care to find out how to spell the name correctly when he wrote his book about Andres, published in 1899.

Indian agent named as George Hunt is misattributed. The real agent was George's brother Col. Philemon Burgess (P.B.) Hunt. Perhaps the most glaring error is in the misspelling of Andres' native name. Andres wrote it as "Andelle"—his signature even appeared in a letter Andres wrote on letterhead of Methvin's school. It would be unlikely that Methvin wouldn't know how Andres spelled his Native name, particularly since both men both worked together in the same school and preached in the same Methodist community.

Andres already had acquired a sufficient education to write well in English and teach in Methvin's school by the time the preacher wrote the book. Given the errors, it seems that Andres had no opportunity to review Methvin's work prior to publication. The events of Methvin's tale of Andres are believed to be true.

It is unclear, however, why Andres, at age 55, wrote his own version of his captivity. He advertised his own book under a headline *"Indian Life"* in early 1910 in the *Anadarko Daily Democrat*. The ads promote "a true story of Indian life" written by Andres about his captivity. The books, available for purchase at the local Post Office bookstore, must have attracted little interest since these ads appear to be the only records that his autobiography ever existed. Although his book failed, Methvin's was republished in 1927.

ANADARKO DAILY DEMOCRAT
VOLUME IX.—NO. 32   ANADARKO, OKLAHOMA WEDNESDAY MARCH 16, 1910   PRICE 2 Cents

Indian Life.

A true story of Indian life, written written by Andre Martinez, who was captured by the Indians when a boy. His little brother was killed and he was adopted by the chief. He grew up as an Indian. 21 years of experience among them. Intensely interesting. Book on sale at the Postoffice Book Store.   d-w-k-y-14tf

Andres authored his own story of his captivity and life but it appears there was little interest in his version. Although this newspaper ad from March 1910 mistakenly identified his relative Pedro as his brother, this notice provides the only known record that Andres even wrote his autobiography.

Andres made a homestead with his allotment of Indian land where he farmed and raised livestock on a ranch. An advocate for Native rights, Andres also helped in managing Indian affairs. He became known as a respected citizen with great influence in the community, according a 1918 edition of *The American Indian* magazine. Andres died in December 1935 at age 80 after working nearly 50 years among the Kiowas as a missionary and teacher.

Chapter 16: Methodist Missionary to the Indians: John Jasper Methvin

Methodist preacher/attorney John Jasper (J.J.) Methvin was a man of contradictions. When he came as a missionary to live on Indian land, he told the Kiowas and other Natives on the reservation that he "was not there as a cattleman nor the Indian trader to make money." Yet, his speech and his actions proved otherwise.

Methvin arrived as a wandering (itinerant) preacher assigned to the reservation at Fort Sill by a Southern Methodist Indian Mission Conference.

"We have three kinds of work. First, the work among the white people; second, full bloods and blanket Indians; and third, Indians of mixed blood," noted Dr. I.G. John, during an 1896 Indian missionary conference. "The work among the blanket Indians is as truly missionary work as any in China or Japan. These Indians are heathen, and we should have more men and money here if we expect to continue working among them and make it a success." At that time, the organization was divided among nine elders, each of whom presided over a district. With 550 preachers, it had a congregation of 17,200 people (27% were Natives).

Methvin was among its preachers when he arrived in Anadarko in October 1887. In his early 40s, he brought a wagon packed with his wife, five children and their belongings. All real estate was owned by the government or the Natives. Without a place to rent, the Methvins moved into a government mess house. They lived there until moving into a three-room house

John Jasper Methvin after his arrival as a Methodist missionary to the Kiowas. Photo courtesy of the Oklahoma Historical Society.

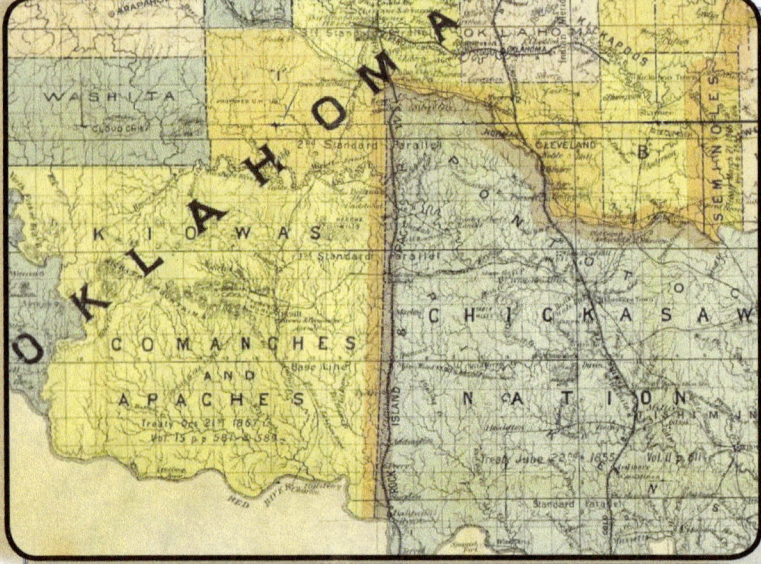

Part of a map showing the reservation for the Kiowas. The area was contained within a land parcel designated also for Comanches and Apaches (upper left). The U.S. government called this region Indian Territory because it was set aside for the relocation of Native tribes. The expanse covered a broad section of the Midwest until the government reduced it in increments during the 1800s for white settlements. The former Indian Territory is now mostly in Oklahoma. Map of the Indian and Oklahoma Territories (1893), courtesy of the University of Texas at Arlington Library.

owned by a trader, who used the quarters for cooking and dining.

The government agency in charge of the Kiowas was in chaos when the preacher arrived. "The agent himself had been removed, the superintendent of one of the Indian schools was suspended for drunkenness, one of the government employees in a drunken carousal had shot himself and was suffering from a severe wound, and some of the clerks had been drinking. An investigation was going on and things were in a stir," Methvin recalled. "Through the influence of the politicians, it seems that many had been appointed to the Indian service without regard to mind or matter, creed or conduct. There were some exceptionally excellent characters among them, but as a rule it was a crude and crusty crowd and as clever as they were crude."

Based on that description, it is easy to envision how a person with a legal mind and meager funds, like Methvin, could take advantage of the government benefits earmarked for Indians on the reservation. The Natives were in a complete state of dependency on others in

Three Natives (right) stand next to a Kiowa camp near Fort Sill. Photo by J.E. Irwin (circa 1898), courtesy of the Beinecke Rare Book and Manuscript Library, Yale University.

> The north side of the old post headquarters at Fort Sill. This building was a focal point at Fort Sill from 1870 until 1911. Photo courtesy of the Library of Congress.

the reservation since they couldn't read or write English. Not only did the Indians need others to translate for them, but words had to be explained properly. There were many instances that Indians found themselves taken advantage of in legal situations and unable to reverse the terms they mistakenly had agreed to because of improper translations. In fact, most Natives were unable to write their own names on treaties and signed official documents by marking an "X" next to their names, which had been written by someone else. Another problem at that time were Indian names. In general, Natives only had a first name and lacked a surname, which placed them at a further disadvantage in U.S. society and official dealings.

Fort Sill on an 1879 map, courtesy of the University of Texas at Arlington Library.

In less than five years after arriving among the Kiowas on the reservation, Methvin had himself legally declared a member of the tribe so he could receive the same land allotment as the other Natives. He had no compunction about taking what little land the Natives had after being forced to live on a reservation. He was among 5 other whites (including the officer in charge of Fort Sill and the reservation) who felt no shame in having themselves legally designated as "friends" of the Indians for rendering valuable services. This legal determination meant Methvin and the other four people could each select a 160-acre tract of land to own.

Besides Methvin (aged 45), the others legally entitled to each get 160 acres of land were:

- **Zonee Adams** (1 year old)—whose mother (Miss Whittaker) was a missionary and father had been former government Indian Agent Charles E. Adams of Baltimore, who served from 1889 to 1891 before he resigned;

- **Emsy S. Smith** (24)—who interpreted for the Comanches supposedly without compensation;

- **David Grantham** (40)—who lived with Quanah Parker for a decade and claimed to have taught Comanches how to farm, despite being Quanah's sharecropper/handyman; and

- **John T. Hill** (55)—described officially as someone who spent time with Indians, but who was a con man that helped trick Natives into selling their land at low prices.

> **ARTICLE X.**
> It is further agreed that the following named persons, not members by blood of either of said tribes, but who have married into one of the tribes, to-wit, Mabel R. Given, Thomas F. Woodward, William Wyatt, Kiowa Dutch, John Nestill, James N. Jones, Christian Ke-Oh-Tah, Edward L. Clark, George Conover, William Dietrick, Ben Roach, Lewis Bentz, Abilene, James Gardloupe, John Sanchez, the wife of Boone Chandler, whose given name is unknown, Emmit Cox, and Horace P. Jones, shall each be entitled to all the benefits of land and money conferred by this agreement, the same as if members by blood of one of said tribes, and that Emsy S. Smith, David Grantham, Zonee Adams, John T. Hill, and J. J. Methvin, friends of said Indians, who have rendered to said Indians valuable services, shall each be entitled to all the benefits, in land only, conferred under this agreement, the same as if members of said tribes.
> **ARTICLE XI.**
> This agreement shall be effective only when ratified by the Congress of the United States.

> Missionary to the Kiowas and Methodist preacher John Jasper (J.J.) Methvin had his named added in 1892 to names of 562 male adults in the Kiowa, Comanche, and Apache tribes so he could receive a free tract of 160 acres of land from the U.S. government. Methvin's new family acreage was part of an Oct. 1867 treaty the government made with the Natives when they forced them from their nomadic homelands onto a reservation. Under terms of the treaty, Methvin got to choose his own tract, which was a prime piece of real estate he named Methvin Canyon.

Congress disapproved two names for inclusion into the tribe: the current Indian agent at that time George D. Day (43), and Lt. Hugh L. Scott (40) from Fort Sill. Otherwise two other white "friends" of the Natives would have grabbed a share of land. Hill was a West Point graduate who grew up in Princeton, N.J. In his memoirs after achieving fame and fortune, Hill mentions about how he failed to find promotions with salary increases in his early military career. "I was 19 years a lieutenant and 5 years at the head of the first lieutenants without gaining a single file. But this was never allowed by either my wife or myself to sour our dispositions as some have permitted slow promotion to do, and we enjoyed our daily life on little money," Hugh commented.

While maintaining his bright outlook on life, Hugh discussed how he happily collected Native heirlooms as curios at Fort Sill and would have shamelessly helped himself to Indian land and taken the clothes off their backs if given the opportunity.

Oklahoma newspaper the *Hobart Weekly Chief* questioned in January 1902 the land given to the baby Zonee. Under the headline asked: **"How was it done? Who did it? Was it fraud? An Infant given an allotment as a friend of the Indians."** It questioned what valuable service a 1-year-old, then living in Oregon, could have rendered. "It is charged that someone made the selection of the allotment for Zonee and that she obtained a nice quarter of the land. Who it was that obtained the allotments for these parties no one seems to know," the newspaper declared, adding that Indians were "free to denounce the deal as a large juicy graft."

It was well known that the Indians, previously nomads, had no experience and little knowledge about how to select the most valuable tracts of land on the reservation. Methvin, however, had no trouble selecting his 160 acres. His land, which he named Methvin Canyon, was described by a local newspaper for its beauty "with its dense shade, trickling springs, and ferny dells" in idyllic recreational surroundings.

He did much more than make money off the Indians—he took their land, which was something that they could not replace.

It is difficult to imagine what great contribution Methvin had made in his five years there when he got the large tract of land. His new school was built upon more free reservation land gifted by the U.S. government and had low enrollment compared to other religious schools. The numbers of students at Methvin's school (named the Methvin Institute) vary greatly between his descriptions and official reports. Some say his school opened in 1890 with 15 students, while other reports mention 35 students. Methvin reported that his school in 1896 had "a prosperous year" with a student enrollment of 36 Kiowas, 7 Comanches, 4 whites, and 1 Apache. (The white students probably included some of his 5 children.)

Two government schools were already on the reservation when Methvin decided to build a Christian school with a vocational slant. Not only would Native children learn to read and write, but they would be taught trades.

Journalist Richard Harding Davis visited Fort Sill in 1892. He described how Native parents visited schools to proudly watch their children as they learned to bridge between both cultures by speaking and understanding English. Despite unsuitable educational materials provided by the government, the Indian pupils impressed Davis with their knowledge.

"The teachers are not permitted to study the Indian languages, and their charges in consequence hear nothing but English, and so pick it up the more quickly. The young women who teach them seem to labor under certain disadvantages; one of them was reading the English lesson from a U.S. history intended for much older children—grown-up children, in fact," Davis said. Teachers were unable to select grade-appropriate materials.

These Kiowa girls (right) and boys (left) at Fort Sill were prime candidates for cultural assimilation into the white world in mandatory education on the reservation. Photo of the girls was by J.E. Irwin (circa 1898), courtesy of the Beinecke Rare Book and Manuscript Library, Yale University; and of the boys by Horace P. Robinson (circa 1890), courtesy of the DeGolyer Library, Southern Methodist University, Texas.

He witnessed a teacher turn Native parents out of their chairs to sit on the floor so he and other white people could be seated. The teacher justified this discriminatory act by saying the Indian parents were accustomed to sitting on floors. "She afterwards added to this by telling us that there was no [positive] sentiment in her [towards the Native children], and that she taught Indians for the $50 there was in it," he noted.

As Davis toured Indian schools, it is likely he visited the Methvin Institute.

Methvin's school was built with various donations. Methvin used his legal expertise to have the U.S. Commission of Indian Affairs equip his school with supplies meant for Native children. When the government refused his initial request to be provided with school supplies, Methvin invoked the terms of the Medicine Lodge Treaty and rights for Indians. Rather

> **Methvin Institute.**
>
> An Indian Mission School under the auspices of the Woman's Foreign Missionary Society of the M. E. Church, South.

Letterhead of the Methvin Institute, a Southern Methodist school founded by preacher John Jasper Methvin. The school was created on the Kiowa, Comanche, and Apache reservation near Fort Sill to convert and educate Native American children from elementary school through 8th grade.

than give supplies "to the Indians as they ran wild over the reservation," he suggested a portion of supplies be sent to his school instead. He promised to distribute the supplies to Native children in attendance. The government agreed.

There is no way to know if Methvin's school warehoused supplies for future use. One student who attended the school told of being given shoes to wear that were too large for his feet. This anecdote may indicate items that could have been put into the hands of needy Native children went on a shelf at the Methvin Institute.

According to an 1895 report by the Board of Indian Commissioners, the Methvin Institute was "doing a good and needed work among the wild tribes…There are 160 acres of land and several good buildings, and numerous farm implements and stock (the school is an industrial one) connected with the institution, the whole valued at $10,000." The school had two literature teachers and three in the industrial area.

Despite such a glowing assessment, the school closed 13 years later. Enrollment was low and the land it was located on became valuable for sale in development lots. The school closed in 1908. In October of the same year, the school land was sold for $45,000 to land speculators. Natives received no funds from the sale of the school, and the land became a large part of Anadarko's residential district.

The location of Methvin's Methodist mission is circled on part of a 1901 map of Oklahoma and Indian Territory. The curving red line follows the nearby Washita River. Map courtesy of the University of Texas at Arlington Library.

Methvin remarked that the only remaining relic left was a lone cedar tree standing on one side of a street. The tree had been carried from Methvin Canyon to be planted at Methvin Institute.

Ida A. Roff was employed at Methvin's school from 1891-1901. During that time not only did she teach Kiowa children, but she obtained their handmade toys as souvenirs.

The items made by Kiowas are shown right: a miniature beaded cradleboard, a boy and girl doll with real hair (made by Lone Wolf's sister Laura Pedrick). She also obtained valuable children's articles: a Kiowa baby's high-top moccasins, a Comanche child's pair of beaded moccasins, and silver jewelry for Delaware Indian children (a ring, bracelet, and scarf holder).

No doubt these items had sentimental value, especially the toys. Since Indians were on a reservation, they had no access to many of the items used to make these articles, which increased the value of the items.

What is clear is that children were deprived of the use of their toys, clothing, and jewelry by a woman who supposedly went to the reservation to teach them a better way. It is ironic that in school the children were taught that their Native culture had no value, but in reality both white men and women realized the potential importance of Indian goods and had no problem taking personal items away for private and commercial use.

Methvin's writings and extensive interviews taken in oral histories display an absence of kind words or concern for the Native children under his care, or even the adults on the reservation. He frequently makes mention of his 50+ years of work among "the Wild Tribes" and his attempts "to teach them the right way to live."

In 1937, at 90 years old, Methvin reviewed his missionary accomplishments among the Natives. He discussed his achievements, which included a parsonage, rock church, and dining hall. The structures were built on 40 beautiful acres surrounded by mountains on nearly every side and overlooking the blue waters of Lake Lawtonka. He selected that prime piece of real estate from land

Captives of the Southwest

A Kiowa woman (left) makes lace at the Methvin's Methodist school. Since the institute was a vocational school, missionary teacher Ida Roff was hired mainly to teach Kiowas to make lace. Many Americans avoided this tedious menial labor; yet this skill was transferred to Native women. Methodist missionaries thought lacemaking would provide Natives with high profits ($39 per month), and the work would lead the Indians to higher Christian spirituality.

that once belonged to the Natives. The church was built on a field belonging to the Methvin school.

> By reaching these Indian women industrially, she is gradually reaching them spiritually.

This statement about Ida Roff's lacemaking venture for Kiowa women at the Methvin Institute was noted in an 1891 report on missionary work by the Protestant Episcopal Church.

"Here a congregation of enthusiastic Indian worshippers, all dressed and in their right minds, greeted me last Sunday," the preacher recalled. "They were chiefly the descendants of those to whom I first broke the glad news in those other days of long ago. There was no paint on their faces, no rings in their ears, no fantastic paraphernalia, no discordant 'hi-ya' of the Indian song. But all were neatly dressed and ended the day's worship with a true devotion, singing the songs of redeeming grace."

His condescending remarks about people he spent the majority of his life with indicate what a low view he had of Natives. His cold attitude demonstrates how Methvin was an opportunist rather than the compassionate Christian educator that he presented himself to be.

> It is from this mission that the pieces of the beautiful work which are to be found in New York homes have come. The isaithmah, or sewing women, as the lace makers are called, come from all parts of the reservation to the mission school, which is near the center, and are instructed in this work by Miss Ida Roff, who has been in charge here about four years. Despite the fact that many of them do not understand or speak our language, all learn to do the work well enough for sale. The ability to imitate which is possessed to a high degree by the Indian races is the quality which enables them to become adepts at lace making.

New York homes had lace made by Kiowa women at Methvin's school. They mastered the prized, 15th-century Italian "Reticilli" stitch. Their handiwork included pillow edgings, table centerpieces, and tea towels—none of which had any practical relevance for nomadic Native women. The Kiowas were struggling financially in their forced subjugation on an Indian reservation. Although the Kiowa women earned money from lacework sales, there was no mention how the lace traveled to fancy East Coast homes in the 1901 *"Our Day"* magazine article. Undoubtedly, a middleman profited from sales of Kiowa lace. Roff had from 40 to 50 women working for her.

Other contradictions about Methvin can be found in his Civil War dealings. In January 1934, he sought money in Oklahoma by filing an

"Application of Indigent Soldier or Sailor of the Confederacy" to receive a pension. He wrote that he was needy because his yearly income amounted to $200—a combination of free-will offerings, Methodist Old Minister's relief funds, and real estate income. Although he listed real estate worth $2,040, Methvin claimed his income failed to pay for his mortgage and back taxes.

Claiming he was indigent, Methvin filed this successful application to receive a pension as a former Confederate soldier. The Oklahoma pension was for veterans in financial need.

Although he wrote several books, he made no mention of any royalties received for:

🖋 3 volumes of poetry: *"The Lone Cedar and Else," "The Divine Tragedy for the World's Redemption—An Easter Poem,"* and *"Fig Leaves and Else: A Collection of Homemade and Prose Composition."*

🖋 *"Andele, the Mexican-Kiowa Captive: A Story of Real Life Among the Indians,"* published in 1899 by the Pentecostal Herald Press and reissued in 1927 by Plummer Printing Co.;

🖋 *"The End of the Trail,"* published (date unknown) by N.T. Plummer Print Co.;

🖋 *"In the Limelight: or History of Anadarko and Vicinity from the Earliest Days,"* published in 1923 by Walker-Wilson-Tyler Co.; and

🖋 Articles for Christian and historical magazines.

Methvin clearly negotiated his business deals with more than one publisher. His writings indicate he had a second career as an author and may have published other books that are unknown at this time. He penned his autobiography in 1930, with limited copies distributed.

Despite his assertions of financial need, he used stationary from A.E. Baldwin to write to the Confederate Pension Dept. in Oklahoma. The A.E. Baldwin company was involved with securities, investments, and life insurance. Methvin's letters contained information about his pension request and complaints when he failed to receive his quarterly payments. If Methvin was truly poor, it is a wonder he had access to letterhead from a company that handled people's wealth and financial planning. A more likely scenario is that he had investments and/or life insurance with A.E. Baldwin.

The Confederate Pension Dept. informed Methvin in February 1934 that his pension was granted immediately after he filed the application; he would receive $324 per year in payments of $81 per quarter. In Oklahoma, Confederate veterans or their indigent widows could qualify for a pension in Oklahoma if they owned less than $2,000 worth of property and earned no more than $500 yearly. Proof of an honorable discharge also was required.

Methvin's Civil War service itself presents another cloudy area due to his apparent misrepresentations. The preacher described himself as a boy-soldier of 16 who gallantly served the Confederate Army for two years in noteworthy battles in and around his home state of Georgia until the South's defeat in mid-1865.

This portrayal of Methvin was repeated in his obituary, written by long-time friend and fellow Methodist preacher Dr. Sidney Babcock. Both Methvin and Babcock came from the same area in Macon, Ga., moved in the same religious circles, and were leading church elders in Oklahoma for decades. It would be easy to conclude that Babcock merely got his facts wrong if he hadn't known Methvin well. However, Babcock clearly knew intimate details about Methvin's life that only the latter could have provided. Babcock wrote Methvin's 1941 obituary for the Oklahoma Historical Society's scholarly magazine, which contained 6 pages of detailed accolades.

Methvin's stint as a rebel soldier was depicted as: "These years were the most horrible years of the war and he engaged in some of the hottest battles. However, he seldom referred to the war. When he did he characterized it as 'that senseless war.'"

Methvin wrote letters to the Confederate pension office on stationary belonging to investment and life insurance companies. His handwriting can be seen on the back side of the letterhead (top). If he was truly poor, it would be unusual for him to have access to such stationary.

The reality of Methvin's service record differed. He was not a boy-soldier, but was well past 17 years old when he enlisted as an infantry private in the 57th Regiment Georgia, Company D (the Smiths Guards). His service in the Confederate States of America lasted from April 1864 to the surrender of his unit in April 1865, which is nearly one year to date, rather than two. Methvin

Confederate soldiers in Georgia look east to Atlanta. Methodist preacher John J. Methvin served in the Confederate Army in his home state of Georgia. Photo by George N. Barnard (1864), courtesy of the Library of Congress.

was captured by Union trips while making his way home. Members of his unit included his two older brothers William Kelly (W.K.) and Thomas Jefferson Methvin, who both enlisted in 1861.

In a letter to the Confederate Pension office, Methvin described "fighting the blue coats" during all "the chief battles" and skirmishes in Georgia, Tennessee, and the Carolinas.

"I was wounded in the battles around Atlanta, flesh wound, and my brother was shot down by my side, killed instantly, the ball through his head. That was the first day of September 1864. Those tragic days still linger with me. That was the day that [General William T.] Sherman got into Atlanta. Then followed days of weary marching through hunger and cold into Tennessee, spilling blood like rain at Franklin, and Nashville, and Murfreesboro and other places, and on until defeat came to our cause and the 'Bonnie Flag' was folded tenderly," Methvin wrote. "And we marched more to endure the vicious reconstruction period. But the Bonnie Blue Flag still stirs our hearts, and we still shout response when the band plays 'Dixie.'"

His patriotism for the Southern cause in this letter and in writings from his autobiography is evident. The only regret he mentions is the death of his brother—rather than the senselessness the war or even the doomed Southern fight for racial superiority and their rights to slavery.

Another murky issue is how Methvin blurred the facts about the death of his brother, Thomas, and the fall of Atlanta as both having occurred on the same day. Thomas died Aug. 31, 1864 amid heavy Confederate losses during the Battle of Jonesboro—which led Atlanta to fall into Gen. Sherman's hands on Sept. 2, 1864. Methvin's version skews the truth to link the tragic fate of his brother with the shocking milestone of Atlanta's passage into Yankee hands.

Perhaps the most troubling part of Methvin's Civil War tales is his failure during the majority of his life to mention his role as a prison guard at the notorious Andersonville Confederate prison. Built as Camp Sumter in Georgia, the prison was meant to hold no more than 10,000 Union prisoners of war. Some 13,000 prisoners died there of the 45,000 held in captivity for a little over a year during the prison's operations. Union soldiers who arrived were ushered into an open area called "the pen" that had little protection from the sun and cold. Confederate surgeon Dr. J.G. Roy estimated that from 30,000 to 35,000 prisoners (most suffering from scurvy, chronic diarrhea, malaria, and starvation) were confined there. Dr. Roy said it "was dangerous for a man to open his mouth at sundown" due to insects—such as white-winged ants—and from maggots living in "animal and vegetable matter" in the swamp near the prison. Federal prisoner Martin E. Hogan described half-naked men crawling on the ground in search of food, while others burrowed into the ground for shelter. Hogan saw a prison "dissecting room" where he "saw students in the pursuit of knowledge sawing open the skulls of deceased prisoners and opening their bodies."

Methvin's view about Andersonville was that the prison had been portrayed unfairly, according to a magazine article written by one of his relatives, journalist Eugene Methvin.

In previous writings, the preacher made no mention of his time at Andersonville until the age of 84.

"Much has been said about the treatment

A view of the southeast side of Andersonville Prison in Georgia. Captured Union soldiers were held in the interior section called the pen. Surrounding the pen was a perimeter called the "dead line" where guards shot to death any prisoners who crossed over the uncovered section. Union prisoner J.D. Kieser saw a Confederate guard shoot a starving man in the head when he reached over the dead line to retrieve a piece of moldy food. A Confederate had thrown a rotting piece of bread or cake, which was supplied from the Union. Wooden stockade fences and banks of cannons surrounded Andersonville. As a guard, Methvin's duties would have included punishing prisoners. Guards often fired their guns at night to scare the prisoners. The guards lived beyond the wooden walls (lower right) in huts and tents. Illustration (circa 1890) courtesy of the Library of Congress.

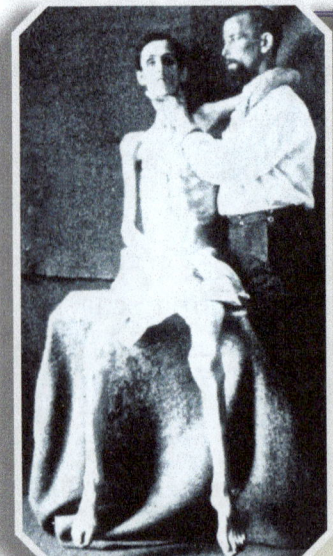

A former Union prisoner from Andersonville is examined. Prisoners were exchanged between the North and South during the Civil War. Annapolis physician B.A. Vanderkieft treated over 2,000 prisoners from Andersonville after they were traded. The doctor said many were handed over both in a dying condition and as living skeletons. Photo (1861–1864) courtesy of the Library of Congress.

of prisoners at that place, and much that was untrue," the preacher said.

Yet, Andersonville commander Capt. Henry Wirz was convicted of war crimes in 1865 by a military tribunal after the Civil War for ordering guards to shoot prisoners to death; murdering several prisoners (i.e., kicking to death); sending dogs to hunt escapees; injuring and destroying lives through torture and suffering; providing insufficient and unwholesome food to Union prisoners; and exposing prisoners to inclement weather, including the dews and burning summer sun. Capt. Wirz and another man were the only two Confederates to be convicted of war crimes. Wirz died on the gallows in November 1865.

Despite widespread national condemnation of the horrors at Andersonville, the preacher Methvin wrote: "Prison life is always hard, especially in war prisons. But federal prisoners were not treated with any intentional cruelty, and they suffered no more than Southern men in Northern prisons."

What makes this statement all the more outrageous is that Methvin's older brother William was captured during the war and incarcerated in Johnson's Island Union prison in Ohio. There Confederate prisoners lived in barracks, ate in mess halls, had latrines, and could amuse themselves in projects, shop in the sutler's store, or read newspapers. It is difficult to imagine that Methvin failed to contrast his experience of the horrors of prison life at Andersonville with the almost hotel-like confinement of his brother at

Thirteen thousand of our men died in the Andersonville prison pen.

Union prisoners were kept out in the open without barracks in inhumane conditions. Up to 35,000 prisoners were kept in overcrowded conditions. With no shelter from the hot sun or winter cold, prisoners burrowed into the ground for cover. Each hole could hold up to 4 men. The bodies of 13,181 dead Union soldiers were buried at Andersonville Prison. This newspaper notice (above) was published in May 16, 1865 in the *Evening Star* in Washington, D.C. (circa 1890) courtesy of the Library of Congress.

EXTRA

Execution of Henry Wirz.

The Andersonville Jailor Expiates His Crimes on the Gallows.

The curtain has fallen upon the WIRZ tragedy. That graceless wretch has paid the penalty of his crimes so far as this world i[s]

News of the military trial, conviction, and hanging of Capt. Henry Wirz made headlines around the United States. The *Daily National Republican* published the above headline after the execution in Washington, D.C. on Nov. 10, 1865. The death sentence was read to Wirz along with the verdicts of 11 charges which included: torturing prisoners (hanging by their thumbs); injecting poison substances under the pretense of vaccines into prisoners (causing them to lose the use of their arms or die); setting dogs upon escapees to seize, tear, and mangle them.

Johnson's Island.

In regard to Andres Martinez, the preacher ensured he maximized this relationship to his advantage. When Andres returned to the Kiowa reservation, he was at a critical point in his life. The former Hispanic captive was no longer illiterate, no longer viewing himself as a Native, and no longer living a passive life of subsistence as a menial laborer in a blacksmith's shop. Andres was among the Kiowas he loved while looking to make his place in the white man's world.

A soldier tests the trap door on the gallows before the execution of Andersonville commander Capt. Henry Wirz for war crimes (1865). Other soldiers stand in the background in tree branches. Photo by Alexander Gardner, courtesy of the Library of Congress.

Methvin seized the chance to use Andres and his established trust with the tribe to expand the preacher's reach into Native lives. First, Methvin hired Andres as an interpreter and then as a vocational teacher at the Methvin Institute. Then Methvin converted Andres, presided over his church wedding, and helped the Hispanic become a fellow preacher on the reservation.

As a Methodist, Andres understood better than Methvin how to fit that brand of Christianity into Native culture. If Methvin viewed Indians and their traditions as inferior, Andres did not. Therefore, Andres was an important instrument in Methvin's success as a minister and educator in the cultural assimilation of Natives. As a reverend, Andres assisted Methvin in his ministry. A local newspaper in Oklahoma mentions Andres assisting at a funeral conducted by 86-year-old Methvin in September 1933.

Later in his life, Methvin spoke about how important Andres was in the missionary work with the Natives.

"Martinez is and has been for these years a greater force for the uplift of the Indians than any other force in their midst, either of church or government. It is a long way from the tepee and tom-tom steeped in superstitious worship to the temple of God with its songs of prayer and praise. Martinez is now a minister of the gospel," Methvin remarked.

Of all Methvin's religious converts, Andres became the most famous due to Methvin's book about the Hispanic's captivity as a youth. Methvin called Andres a friend, but never gave him credit in the book, which the preacher dedicated to young Methodists.

In demand for sermons and speeches, Methvin was known for his faithful attendance at annual Southern Methodist conferences. "No conference was quite complete without him and his friend, Andres Martinez," recalled fellow Methodist preacher Sidney Babcock.

With Andres at his side, Methvin could demonstrate publicly his success among the Native people, with whom he viewed as inferior.

"There never was a people, perhaps, in whom there was so little upon which to base a hope of building a civilization," Methvin wrote. "No homes or home life, no enterprise, no written language, but wild, nomadic, barbarous, savage, their glory the glory of war and plunder, their religion that of bloody revenge, the conscience and moral instinct dead."

It mattered little that Andres was not an Indian. His longtime association with the Kiowas and knowledge about their culture was sufficient. Methvin exploited Andres, using him as a prop in demonstrations of Methvin's religious power to convert undesirables.

John Jasper Methvin, Methodist preacher to the Kiowas, Comanches, and Apaches in Oklahoma, died at age 94 in 1941. His efforts to eradicate important cultural traditions of the Plains Indians on the reservation were opposed by famed Comanche chief Quanah Parker.

Chapter 17: Indian Captives

Often untold are the fates of Native women and children captured as war bounty and turned into slaves in New Mexico. Most of these people vanished into time. Indian women who were mature and brave enough tried to escape and journey by themselves to return to their people. Their children had less of a chance to rejoin their tribes. Only on rare occasions would they be traded back to their people. Instead, they lost their cultural identities and faced a hard life performing domestic work or manual labor for people who exploited them. Some formed their own communities as Genizaros under the Spanish Crown.

To better understand the plight of many of these Indian captives in New Mexico, it is useful to examine how they fared under the Hispanics and the Americans. There were differences in how some Native captives were treated under each invader.

Under the Conquistadors

Native people who lived in and roamed through New Mexico experienced hardships—including oppression, murder and capture—during conquests of the area by Spain, Mexico and, finally, the United States. The Indian tribes were composed of two types: villagers (whose homelands extended into what is now Arizona and Colorado, but were mostly located alongside the riverbeds of the Rio Grande) and nomads (who roamed in certain geographic areas or ventured onto another's turf). Despite

This Spanish morion helmet (made to protect from blows to the head and provide a shield from the sun) was found near Grants, N.M. near Navajo lands. It is engraved on each side: with Jesus on the cross, and with Our Lady and the Christ child. It is on display at the Palace of the Governors in Santa Fe. Oñate listed armor in the inventory of items he brought to N.M. in 1598. A full suit weighed about 60 pounds.

This backplate (below) was found along the Rio Grande near Socorro, near traditional Apache hunting grounds. The bullet hole shows the Spanish soldier was shot below the left shoulder blade. It is shown in the Albuquerque Museum. Photos by Noël Fletcher.

An illustration of the fortified town of Alburquerque, in the Extremadura region of Spain, by Alain Manesson Mallet (1696), courtesy of Wikimedia Commons.

similar core beliefs and customs, not all tribes spoke the same language or shared the same traditions. Nomads raided villagers. Hard feelings could lead tribes to join with foreigners in such roles as scouts in the military or local retaliatory actions against nomadic tribes.

Spanish settlers moved into New Mexico after Conquistador Don Francisco Vasquez de Coronado claimed it in 1540 during the first La Entrada (entrance). Most Spanish settlements in New Mexico were located along the Rio Grande (which was also called Rio del Norte) adjacent to Indian villages (called Pueblos).

Many explorers (Hernan Cortes, Vasco Nunez de Balboa, Francisco Pizzaro, Hernando de Soto, and Francisco de Orellana) as well as my Perea family members came to the New World from a mountainous region of Spain called Extremadura, also known as the Cradle of the Conquistadors. I was born in Albuquerque, which takes it name from a city (Alburquerque) in Extremadura, also the site of Moorish castle and other architecture dating back to the rule of Muslim invaders. The Pereas, who made their home along the banks of the Rio Grande between Albuquerque and Santa Fe, were descended from Spanish Arabs and took their surname from an Arabic word "Bariya," meaning wilderness east of the River Jordan.

In January 1598, 200 Spanish colonists (including soldiers, wives, and Catholic priests) came in an expedition and formed communities along the Rio Grande. Other expeditions followed. The Spaniards lived in great isolation in small communities and far away from others, including supplies and military reinforcements. Nearly 100 years after settling in New Mexico, there were less than a total of 3,000 Spaniards living in communities including the capital city Santa Fe. [One indication of the isolation of Spaniards in New Mexico (compared to other colonies in California, Texas, and Florida) is that the Spanish language there is archaic — with words

A statue of Don Francisco Cuervo y Valdes, who founded Albuquerque, N.M. on April 23, 1706 stands outside the old Spanish community called Old Town. (Sculpture by Buck McCain, 1988). Photo by Noël Fletcher.

dating back to the 1500s and 1600s used today in New Mexico, but no longer in Spain. The Hispanics in New Mexico spoke Spanish without the influence of Mexican dialects and preserved the words in use hundreds of years ago by the Conquistadors. This rarity continues to interest present-day Spanish-language scholars.]

Today, many Hispanic families in New Mexico can trace their relatives to the conquistadors. Several of my family members came to New Mexico with Don Juan de Oñate in 1598, including my two grandmothers Catalina Perez de Bustillo and Catalina Lopez. On my Candelaria grandfather's side, three of his ancestors (a soldier and his two brothers) also joined Oñate during his exploration up the Rio Grande. Pausing during their journey, the explorers stopped at a spring beneath a massive sandstone cliff called El Morro, today a national monument. There, my ancestor Jose de la Candelaria carved his name alongside Oñate's. During the late 1600s, my grandmother's Perea family joined Diego de Vargas in Spain's reconquest of Santa Fe after numerous Pueblo Indians rose up in a revolt against the Spaniards.

During what is known as the Pueblo Revolt of 1680, Native male runners carried knotted yucca cords to each Pueblo village and told them to untie one knot each day until a single date when all would revolt. The knotted rope (a symbol of Pueblo strength and unity) and the Pueblo Revolt are celebrated by Natives today as the first successful revolution of indigenous people against a North American colonizer that preserved their way of life and sovereignty.

On Aug. 10, 1680, natives from several Pueblos simultaneously attacked Spanish colonists, including 2,500 warriors who besieged Santa Fe for several days, killing five Spanish captains and wounding others. During the insurrection, the Natives massacred nearly 400 men, women and children. Among the dead were 73 men capable of bearing arms, 68 children, 45 women, 12 Indian servants, and 21 Franciscan priests. The survivors were driven 330 miles away to present-day El Paso, Texas.

Today, it is common to condemn all early Spanish settlers in New Mexico's history for crimes against Natives while ignoring the fact that blood was shed by both Indians and Spaniards. I don't condone the wanton slaughter of anyone. Some Spaniards mistreated and enslaved Natives, but not all relations between them were bad.

For example, Hispanics in the town of Bernalillo, where many of my Perea family members settled, celebrate an important religious feast day in their Catholic faith to their patron saint, St. Lawrence (San Lorenzo). The Spaniards were on such good terms with their neighbors at Sandia Pueblo before the Pueblo Revolt that the Indian villagers warned them to flee or be killed on the day of the uprising, which was St. Lawrence's Feast Day. The Spaniards abandoned Bernalillo (located between Santa Fe and Albuquerque), praying to St. Lawrence for their safety, which they obtained and commemorate to this day with an annual town celebration on his Aug. 10 Feast Day.

The Spaniards retook their lost territory 12 years later and freed 88 captives. Among those were 19 Spanish women who had been held captive by Natives for 12 years and had *Mestizo* (mixed race) children born during that time.

The Spanish Crown acknowledged Pueblo sovereignty, in the

Spanish explorer Francisco Vasquez de Coronado and his soldiers camped in what is now Bernalillo, N.M. between 1540 and 1542 during his search for the Seven Cities of Gold. Photo by Noël Fletcher.

A much-loved statue of St. Lawrence, the patron saint of Bernalillo, that is kept by a chosen family for one year, starting on his feast day Aug. 10, also the date of the Pueblo Revolt. This statue is paraded through town by the Catholic devotional group called the Matachines dancers (*danzantes* in Spanish). Photo by Noël Fletcher.

first international recognition for the Native communities as semi-autonomous municipalities with inherent self-government rights. Canes were presented to each Pueblo in recognition by the Spanish Crown for their land grants and governmental rights.

So few Spanish settlers were surrounded on all sides by indigenous Natives, who could have easily wiped them out if the two groups had not learned to coexist. The settlers had a limited amount of munitions, supplies and reinforcements. They had to learn to get along with the Natives. For hundreds of years, Spanish became the language of trade and commerce between the Natives and the settlers.

The entrance to the sanctuary of St. Lawrence in Bernalillo, which was built around 1857 by members of my Perea family to serve the community. Many of the Pereas, including Jose Leandro Perea and his wife, were buried under the floor of this former church. It is now used by the Matachines, who are raising money with their dances to restore it. Photo by Noël Fletcher.

Matachines dance on the Feast Day of San Lorenzo on Aug. 10, also the date of the Pueblo Revolt. Toros (bulls) dressed in red and black (left) symbolize paganism, evil and temptation. The danzantes (right) wear crowns of their patron saints and through their dance overcome their temptations. The Matachines is of ancient Spanish-European origin, and was influenced by Arab traditions during the Moorish occupation of Spain. The custom of veiling the face and eyes is Arabic. Photo by Noël Fletcher.

Genizaros

After the Pueblo Revolt and the Reconquest of New Mexico, the Spaniards and Pueblo Indians lived in relative peace with each other. However, there were military expeditions conducted from time to time against nomadic Native tribes (such as Apaches, Comanches, Utes, and Navajos) and in retaliation for raids upon Spanish settlers as well as theft of their horses and livestock.

During the 1700s, the Spanish settlements prospered and Royal Roads (known as *Camino Real*) were established linking Santa Fe to Mexico City in trade routes. The Spaniards also kept census records of local populations and churches made detailed accounts of the backgrounds of people who married, which helped prevent close intermarriages. My Perea family, for example, counted themselves among less than a dozen families who were business, political and community leaders. Many of these families, mine included, were particular about their bloodlines and arranged marriages between those of Spanish descent. Others wed Natives (called *Indios*) and those of mixed blood (known as *Mestizos*). The Catholic Church carefully recorded the races of the people who received the Sacraments of marriage and baptism.

A Spanish "casta" (caste) painting from Mexico showing 16 racial classifications from colonies in the Americas, circa 1700s. Courtesy of Wikimedia Commons. The 1790 Spanish census for the Province of New Mexico lists 8 ethnic types: *Coyote* (3/4 Indian, 1/4 Spanish), *Color quebrado* (broken color in Spanish for mixed-race), *Lobo* (wolf in Spanish for 1/4 Indian, 3/4 black), *Mestizo* (usually Spanish, Indian mixed race), Spanish, *Genizaro,* and Mulato (1/2 black, 1/2 white).

In New Mexico, the Spaniards used a little known term called *Genizaro* to define a displaced person whose parents came from diverse nations. *Genizaros* were usually captive Indians and others, such as people rescued during an encounter with a nomadic tribe, who found themselves caught between two worlds—the Spanish and tribes. Scholars contend that not even in Mexico or other regions in Spain's New World was the term *Genizaro* used for such displaced people as those found in New Mexico. *Genizaros* could also be used to describe nomadic Native children taken from ancestral lands during military raids and brought back to live among the Spanish as servants and laborers.

In colonial New Mexico, 60 families of *Genizaros* were known to live in two settlements south of Albuquerque called Tomé and Our Lady of Belen. In these frontier towns, the *Genizaros* had their own communities to help provide armed protection against marauding tribes.

For example, a 1790 census of a *Genizaro* settlement in Belen listed a plaza area under a commander named Marcos Velasquez (a *Mestizo* shoemaker) who had jurisdiction over 35 Indian families living there who had converted to Christianity as adults. A commander such as Velasquez could protect his outpost from attacks.

These Native and mixed-race *Genizaros* lacked a unifying tribe so they lived under Spanish protection as a separate class of citizens until increased intermarriages with Hispanics ensued in the 1800s and records stopped tracking *Genizaros*.

RACIAL PREJUDICES

Growing up among Hispanics in New Mexico, I was aware that many of them view Native Americans poorly, so much so that one way to insult another for being uncivilized is to call that person a *Navajose* (Navajo) in Spanish. Although Hispanics have lived side-by-side with Indians for centuries, both cultures tolerate each other and can work together but their personal lives are mostly kept apart. There can be mutual suspicion.

Also Hispanics and Native cultures pass down oral histories in families. These personal stories can include instances of mistreatment at the hands of another race. For example, my great-grandfather was a young boy with his mother at his family's ranch when a war party of Apaches in the mid-1800s came to their home while the men were afield. His mother recognized danger. When a scout peeked in her window and asked her in Spanish for a *sopaipilla* (deep-fried bread), which she was making, she turned as if to get him one and flung a pan of hot grease in his face. She scooped up my great-grandfather, threw him on the back of her horse and rode away for their lives.

The Pereas' ranch land extended from the middle ground range (shown above) to the Rio Puerco, a tributary of the Rio Grande, not far from the base of this mountain range where Mount Taylor, a stratavolcano, rises in the distance. Nomadic tribes would ride from the western ranges around the mountains and cross the plains into ranches like my great-grandfather's home, which was burnt to the ground by an Apache war party. Photo by Noël Fletcher.

When my great-grandfather turned around, he saw his home in flames and surrounded by a war party. From that time, he had no love for Indians of any kind. I don't condone this type of thinking, but I can understand how this trauma could taint his views.

On the other hand, I also understand anti-Hispanic discrimination by some Natives. As a young teen, I briefly dated the son of a prominent Pueblo artist.

My great-grandfather and his mother would have fled on horseback from the Apache war party through terrain like this, which is located close to where their ranch would have been. Photo by Noël Fletcher.

A 12-year-old Native girl from an unknown tribe is shown as a servant in a Taos, N.M. household in 1860.

He belonged to two different Pueblos: half-Acoma and half-Jemez. We went to the movies, got hamburgers together, hung around at school, and talked and laughed together on the phone for hours at night—all pretty innocent. His mother despised me because I was Hispanic. She yelled at him constantly about me. What I didn't hear in the background on the phone, he would chuckle and tell me about. I mentioned this once to a woman acquaintance from another Pueblo. She laughed and told me her mother-in-law broke up a prior relationship her husband had with a Hispanic girl because his family wanted him to marry a Native. Non-Natives spouses are precluded from participating in many ceremonies.

NATIVES AS SPANISH PEONS

One thing that is not spoken about in relations between the two races is the use of Indians as servants in Hispanic households. It was quite a shock for me to discover it in my research, particularly in looking at census records from the 1700s and 1800s. Not only was I aghast to see the names of Native servants listed in the households of some of my family members, but it was equally as disturbing to see them in many other households as well. The ages of Indian servants ranged from 5 to 45 years old.

The practice at the time was to give Native servants the surnames of the head of the household, which can cause confusion for non-New Mexican genealogists who base assumptions on census records. A mistake was made by one such person that has been often repeated; erroneously claiming one of my relatives took advantage of a Native servant and married her. In reality, he married a distant cousin in his household who shared the same last name, which is documented in their church marriage records.

In 1860, one Santa Fe home belonging to wealthy merchant Jose M. Gallegos had over 20 servants including two Natives—a 7-year-old Apache boy and a 35-year-old Ute woman.

In that same year, in the household of Cubero merchant Clemente Sarracino there were six servants, including three Indians aged 4, 6, and 14. In southern Valencia county 44-year-old rancher Rafael Luna, his wife Dolores and their 5 children had 11 servants—including 7 Indians who ranged in age from a 55-year-old woman to a 6-year-old girl.

Equally upsetting was to learn how easily this "local custom" was accepted and practiced by Americans and others who came to New Mexico. In testimony in 1865 to U.S. Army officials about Indian relations, Santa Fe's Catholic Archbishop Jean-Baptiste Lamy, of France, declared: "There are a good many Navajo captives among the Mexican families; they make the best of servants. Some families abuse them, while others treat them like their own children. Most of the Mexican families have them; there are more than a thousand perhaps 2,000 or 3,000. Part of these captives have been taken in war by the Mexicans, and part have been purchased from the Indians, such as the Utes, who are constantly at war with the Navajos. These slaves have been bought and sold in this manner for years…"

When New Jersey-born Gen. Stephen Watts Kearny rode with his troops into Santa Fe in August 1846 and claimed New Mexico as part of the United States, local Hispanics did not perceive slavery as a concern. For hundreds of years, the Hispanics and Natives battled each other in periodic skirmishes and raids. Retaliation occurred on both sides, resulting in lost lives and captured women and children carried off by a victorious party. Sometimes, captives

Jean-Baptiste Lamy, a native of France came to N.M. and became the head of the Catholic Church in Santa Fe from 1853-1885 when its leadership changed from Mexico to the U.S. Although popular among the Americans, Lamy earned a bad reputation among many Hispanics that persists today for mistreating them as inferiors, threatening to excommunicate them for non-religious matters, and viewing their adobe churches as crude. Rather than promoting Hispanic priests, he imported non-Spanish speaking priests from France and Italy to administer to Hispanic communities. Lamy also used land donated to the Church by devout Spanish families and created himself a mountain lodge, elaborate gardens, and resplendent living quarters.

returned to their families via commercial transactions (through ransoming or bartering) or a successful escape. In addition, some Hispanics engaged in slave hunting, making expeditions to capture Southwestern Indians for sale as servants. Many Hispanics viewed these practices as a legitimate form of peonage, particularly in northern New Mexican cities such as Santa Fe and Taos.

Known as El Leoncito (Little Lion), Col. Manuel Antonio Chaves (1818–1889) was a distinguished military man and rancher. He described to journalist Charles F. Lummis how his brother Pedro took orders from Hispanics to capture Navajo girls at $500 each to sell as house servants.

A group of villagers would attack a band of hostile Navajos. Then he would get his fellow villagers together to "strike a band of hostile Navajos, kill the warriors and bring the women and children home for servants."

Prevailing attitudes about Indians captured into servitude can be found in oral histories taken in 1936 in New Mexico during a Depression Era federal writer's project.

Col. Manuel Antonio Chaves.

In one, Sarah Garcia told about how Navajos attacked her great-grandfather's home and killed two of her grandfather's brothers. In revenge, her great-grandfather left a month later to attack an Indian village. During the fight, he lost another son, but captured a Navajo girl. "The girl grew up to be a great help to the family. Later she married a Spanish youth. She died only a few years ago, leaving to survive her a daughter, whom we love as if she were our own blood."

Another point of view came from an interview in northern N.M. with Frank Garcia about the town of Questa near the Colorado border. He described the richest man in town in 1830 as being Don Benito, who had 30 Indian servants. "The Indian slaves seemed to enjoy the hard work under their master, performing their daily tasks as faithfully as they could and hoping someday to be highly rewarded by their master. This valley at that time was covered by a dense forest so that the clearing of land was an important occupation for the Indian slaves."

Mountain trees rise from the hillsides around Questa, N.M., where Indian slaves were used by Don Benito in 1800s to clear the valley of dense forests. Photo by Zita Fletcher.

In the town of Las Vegas, Mary Elba C'de Baca talked about how her grandparents bought a sawmill and had "two Indian companions" Maria and Sabina. "She says that they were forced to work very hard. They arose at 4:30 every morning and prepared breakfast for the peons, who worked at the sawmill, and spent the rest of the day doing housework and other duties."

As a U.S. Army chaplain and Baptist missionary, Rev. Hiram Walker Read toured New Mexico in 1851 with paymaster Major John Randall Hagner. Read mentioned stopping 16 miles outside Santa Fe to stay at an old adobe known as Delgado's ranch, where the staff included slaves known as peons.

Writings from the 1800s indicate New Mexican Hispanics believed their treatment of Indian peons differed from that of Black slaves in the South and East Coast. They contended that Indian servants were treated as extended family members, who were allowed to marry whomever they chose, had offspring who were not considered servants, and were free to leave upon reaching maturity. In 1856, Josiah Gregg wrote about his experiences as a frequent traveler along the Santa Fe Trail into New Mexico. He said Native slaves usually were held in bondage until age 21. However, some remained in bondage for their entire life if kept ignorant about their ability to be freed upon reaching the age of independence.

Father Antonio Jose Martinez was a notable Taos priest whose 74-year lifespan saw New Mexico's transition from Spanish rule, Mexican governance, American occupation, and Territorial status. Two years before his death in 1867, Martinez gave his opinion about Indian slaves. "No, they are servants, and are well treated; if they marry, they are free to live in their master's house and pass their life as they please, the same as with the sons of Indians, who, if not married when attaining their majority, become free after their marriage."

Kirby Benedict, an Illinois attorney colleague of Abraham Lincoln, came to New Mexico

Judge Kirby Benedict (1811–1874) was a lawyer and friend of Abraham Lincoln and appointed to serve in N.M., where he was controversial on the bench and a known alcoholic who had enemies and admirers.

as a judge after being appointed in 1853 by President Franklin Pierce. A decade later, Benedict described his personal and judicial experiences with Native slaves. He noted that the majority were female Navajo women and children "taken by force, or stealth, or purchased…They are bought and sold by and between the inhabitants at a price as much as is a horse or an ox."

Benedict recalled presiding over a Valencia County District Court case in 1855 involving a wealthy woman "who claimed possession and services of a Navajo girl then 12 years old, and who had been held by the petitioner nearly 7 years."

The North and South had been battling each other during the Civil War when Benedict encountered another case of Native slavery in 1862. An elderly man took an Indian woman to court for seeking her freedom. She had been "held in service for many years" after being sold as a child to the man. "The right of the master to the possession and services of the woman on one side, and the right of the woman to her personal freedom, were distinctly at issue," the judge remarked.

In both of the above cases, Benedict ruled that the Natives were free. "I held the claim of the master to be without foundation in law and against natural rights. In each of the cases, the party adjudged against acquiesced in the decision, and no appeal was ever taken." He described those having Indian slaves as "easily alarmed at any movements in the civil courts or otherwise to dispossess them of their imagined property."

Although Native slaves could go to N.M. courts to seek their emancipation, they generally did not. Benedict said he thought they "were so influenced by the circumstances which surround them they do not seem to think of seeking the aid of the law to establish the enjoyment of their right to freedom."

Indian slaves could spend most of their lives as servants to a family. This was true for three Native women who spent nearly 60 years waiting on the Romero family in Las Vegas. Serving as a sheriff for two terms starting in 1881, Hilario Romero bought Refugia and Maria for $100 each during a trip to Texas. They performed outdoor work for decades before being freed in their later years. Sheriff Romero gained his third Native servant named Felipa when her father in Mexico sold his daughter to repay a $200 debt. Felipa performed housework for the Romeros for a longer time period than the other servants and lived to an advanced age, according to an oral history in 1936.

A few months before seven Southern states in 1861 adopted the Constitution of the Confederate States of America, a New York newspaper published a blistering attack on New Mexico and its Hispanic population while denouncing pro-slavery elements within the Territory. The newspaper also attacked the peonage system in New Mexico, calling it debasing and a form of "modified slavery."

Miguel Antonio Otero penned an impassioned response from his post in the U.S. House of Representatives in Washington, D.C. that was reprinted in Santa Fe. In it, Otero denied peonage was a form of slavery. "It is merely a system of apprenticeship or temporary voluntary servitude, whereby a man is enabled to borrow money, or otherwise create a debt, and to give his personal service, at a stipulated rate of hire, as a security for the payment," Otero declared. The law allowed peons to change "from one temporary owner of his services to another whenever he becomes oppressed or unfairly treated." He objected to the term "debasing" because peons retained their civil rights and their families weren't under the same terms of servitude. "The social and political status of an individual is not affected by his entering into the condition of a peon," Otero said. "It is simply a voluntary engagement to render personal service at a stated hire for a valuable consideration."

Miguel Antonio Otero, a N.M. representative who served three terms in Congress, shown in his 2nd term in 1859. Photo by Julian Vannerson, courtesy of the Library of Congress.

It is important to note that although Otero denied peonage was a form of slavery, he held pro-slavery political views.

Chapter 18: Native captives under the U.S. Military

While researching this book, I read numerous military reports from U.S. Army officers in New Mexico's forts that discussed battles with nomadic Indians. Details included how many miles marched, efforts to locate Indians, skirmishes, livestock lost or found, soldier casualties, and the numbers of Native men killed—and the number of female captives taken. I wondered what the military did with the imprisoned Native women, particularly the Apaches and Navajos. Soldiers had orders to shoot any male Native old enough to bear arms. Rarely were nomadic Indian men taken prisoner. Usually they were killed on sight after the U.S. military declared war on a tribe.

I was taken aback to learn that members of the U.S. military in New Mexico were enslaving captive Native women and children and engaging in human trafficking.

In 1821, Spain transferred New Mexico to be governed by the new Republic of Mexico after it gained independence. Under the Plan of Iguala, all social and ethnic groups within the new republic (including Natives in New Mexico) were equal. And as Spain had done beforehand, Mexico presented special canes to each Pueblo in recognition of their sovereign status and right of self-governance over their lands. Government relations with the Pueblos were peaceful. However, Mexican soldiers fought from time to time with nomadic tribes such as the Navajos, Apaches and Comanches, with the latter tribe notorious for traveling to southern New Mexico and across the Mexican border to steal horses to use and trade.

Life changed little for Hispanics and Natives in New Mexico who lived under the Mexican flag for some 25 years until the United States annexed Texas from Mexico in 1845. This led to the U.S. Army's invasion of northern Mexico a year later, after General Kearny seized New Mexico.

A soldier at Fort Stanton in southern New Mexico takes a break in 1885. Source: Palace of the Governors.

As the Territory of New Mexico struggled to govern itself under American occupation, the legitimacy of black slavery emerged as the states began to take sides on the issue in the years leading up to the Civil War.

Black slaves were rare in New Mexico and introduced into the area by U.S. military officers, who brought their black servants with them to live in forts. In the early 1860s, for example, only 22 black slaves were listed as being in New Mexico. In fact, the U.S. war with the Navajos began after a warrior rode into Fort Defiance in 1858, after a fight with his wife, and shot a fatal arrow into the black slave "Jim" who served then-Major William Brooks. Rather than surrender the killer to the fort, the Navajos sought to pacify Major Brooks. "The Indians have offered Major Brooks several thousand sheep and 1,000 ponies to indemnify him for the loss of his Negro," noted an Ohio newspaper in September 1858. It described a battle that followed between Brooks and the Navajos, who previously "declared they would not fight and, in case of their refusal, the Major intended burning and destroying their wheat and corn fields, which, if done, would doubtless cause a collision between them and the troops."

William Thomas Harbaugh Brooks (1821-1870) born in Alabama and a West Point graduate. His refusal to let Navajos make amends for killing his black slave led to a prolonged U.S. war against the Navajos that resulted in thousands of deaths. Photo courtesy of Wikimedia Commons.

Despite prior peace treaties, a series of retaliatory attacks ensued that evolved into the U.S. military embarking into an all-out war on the Navajo people.

In 1848, 12 prominent N.M. political representatives, including one of my relatives named Juan Perea, assembled under governor Donaciano Vigil in Taos and created a petition to Congress. They asked for a civil government, to be kept from merging into Texas (which was pro-slavery) and protected against the introduction of slavery—which is ironic, given that Native captive servants were not considered slaves.

The plight of enslaved captive Indians was arguably more difficult than for blacks in the South because the Natives remained in captivity during a bureaucratic debate over a definition of slave vs. peon and were not freed until long after the Emancipation Proclamation.

Human trafficking of Indians was widespread. The peons were primarily captured nomads,

Juan Perea (above) and Donaciano Vigil (below).

including many Navajos.

"A healthy, intelligent girl of 8 years was worth $400 or more. Their children were not regarded as salable property, but treated as citizens," noted a federal government report.

On June 19, 1862, Congress endorsed a measure prohibiting slavery in United States territories, outlawing slavery in New Mexico.

At the end of the Civil War in 1865, government officials in New Mexico generally viewed the capture and enslavement of Natives as a legitimate form of peonage (not slavery) and/or rightful war booty that the victorious were entitled to take.

A military letter to the Inspector General in N.M. in September 1865 defended peonage as a voluntary service sanctioned by the President and law.

A Report to the Secretary of the Interior on Peonage in August 1865 noted 400 Indian captive servants in Santa Fe alone in a practice recognized as a way to obtain physical labor. "Their treatment varies with the whims and feelings of their holders. Sometimes they are, doubtless, better off than when free. The arguments to sustain the system are the same as those formerly used in behalf of [black] slavery. In spite of the stringent orders of the government, the system continues, and nearly every federal officer held peons in service. The superintendent of Indian Affairs had half a dozen. The practice of federal officers sustained it."

In fact, testimony before Congress related that most military and government officials, including Indian Agents, owned captive Native slaves.

One surprising discovery I made about Americans who held captive Indian slaves involved Kit Carson. Not only did he help track and kill Indians in New Mexico, but he had a 22-year-old female Native servant named Juana Maria Carson living in his household in Taos as a captive slave for his wife and children. When I visited Kit Carson's Home & Museum in Taos, I was told by workers that he was so friendly with Natives that he and his Hispanic wife Josefa ransomed 3 captive Navajo children, who were raised as part of the family. In fact, this information is even on the museum's website. Yet, when I asked for details about the names of the children, wondered where their photos were among the family photos on display, and inquired what happened to them, the staff could provide no answers. It makes no sense that since Kit Carson led a military hunt against Navajos, particularly at a time when they would be at their weakest, he would "rescue" 3 of their children. Who did he save them from? A year earlier, he was promoted to the rank of 2nd Lieutenant in the U.S. Mounted Riflemen as part of the military effort to kill Navajos. I have met many Hispanics in New Mexico whose families date back to the Conquistadors, like mine, and have heard their oral histories ranging from the 1700s to the 1800s about how an Indian child was adopted into a family and raised among them. They always know who he or she was and what happened to them because those Natives became part of that family's history. But I found no such evidence with the Carson family. The fact that Kit Carson had a captive Native slave/servant in his home in 1860 as he was making a

Entrance sign in Taos to the adobe home where Christopher "Kit" Carson lived with his third wife, Josefa, after he married into her wealthy Hispanic family. Photo by Noël Fletcher.

Interior courtyard (left) of what is now the Kit Carson museum in Taos. A hide faces the wall in the living room (*sala* in Spanish) next to a fireplace in Kit Carson's former home near the downtown Plaza in the city. Photos by Noël Fletcher.

name for himself as a famed Indian killer doesn't match with the popular myth of this man.

Some may view Carson as a hero, but I do not. It was disturbing to read his exploits against the Navajo (who traveled in nomadic groups with their women and children), how he relentlessly chased them starting in mid-1863 through the cold desert winter into 1864. It was Carson's idea to destroy their food sources, including numerous peach orchards that took years to grow in the wild, capture their livestock, and ruin their dwellings. I wondered how it was possible that such a brutal man could have lived among other Native tribes, even taking two Indian wives, yet use this intimate knowledge of how these indigenous people live and what they hold sacred to use against them.

I read numerous documents attributed to Carson and learned he was illiterate, taking great pains to hide this fact. Therefore, he pretended to write reports that he dictated to others, putting his name on them to rise high to the rank of Colonel and command men. I believe his illiteracy was but one indication of his duplicitous nature. His possession of an Indian slave in his household is yet another example of his bad character.

A few officials tried to free captive Natives at the end of the Civil War. For example, in 1865 in northern New Mexico and Colorado, a local Indian Agent and deputy marshal visited white people who owned Indian slaves and ordered that the Natives be released, including Navajos who were to be returned to their people.

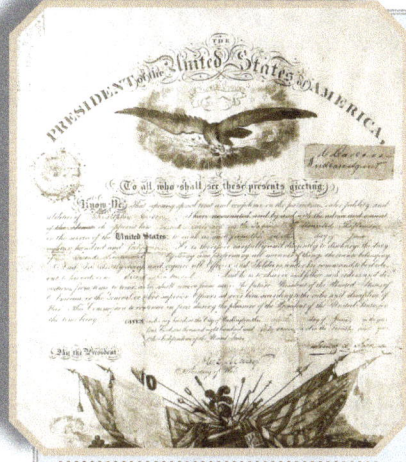

Kit Carson's certificate appointing him June 9, 1847 to the rank of Second Lieutenant in the U.S. Regiment of the Mounted Riflemen. It is displayed at the Kit Carson museum. Photo by Noël Fletcher.

The 1860 U.S. Census listing Christopher "Kit" Carson, his wife, children, and Indian servant/slave Juana Maria Carson, aged 22, from an unknown place of birth. She had Carson's surname, which was customary at the time to add to the names of captive Native slaves. It unknown what tribe she came from. In other 1860 surveys in N.M., next to the names of many captive Indians it listed their tribe, such as Ute, Apache, or Navajo.

However, the government was unsure what to do with orphaned Ute children, who were homeless. "There are captives here who know not their own parents, nor can they speak their mother tongue, and who recognize no one but those who rescued them from their merciless captors. What are we to do with these?" asked Lafayette Head, a U.S. Indian Agent.

Despite such efforts, the practice continued. An 1866 government report on Indian affairs listed 2,000 Natives held as captives or peons in New Mexico. It noted a practice, sanctioned by Territorial law, in which whites were encouraged to conduct voluntary campaigns against Natives and could keep any "plunder" obtained as a reward for their services. They were instructed to report all Native captives seized to Territorial officials, but "the captives are either sold, at an average of $75 to $400, or held in possession in practical slavery. This state of things of course keeps up a state of hostility among the Indians." The report asked for Congress to intervene to stop this form of slavery.

One Indian Agent reported that Navajos told him of several cases of their children being held as peons, and failed attempts by parents and tribal leaders to recover the captured children. "Although this is directly contrary to existing laws, I am convinced that any litigation would go against the Navajos" due to prejudice from local civil officials, the agent wrote. "I earnestly request that, if possible, some steps be taken to do away with this system of peonage and have the children that are held against their will returned to their parents, as the Navajos love their children and I think (and they claim) that they are entitled to the same as any other race of

> **OFFICE SUPERINTENDENT OF INDIAN AFFAIRS,**
> *Santa Fé, New Mexico, May 19, 1863.*
>
> SIR: I have the honor herewith to enclose a translation of a letter received from San Isidro, in the county of Santa Ana, informing me that some friendly Navajo Indians have been murdered in the neighborhood of that place. Besides the child which is mentioned in the letter as having been sold at Corrales, I am informed that another has been sold in the Rio Abajo, and that they are both the children of two of the murdered Navajoes.
>
> Whilst this condition of things exists, your excellency will readily perceive that it will be impossible to keep peace with the Indians.
>
> If the citizens are permitted to commit these enormous outrages upon the Indians with impunity from punishment by our courts, we must expect that the Indians will seek their own redress in their own way, and thus make the innocent suffer with the guilty. This should not be; the authority of the law should be imposed to prevent its longer continuance, and the duty of seeing that the laws are faithfully executed being devolved upon you as the executive officer of the Territory, I demand that you require the proper officers to arrest those guilty of these murders and the robbery and sale of those children, and hold them to answer before the courts for the offence.
>
> I am informed that one of the children before mentioned was sold in Corrales, in Bernalillo county, and the other in or near Albuquerque.
>
> Very respectfully, your obedient servant,
>   J. L. COLLINS,
>   *Superintendent Indian Affairs, New Mexico.*
>
> His Excellency W. F. M. ARNY,
>   *Acting Governor of New Mexico.*

This letter shows that some U.S. officials were concerned about the slavery of Natives. The children mentioned were sold following the murder of their Navajo parents. I was shocked to learn that one child was sold in Corrales, where my Perea family lived since 1780.

people."

While the federal government and its Indian Agents grappled with the issue of Indian slavery, Congress began to take note. Insightful testimony was given to Washington lawmakers by Georgia physician Louis Kennon, who had lived in New Mexico for 12 years and was familiar both with the system of peonage and black slavery. "I think the Navajos have been the most abused people on the continent," declared Dr. Kennon, who said the system of peonage in New Mexico was worse than slavery in the South because there was "no obligation resting on the owner to care for the slave when he becomes old or worthless."

Eventually Congress passed the Peonage Abolition Act of March 1867 that outlawed this form of slavery and servitude in New Mexico. People were so reluctant to give up their Native captives that Herman Heath, acting governor of N.M., issued a proclamation in June 1868 promising to punish anyone found in violation of the laws who retained peons.

An Indian girl, mostly likely a captured servant, stands next to Lydia, the wife of Lt. William Bartlett Lane, and her 2 daughters in front of their quarters at Fort Union, N.M. in 1867. Mrs. Lane wrote a book published in 1892 called *I Married a Soldier, or Old Days in the Army.* Penned under Lydia Spencer Lane, the book is famous for depicting her life as a military wife on the Western frontier. Photo courtesy of the Daughters of the U.S. Army Collection, U.S. Army Heritage and Education Center, Carlisle, Pa.

This advertisement appeared in *The Santa Fe Weekly Gazette* on April 29, 1854. It shows the $30 value of a child slave, owned by Capt. Issac Bown of N.Y., who was stationed at Fort Union, N.M. and attached to the commissary department. He died in 1858 in Louisiana.

FIFTY DOLLARS REWARD.

A Reward of FIFTY DOLLARS will be paid for the apprehension and delivery, at this place, of Marcelino Fierro, and a woman calling herself Francisca, living with the said Marcelino, who left this place on Saturday the 22d instant, taking with them a boy about three months old, the child of a servant girl the property of the undersigned, and also a boy of their own, about fourteen months old.

The above reward will be paid for the delivery of the above mentioned persons with the child, or thirty dollars will be paid for the child alone.

ISAAC BOWEN,
Capt. U. S. A.

Alburquerque New Mexico,
April 27 1854, 2w-

Lt. W.T. Sherman issued a military order in September 1868 to reclaim from peonage the Navajo women and children held in slavery in New Mexico, who were in need of "the friendly assistance of the officers of our government." It declared that help would be provided to a tribe or individuals who wanted to search for missing women and children thought to be in bondage. "If any woman be married away from her tribe, she should be permitted to have free choice of action. If unmarried and held as a servant, the officer should explain to her her rights under the law and leave her free to choose, satisfying himself that she receives wages and understands her true position." The order also provided instructions about how to repatriate former captive children to their tribes.

Unlike with the nomadic Native tribes whose homelands were in New Mexico, President Abraham Lincoln presented this silver-handled cane to the governor of Cochiti Pueblo and 18 other Pueblo (village) governors to acknowledge their sovereign rights to govern their tribal lands. This photo is on display at the Indian Pueblo Cultural Center Museum in Albuquerque.

To get its message across, the government publicized arrests in local newspapers for people who continued to hold Indian slaves. For instance, a local senator from Taos County named Juan Benito Valdes was arrested for holding 10 Indian slaves in violation of law and brought before the U.S. District Court. In another action, from 200 to 300 people from Taos and Rio Arriba were summoned to the same court on charges of illegally holding Navajo captives. However, the Grand Jury didn't indict anyone on the charges.

In the concluding chapters, I provide cases of captured Natives whose stories have been documented. While some of these people weren't from New Mexico, they undoubtedly shared similar fates as those taken from New Mexico. It is my hope that providing this information about the tragic fates of these lost and abused people will promote greater understanding, tolerance and goodwill among people of all races.

Chapter 19: Wilson Graham: Captive Arapaho boy found in Circus

A young Arapaho boy shown in his village in 1892. Photo by James Mooney, courtesy of The Smithsonian Institution.

Often the fates of captive Native children went unknown. Although the following case involved an Arapaho boy who was not from New Mexico, what happened to him may have occurred with other captive Indian children.

In late 1876, General Winfield Scott Hancock was tasked with locating two Native children (a brother and his sister) who as babies were thought to be the only captive survivors of the Sand Creek Massacre in Colorado Territory. The massacre occurred when Col. John M. Chivington led nearly 700 U.S. Volunteer Cavalry soldiers with howitzers to attack a village containing peaceful and friendly Indians: hundreds of Cheyenne and Arapahos. The camp was occupied at the time of the attack by mostly the aged, women and children. Atrocities were committed against the 200 Natives who were murdered.

"I tell you Ned it was hard to see little children on their knees have their brains beat out by men professing to be civilized…They were all horribly mutilated…You would think it impossible for white men to butcher and mutilate human beings as they did there, but every word I have told you is the truth, which they do not deny. It was almost impossible to save any of them (the Indians)," wrote Capt. Silas S. Soule, who refused to fire during the

A ledger drawing of the Sand Creek massacre by a Cheyenne eyewitness and artist named Howling Wolf, who was 15 years old at the time. The troops (shown on the left) attacked the camp while the warriors were away hunting. Mostly women and children were butchered and their were corpses mutilated. Image courtesy of Wikimedia Commons.

massacre and wrote about it to his former commander Major Edward "Ned" Wynkoop to seek justice for the slain Natives.

Years later, a band of Cheyennes went to the U.S. military to seek the two surviving captive children. The boy was thought to be the heir of the tribal chief, noted Gen. Hancock's wife Almira, who wrote about the incident in 1887. A sergeant, who had been placed in charge of the children after the battle, said the girl died and admitted to giving the boy to a circus.

"The government, after considerable trouble, discovered him [the missing Native boy] in a traveling circus and he was sent to General Hancock to be duly delivered to the tribe that claimed him as chief," noted the *Philadelphia Evening Public Ledger*, in January 1921.

The child Wilson Graham was found in an acrobat's outfit. He had been named after Wilson and Graham's circus, where he was put on display as a curiosity and made to perform skits.

"Instinctively, this little fellow felt degraded by his association with the circus and would fly into a passion, with murderous intent depicted upon his face," if someone discussed the circus or asked him to impersonate Napoleon, George Washington, or other famous people, which were among the roles he had to fill in the show, wrote Almira, adding that he would

Capt. Silas Stillman Soule (1838-1865) was born in Kansas and opposed to slavery. He joined the Colorado volunteers under the Union Army. While in command of Company D, he was at the Sand Creek Massacre and refused to allow his men to fire at the Natives who were camped there under a Union flag as a sign of peace. He was horrified by the slaughter and mutilation of mostly women and children. He wrote a letter describing the atrocities he saw and sought to hold John Chivington, who led the massacre, accountable. Capt. Soule was shot to death a week after he testified against Chivington, who was never held accountable for the massacre. Photo courtesy of Wikimedia Commons.

not be bribed or forced to talk about the men in the circus. His only response was: "They are bad, wicked men. I want the General to kill them with his big guns."

Cheyenne leaders failed to recognize Wilson, who later was identified as an Arapaho and reunited with his tribe. A year later, an Army officer saw the boy, and Almira wrote about it.

She said "our former protégé, the little savage, [was] in a perfect state of nature, and with his hair to his shoulders. … this wild, untamed child, with bow and arrow strapped to his back, was none other than Wilson Graham, who had become a cruel, wicked fellow, and who was totally without sympathy for those [whites] who could have protected him had he been disposed to pursue other than the life that seemed to belong to his nature. Upon learning these facts it quite reconciled us, and totally dispelled the regret, and indeed the pain, that it cost General Hancock to give this poor little Indian boy up to his tribe…"

General Winfield Scott Hancock (seated) with his division commanders (circa 1861 to 1864). His wife wrote a book that discussed her husband's directive to find the missing Native boy who survived a massacre. She temporarily took the child (named Wilson Graham after the circus where he was forced to join) into her home. She had nothing but negative comments to make about the boy and lacked compassion. Photo courtesy of the Library of Congress.

Chapter 20: The Tragedy of Apache May

Moved by pity at finding an Apache baby left behind by her fleeing mother, a hardened Indian fighter, lawman rancher and killer of desperados saved the child from injury and possible death by vengeful Cavalry soldiers. Yet, John Horton Slaughter's compassion fell short of returning the rescued child to her people, who were being held against their will on an Arizona reservation.

Hatred against Apaches fomented throughout Arizona in May 1896 as Slaughter, who helped track Geronimo and assisted in the notable leader's surrender, joined an expedition with the 7th Cavalry to hunt for Natives thought to be responsible for the March 28, 1896 murder of Alfred Hands, a 23-year-old Englishman.

"The settlers here are wrought up to a high pitch over the murder," blared the *Arizona Republican* of Phoenix on April 2, 1896. News of Alfred's murder spread within days from surrounding New Mexico and Utah to as far away as New York and Washington, D.C.

Apache May after she was captured by John Slaughter after a cavalry raid on an Apache campsite in Arizona. Photo courtesy of Wikimedia Commons.

Alfred had a speech impediment and physical disability that rendered him partially paralytic. He stayed on the ranch and worked with the livestock while his brothers Frank and Edward conducted business and prospected. After returning from a one-day trip, they found their cabin ransacked, several horses stolen and Alfred's body outside. His head was smashed by rocks, his stomach cut open and his corpse riddled with bullet holes.

He was outdoors tending goats near Cave Creek when he encountered a band of several Apaches. The Hands ranch was located within an old Indian trail used for travel to and from

> **APACHES AGAIN.**
>
> **A Settler Is Killed and His Place Robbed.**
>
> SAN SIMON, Ariz., April 1.—The settlers here are wrought up to a high pitch over the murder of Alfred Hands by Apaches. Hands' head was crushed by rocks and his abdomen cut open. The Indians robbed his cabin and destroyed what they could not take away. Cowboys and a detachment of cavalry under Lieutenant Rice are in pursuit.
>
> The settlers will ask the territorial government to form a band of rangers to help exterminate this band of Apaches.

The murder of Alfred Hand, a disabled Englishman who tended to livestock at his ranch, was announced in the *Arizona Republican* on April 2, 1896.

Mexico. Initial reports speculated that Alfred's killers were disgruntled Apaches who had escaped the dreary life at the San Carlos reservation, where the former nomads found themselves under lockdown and no longer free to roam as they had done for centuries.

During the same time as Alfred's murder, a newspaper described a camp of "renegade" Apaches consisting of 3 men, 5 women, and a baby, who left the San Carlos reservation a few months earlier. The Apaches supposedly said they never intended to return because they didn't want to live near so many soldiers. Their camp consisted of huts, with their ponies grazing nearby. "Just beyond where they are camped is an almost inaccessible mountain country, just the place where these murderous Indians are wont to infest, and a regiment of soldiers could not dislodge them," said the newspaper.

Not all Apaches who fled the reservation became violent. However, when Natives were suspected of committing crimes, non-Native residents frequently sought to punish the first Indians they could find regardless of whether or not they had done anything wrong.

Led by Lieut. Sedgwick Rice of Minnesota, troops and scouts from C Troop of the 7th Cavalry rode over 50 miles from Fort Grant to investigate Alfred's death. Evidence indicated the presence of 7 to 8 Apaches. Another cavalry group with 58 men, including 12 Apache scouts, left Fort Huachuca to join the other soldiers. They were equipped with 30 days' rations. News reports provided updates in the search. Soldiers picked up a trail showing four warriors and one woman traveling with eight horses. Upon discovering a campsite, soldiers found items from the Hands' ranch strewn across the area: a packsaddle, a coat and vest belonging to Alfred Hands, silver coins, and a $20 gold piece. Excitement mounted

Lieut. Sedgwick Rice in 1891. Photo by John C.H. Grabill, courtesy of the Library of Congress. Retiring as a colonel, he served for 42 years in the military and is buried at Arlington National Cemetery.

Apache women and children await rations to be issued on the San Carlos reservation in the late 1800s. Their dwellings are located in the distance. Being forced to live on a reservation changed their whole way of life and some could not adjust and escaped. Photo by Camillus Sidney Fly, courtesy of The Smithsonian Institution.

as the cavalry reported they were gaining on the group and only 10 hours behind the Apaches, who left signs along the trail that they traveled mostly at night. A second empty campsite was encountered with more abandoned articles.

Apache warrior Massai in 1880. Photo by Camillus Sidney Fly, courtesy of Wikimedia Commons.

One theory was that band of Apaches was led by Massai, a Chiricahua warrior who escaped from a train taking him and other Apaches to be held as prisoners of war in a Florida fort with Geronimo. Massai and a Tonkawa Native named Gray Lizard left the train near St. Louis, Missouri and journeyed 1,200 miles by foot to an Apache tribal area in New Mexico. From there, Massai lived on the run and eventually would disappear in time.

Soldiers pursuing the Apaches were convinced that the same group was responsible not only for Alfred's death, but also for an earlier double-murder that shook Arizona.

On the evening of Dec. 7, 1895, cattleman J.L.T. Watters was riding through a valley to his home near Duncan when he caught sight of two horses attached to a farm wagon near Ash Springs. One horse (a colt) was tangled in the harness and lying pinned to the ground beneath the wagon pole.

Creeping closer to investigate, he found the body of Mormon farmer Horatio H. Merrill, of Pima. The farmer's head had been shot with bullets that passed through his mouth and heart. Closer to the wagon was his 16-year-old daughter Eliza, shot twice through her body.

Watters believed the pair had been dead for no more than an hour as both bodies were still warm. Neither body was mutilated. A short distance away from Eliza were her belongings, ripped apart from inside a satchel. She had packed a dress, underwear and other clothing, which was torn and scattered. The father and daughter were walking beside the two-horse wagon on their second day of a journey to take their produce to market when they were ambushed by a group of Indians. Tracks from two horses and two people in moccasins were found.

The cattle brand of John Slaughter, posted in the *Tombstone Epitaph* in 1898.

Watters covered the bodies with blankets and went to alert authorities. Later that night, a sheriff, judge, posse, and 9-man jury set out to examine the crime scene. The group "started for the dark and bloody ground" on the public road. There they encountered a "picture presented in the moonlight, the death like silence, an old man and young girl in the rigid embrace of death, [which] moved every heart with the solemnity of the surrounding," described the *Graham Guardian*, of Safford, Ariz. On Dec. 6, 1895. The cause of death was determined to be gunshot wounds fired by persons unknown, supposed to be Indian.

By the time April arrived in 1896, sentiment was growing against all Apaches. Alfred had died a terrible death. And, the *Tombstone Epitaph* noted that the federal government was less concerned for public safety and welfare than granting "unreasonable and dangerous liberties" to the Apaches. It reprinted correspondence from Arizona Congressional delegate Nathan Oakes Murphy, who requested that all local White Mountain Apaches be disarmed and banned from using firearms (also widely used for hunting game), which Secretary of War Daniel S. Lamont rejected as inadvisable.

John Horton Slaughter (1841–1922). Photo courtesy of Wikimedia Commons

Among the civilians who joined military efforts to capture the killers was former Cochise County sheriff John Slaughter, who had been born on a Southern plantation in Louisiana in 1841. He left to become a cowboy in Texas, where he became a famed Texas Ranger and joined the Confederate Army during the Civil War. His life was one of fighting others—Mexicans, Yankees, Indians, and outlaws. Slaughter moved his family to Arizona to ranch. After his wife died, he was aged 37 with two children when he made a business trip to Tularosa, N.M. There he met Cora Viola Howell, 18 years old, who was a descendant of Daniel Boone. They married despite her parents' opposition. They had no offspring but readily took children in need of a home into their 40,000-acre San Bernardino ranch at the Mexican border.

It was already May 15, 1896 and Slaughter was among the cavalry troops chasing the Apaches when news broke in the *Arizona Republican* about a military battle with 11 warriors and 7 women in a camp on the Sonora line. Two Apaches were thought wounded. After the altercation, the military party took everything in the campsite left by the fleeing Apaches—including their provisions, livestock and a baby. This is the first public appearance of the captive child who would be known as Apache May.

Slaughter is said to have seen the baby and feared that other members of the military party would injure or kill her in an act of vengeance. He determined to rescue the child so he took her home to raise her.

The military continued its pursuit and conducted another

> Apache May wore this dress when she was rescued by John Slaughter. The dress was crafted from a white cotton election poster taken from Alfred Hands' house when he was murdered. The poster had the names of candidates in blue ink. The dress was made from cut pieces of the poster, fashioned with both vertical and horizontal words. The leather vest was modified with straps to serve as a child carrier. The vest was identified as a bodice belonging to slain teen Eliza Merrill when she was gunned down. Photo courtesy of the Arizona History Museum.

> **CAUGHT THE APACHES.**
> A Military Command's Battle With the Redskins.
>
> TUCSON, Ariz., May 14.—Advices from San Bernardino ranch, located on the Sonora line in southeastern Arizona, say Lieutenant Averill's command overtook a band of eleven Apache bucks and seven squaws in camp in the Chiricahuas.
> There was a short engagement. Two Apaches are believed to be wounded.
> A pappoose and a lot of stock and the camp outfit of the redskins were captured.

> The first news about the capture of the Apache baby, who would be called "Apache May" in the *Arizona Republican* on May 15, 1896.

Cora Viola Slaughter (1860–1941). Photo courtesy of the John Slaughter Ranch Museum.

raid a few weeks later. The *Oasis* newspaper provided details about the raids on June 13, 1896. "In both instances, the camp was located at night and attacked at the first breaking of the dawn, the first intimation the renegades had of the proximity of the troops being the crack of their rifles," it noted. "On both occasions, the Indians abandoned their camps with everything in them, including their clothing, provisions, ammunitions, arms and field glasses—articles indispensable to the renegade. In the first camp was found clothing known to have been worn by Miss Merrill at the time she was murdered... In the other camp was found the property belonging to Hands, who was killed."

At the camp on June 13, officers discovered 4 warriors, 3 women, and 2 boys. The military captured one of the boys, about 7 years old, eight horses, saddles and the complete contents of the camp, noted the *Arizona Silver Belt* on July 2, 1896. It remarked that the troops destroyed items deemed worthless and the captive boy was taken by Slaughter, who already had Apache May at his home. It is unknown whether this second group of Apaches were involved with the murders or the child called Apache May.

"The boy is now at San Bernardino [ranch], and since he has found company in the person of the other Apache papoose, recently captured by ex-Sheriff Slaughter, takes kindly to his new home and expresses no regrets at not being with the band," declared *The Prospector* on June 27, 1896.

However, Slaughter apparently later returned the boy, described as too wild, to the Apaches on the reservation, but kept Apache May for himself rather than reuniting her with her tribe and possible relatives.

Of interest is that the clothing Apache May wore when she was rescued by Slaughter was made of items taken from Eliza Merrill and Alfred's ranch. She wore a leather vest (crafted from Eliza's clothing) that had been tailored to her small size and attached with long leather straps to enable the child to be carried on someone's back. Although the waistband of the child's dress was made from a flour sack, the skirt had printed writing on it with names of political candidates for 1888. This cloth came from an election poster inside Alfred's ranch.

This clothing is now in an Apache May collection that was donated to the Arizona History Museum in Tucson. Among the items is a two-strand necklace made of red beans, found

Apache May and John Slaughter. Photo courtesy of the John Slaughter Ranch Museum.

in northern Mexico, that Apache May wore when she was captured. A bow and three arrows found in that Apache campsite are also there.

Apache May was thought to be 18 months when she was taken by Slaughter. At that age, she was a toddler old enough to have been recognized by her relatives if she had been returned to them on the reservation. She also may have experienced some trauma due to the violence at the camp and also by the new surroundings that she found herself in. Once at the Slaughter home, she was named "May" since she was taken in that month. It is said that the Slaughters called her by the nickname "Patchy" for Apache. While they may have had been fond of her, this does not seem to have been an affectionate or caring nickname.

It is unknown the type of life she lived on the ranch. She was said to have been taken with the family to places in Arizona, such as Tombstone, where she was viewed as an oddity and made to pose in numerous photos.

In February 1900, her life came to an end when one of her dresses caught fire as she played near a boiling pot. There was speculation that ranch hands deliberately set fire to her dress because of their hatred for Apaches. She died from the burns she sustained and is supposed to be buried in the Slaughter cemetery. It is odd that the unadorned wooden cross from her grave was donated by the Slaughter family to the Arizona History Museum and is located there rather than on her grave.

In the end, the cavalry abandoned the search for the Apaches once the band fled over the hills into Mexico, forcing the U.S. military to turn back. The person who ultimately paid the price for murders of Alfred and the Merrills was Apache May, who had nothing to do with those crimes.

The little Apache girl who was found and cared for by the family of John S Slaughter was fatally burned this morning. So is the report received here.

Chapter 21: Pease Ross: Comanche Boy named after a murder site

The life of a 9-year-old Comanche boy changed forever on Dec. 18, 1860 when he was taken among other war trophies—including the lance, shield and buffalo horns from a dying warrior thought to be a chief—by 40 Texas Rangers who thundered on horseback into a campsite after daybreak where unsuspecting Natives were massacred where they stood or tried to flee.

The attack was led by 22-year-old Capt. Lawrence Sullivan "Sul" Ross, who would later become a Confederate hero, sheriff, state senator and Texas governor. Decades after the massacre, Ross described riding to a hilltop and discovering the Comanches.

"It was a most happy circumstance that a piercing north wind was blowing, bearing with it a cloud of sand, and my presence was unobserved and the surprise complete. By signaling my men as I stood concealed, they reached me without being discovered by the Indians, who were busy packing up preparatory to a move."

Ross had been made a Ranger and charged by Gov. Sam Houston to protect the Texas frontier and kill Indians.

"The attack was so sudden that a considerable number were killed before they could prepare for defense. They fled precipitately right into the presence of the sergeant and his men. Here they met with a warm reception, and finding themselves completely encompassed, everyone fled his own way, and was hotly pursued and hard pressed."

Pease Ross looks uncomfortable in this 1861 photo, which was taken months after his capture and soon before he would accompany Sul Ross and other Confederates to fight Yankees until the end of the Civil War. The boy's hair has been cut since his capture but is messy. His clothes are tattered. Holes are visible in his jacket. His shirt is open and its collar is rumpled. Despite assertions by the Ross family that Pease was adopted and well cared for, the boy's appearance tells a different story. He looks neglected and unhappy. He also was very young to have been used by Sul Ross as his personal valet, especially on dangerous battlefields. Photo by William W. Bridgers, courtesy of the DeGolyer Library, Southern Methodist University.

Ross galloped after a Comanche warrior he identified as Chief Peta Nocona (a claim disputed by the chief's son Quanah Parker and others) and fatally shot a teenaged girl mounted on the same horse behind the warrior. As she died, she fell, pulling the warrior off the horse. A shield slung over the Comanche's back prevented the lethal bullet that killed the girl from passing through him. He sent a volley of arrows towards Ross and they struck the Ranger's horse, causing Ross to accidentally fire a shot that cracked the warrior's arm—disabling him. Ross then shot the warrior twice through the body. Realizing his wounds were mortal, the Comanche walked up to the only tree in sight and sang a death song.

Lawrence Sullivan "Sul" Ross later in life. Illustration courtesy of the New York Public Library Digital Collections.

"At this time my Mexican servant, who had once been a captive with the Comanches and spoke their language fluently as his mother tongue, came up in company with two of my men. I then summoned the chief to surrender, but he promptly treated every overture with contempt, and signalized this declaration with a savage attempt to thrust me with his lance, which he held in his left hand. I could only look upon him with pity and admiration. For, deplorable as was his situation, with no chance of escape … he was undaunted by the fate that awaited him, and as he seemed to prefer death to life, I directed the Mexican to end his misery by a charge of buckshot from the gun which he carried."

During the melee, Ross and his troops seized captive Cynthia Ann Parker and her half-Native baby girl, the sister of Quanah Parker.

> **The Civilian and Gazette.**
> WEEKLY.
> VOL. XXIII. GALVESTON, TUESDAY MORNING, JANUARY 15, 1861. NO. 41.
>
> Capt. Ross has returned to Waco for reinforcements, bringing one of the prisoners, a Comanche boy about 12 years old.

This report from a Galveston, Texas newspaper is among the earliest articles that mentions the captive Comanche boy who Sul Ross would claim as a war trophy and name "Pease Ross." This same article tells about the retrieval of kidnapped Cynthia Ann Parker and the information she provided through a translator. She said the Natives that Sul Ross and his Texas Rangers massacred where composed of 4 tribes who banded together for the winter and had stolen horses. One group was away driving the horses to another location while the people left at the campsite were packing buffalo meat and hides that they had gathered. Cynthia said the Comanches "were in a starving condition" since the buffalo they depended on for food had migrated farther south. Her statements underscore how the Natives at the campsite were no match for the charging Texas Rangers who killed them.

A less famous captive was seized that day while Ross and his men "were assembling with the spoils" and over 400 Comanche ponies. "I discovered an Indian boy about nine years of age, secreted in the grass. Expecting to be killed he began crying, but I made him mount behind me and carried him along."

Ross kept that child for himself and named the boy Pease Ross—because the Pease River in West Texas was the site of massacre, which was called the Pease River "Battle," despite it being an uneven fight in which the Natives had little chance to defend themselves.

To understand the significance of the capture of Pease Ross and the environment he was forced to live in after his family was slaughtered, it is important to look at the household he entered. Three factors are noteworthy:

Portrait of famed Miami chief Brewett by James Otto Lewis (1836). Illustration courtesy of the New York Public Library Digital Collections.

🪶 Sul Ross came from a family of Indian killers: his father Capt. Shapley Prince Ross (who led the Ross Rangers) and older brother Capt. Peter Fulkerson Ross also were Texas Rangers. His namesake—great-grandfather Lawrence Ross—was a young immigrant from Scotland whose parents moved to Virginia; one day while attending school, Indians attacked the schoolhouse, shot him through the shoulder, and carried him off into captivity until age 23, when he was swapped with Cherokees in a prisoner exchange negotiated by Daniel Boone in the first treaty of Limestone in the late 1700s. Although Lawrence spent many years living among Natives, there is no evidence to indicate he had any trouble (as some captives did) readjusting to his former life. In fact, Lawrence married into Kentucky's revered Oldham family, which boasted a Revolutionary War hero and second-cousin to George Washington, Col. William Oldham, who was murdered in 1791 by Miami Indians working for the British and in whose honor a county was named.) In general, people kidnapped by Indians usually either grew to love Native people and were unable to assimilate back into their own race, or they despised Indians and used their knowledge to become scouts to work against and kill Natives in revenge.

🪶 The Ross family was accustomed to being waited on by slaves and servants. Capt. Shapley's "father was a Kentucky planter, and like his father before him, a large

Indian fighter and Texas Ranger, Col. Robert Hall (1814–1899) shown about 1885. He also fought on the Confederate side in the Civil War. Photo courtesy of the DeGolyer Library, Southern Methodist University.

slaveholder," noted an 1893 book on a Texas history of McLennan, Falls, Bell and Coryell counties. When Capt. Shapley moved to Texas, the tradition of family servants remained and included a black named "Old Armistead." Ross himself admits to having a Mexican servant, whose name is listed as 14-year-old "Pablo Ross" in an 1860 census of Capt. Shapley's household. Ross had no problem taking a young teen servant on an expedition and exposing his life to danger, as shown by Pablo's role delivering the fatal shot to the Comanche warrior in the Pease River Battle. Ross also exploited Pablo's knowledge of Comanche customs and language, appearing to encourage Pablo's ill will against Comanches by providing the boy with opportunities to kill them.

Ross made a distinction while naming Pease and a young captive white girl he rescued. In an 1858 battle with Comanches, in which 95 were killed and 350 horses seized, Ross rescued a young captive white girl, of unknown parentage, and took her into his family's household. He named her Lizzie after the woman he had fallen in love with and would wed a few years later. While Ross gave the young girl who was white like himself a name of endearment, he bestowed a name associated with violence, blood, death and racial dominance on a Native child he undoubtedly viewed as his inferior. In fact, naming the orphan boy "Pease" almost seems like an abusive and cruel inside joke.

It was into this household that young Pease Ross was placed to fend for himself as the youngest and most vulnerable person there. The only one who could speak his language was Pablo, a murderous youth a few years older. It is very likely that young Lizzie, aged 12, had harsh feelings for Natives. She was kidnapped at such a young age that she had no idea who she was, where she came from, or what happened to her or her family before her life began with the Indians. If Pease Ross was terrified about his fate after seeing his loved ones slaughtered before his eyes when he was captured, he undoubtedly faced other traumas in his new life among the famous Texas Ranger family.

A Confederate military record for Lawrence Sullivan Ross.

Less than a year after his capture, Pease found himself as a personal servant to Ross, who began his notable climb up the military ladder fighting for the Confederate States Army. On Oct. 18, 1861, Ross was appointed to the 6th Texas Cavalry as a private and would leave a colonel. His regiment was organized in September 1861 with 1,150 men in 10 volunteer companies from his hometown of Waco as well as from Dallas, McKinney, Austin, and Lancaster, and Bell County. Ross is said to have written to his wife about how his fellow Confederates looked on Pease as a curiosity who created "more excitement than a monkey show."

During the Civil War, young Pease (who would have only been 10 or 11 when it started) accompanied Ross as the ambitious Rebel soldier participated in 135 engagements and had seven horses shot out from underneath him in a career acclaimed as "one who displayed most distinguished gallantry," according to *Confederate Veteran* magazine in 1903. His regiment fought in Tennessee, Mississippi and Georgia, participating in the Atlanta Campaign. In 1864, his scouts were behind Union General William Tecumseh Sherman's army "tearing up the railroad, cutting telegraph lines, and capturing and burning trains loaded with supplies for Sherman's army," noted a 1914 issue of *Confederate Veteran.*

Amid the action, Pease served Ross as a valet rather than as a Confederate soldier. Among government documents and records of the men under Ross, there is no military listing for Pease. His young age would not have prevented him from enlisting. My great-grandfather Harrison Fletcher from Iowa enlisted at age 14 for the Union in the Ohio Infantry as a drummer boy (whose duties included carrying the wounded), first in the 149th Regiment and then Company D in the 27th Regiment. Records exist today for many Union and Confederate soldiers, many of whom survived the war and applied for government pensions. Perhaps if Pease had enlisted as a soldier, he would have been able to receive a pension for his military service.

Few details exist about Pease's life. He appears in a Dec. 10, 1881 newspaper article when he was about 30 years old. The *Waco Daily Examiner* reported that Pease, "the Indian," got drunk and was involved in a fight with a crippled Mexican organ grinder. Pease was chased while intoxicated and, unaware of where he was fleeing, "ran plump into the arms of Officers Bell and Miller," who locked Pease up in jail for his own protection.

> **The Waco Daily Examiner.**
>
> —Pease Ross, the Indian, was drinking yesterday, and got mixed up with the crippled Mexican who sets in the front of the Imperial, which so exasperated the organ-grinder that he gave chase to Ross. The latter, in attempting to evade the irate Mexican, ran plump into the arms of Officers Bell and Miller. As a matter purely of protection to Pease, he was placed in the cooler.

Ross discussed Pease in an 1885 interview: "And when in after years I frequently proposed to send him to his people, he steadily refused to go, and died in McLennan County [Texas] last year." This statement appears to be very unlikely. Where would Ross have sent Pease to—an Indian reservation in distant Oklahoma where Comanches were housed? Ross had by this time become a career politician, and this sounds like a hollow statement made to preserve a polished public image. At the time this statement was made, times had changed to be slightly more favorable towards Native people, with Comanche Quanah Parker (whose father Ross had previously claimed to have killed) being a celebrity in Texas.

It is said that Pease married Texana Manning, the daughter of a former black slave. Some members of the Ross family referred to Pease as an adopted family member who was cared for and educated. There is no evidence of this.

However, there are records for a man named Willie Ross who, with Texana Manning, had a son named Samuel David Ross. It would appear that Pease renamed himself "Willie." Government documents for Samuel David indicate the man was a farmer who also lived in McLennan County and identified his race as black. There is no mention of being part Comanche or Native American.

If Pease had married a black woman, their life in the segregated South would have been one that faced much racial discrimination. It has been said that, as a youth, Pease lived in servant's quarters outside the main Ross household with the black slave who cared for stable animals. If that is true, Pease as a Native could have been welcomed into a black community more readily and developed bonds. If his son was Samuel David, as it seems, it is sad that the offspring of this brave Comanche boy, credited as being the sole male survivor of the Pease River massacre, may have lost touch with his rich Native traditions.

Words cannot describe the magnitude of harm that was done to Pease at the hands of Sul Ross when he took that boy captive as an object, a war trophy, rather than viewing that child as a human being.

Chapter 22: Maria the Navajo Baby: A Short Convent Life

After the trampling of horses and smoke from gunfire cleared, when the air was silent from whirring arrows and slashing swords, that was the time Indian battlefield babies entered a new life as they lay among the gore of blood and strewn bodies of their parents. Maria, a Navajo baby, was one such foundling in New Mexico during the 1860s when the Army was doing its utmost to kill and corral onto a reservation a proud nomadic tribe that some American newcomers back then described as having a lively spirit in common with the Irish.

The unrelenting pace of military battles against Natives reached a never-before-seen pitch in New Mexico and the Southwest. After defeating Mexico and seizing new territory, America turned its war machine towards indigenous Natives perceived as blocking its path to the acquisition of new resources. The number of U.S. soldiers (many born in foreign lands) swelled to some 16,000 from less than 10,000 a decade earlier.

A child and three captive Comanche women (left to right, Wap-pah, Marn-me, and Qna-moth-kee) after being taken prisoner by the Army on the Staked Plains spanning New Mexico and Texas. Photo by William Soule (circa 1867–1874), courtesy of Yale University Library.

New Mexico occupied a place of prominence within the military, which in 1860 was organized into seven operational headquarters in each geographical department: New Mexico (which encompassed Arizona and some of Colorado), Texas, Utah, California, Oregon, the West (the Midwest), and the East.

While less than two dozen national arsenals and armories existed throughout U.S. lands, New Mexico had one, which was a temporary facility in 1860 until a permanent structure was built 90 miles east of Santa Fe at Fort Union, located amid the plains in eastern New Mexico along the Santa Fe Trail. During 1858, the national armories manufactured nearly 18,000 rifle muskets, almost 2,500 rifles, over 1,500 cadet's muskets, and 94,800 implements for small arms.

An ordnance report to the Secretary of War from October 1859 provides a glimpse of the types of supplies with which arsenals and armories equipped soldiers in New Mexico for their numerous expeditions against nomadic tribes. These included artillery musketoons, percussion rifles, long-range rifles, and horse artillery sabers. Other items likely included:

- Mortar wagons,
- 6-pound bronze guns,
- Howitzers and their carriages,
- Coehorn (portable) and siege mortars,
- Traveling forges,
- Sharp's and Maynard's carbines,
- Colt rifles, pistols and holsters,
- Adams' pistols,
- Cavalry sabres and swords,
- Bayonet scabbards,
- Ammunition rounds and percussion caps,
- Cartridge boxes and belts,
- Rifle pouches and gun slings,
- Waist and saber belts,
- Horse equipment, artillery harnesses, and saddle blankets, and
- Powder flasks,
- Gunpowder, niter, charcoal, and sulfur.

Future military leaders, instructed at West Point in the finer points of ancient and modern warfare, were sent out in droves to the Southwest to kill Indians

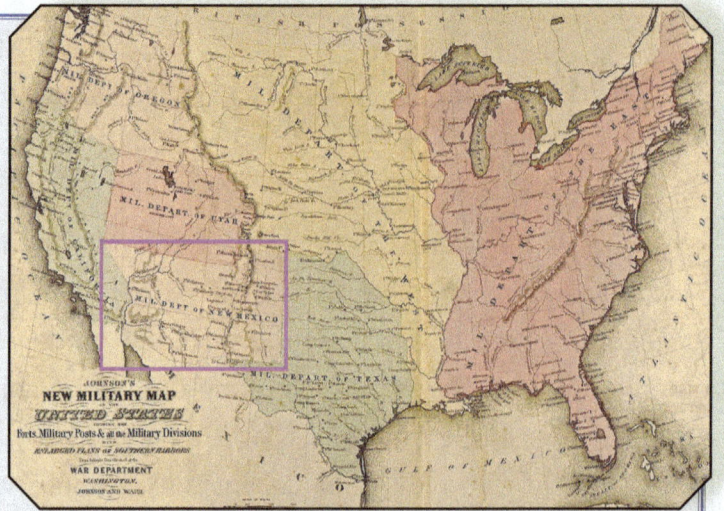

The New Mexico department of the military is shown within a map depicting how the U.S. military divided the country into management districts in 1860. New Mexico was an important Army base of operations against Indians. Courtesy of the Library of Congress.

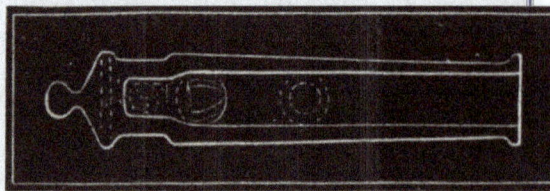

An interior view of a mountain howitzer (above) is shown in a textbook for West Point cadets. The interior workings of a Hale war rocket (below) are depicted in the same book published in 1862. It was written by Capt. J.G. Benton and called *"A Course of Instruction in Ordnance and Gunnery; compiled for the use of the cadets of the United States Military Academy."*

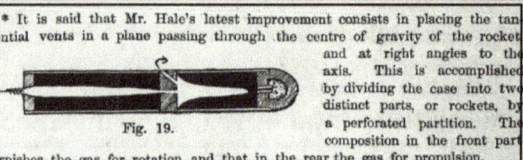

and make names for themselves in their early military careers. At least 204 West Point graduates served as officers on frontier duty in New Mexico's forts from 1848 through 1867.

In another discovery during my research, I learned the U.S. military tested weapons and modern-warfare techniques on Navajos and other Natives, which were perfected and deployed with greater precision during the Civil War. While the Indians mostly used bows, arrows, and lances (formidable short-distance weapons) as well as some rifles, the Army experimented with Hale war rockets, mounted riflemen, and signal communications in New Mexico.

Only a sign stands on the eastern plains of New Mexico where the Fort Union Arsenal once stood near the entrance to the fort's adobe remains. Fort Union was a military stronghold in the Southwest. It was used as an operational base to fight both Natives and Confederates. Ruts from wagon tracks crossing the Santa Fe Trail are still visible today near this sign. Photo by Noël Fletcher.

The War Department tested Hale rockets for more than a year in New Mexico, Baton Rouge, and Washington. Hale rockets (invented in England by William Hale) were projectile war rockets without guide sticks.

"The great difficulty in rocket firing is to get them to start in the right direction," stated an 1863 artillerist manual. "Mr. Hale has striven to overcome this difficulty by placing his rocket behind a strong spring, which holds it until it has acquired force enough both to overcome its own inertia and the strength of the spring."

Hale rockets yielded favorable results except in New Mexico. "The last Mr. Hale attributes to the want of a proper stand in firing the rockets, which may account for it in part, but not entirely, considering, however, all the different trials…," Ordnance colonel H.K. Craig reported to John B. Floyd, Secretary of War in January 1858.

New Mexico's harsh desert climate presented other problems for the Hale rockets, noted the artillerist manual, because the rockets were made with metal cases, which could expand and contract depending on the temperature, causing the rockets to explode like gunpowder charges. "It is stated that in New Mexico, where the climate is very dry, the common sky rocket cannot be kept for any length of time without being subject to the same defect; and they are sometimes restored to their former condition by soaking them for a short time in water, and then drying them," the manual concluded.

Rather than the Hale rockets, Army reports from New Mexico show a preference for firing mountain howitzers during engagements with Indians. This type of short artillery was light enough to be carried on pack animals, could be fired from a low two-wheeled carriage, and could be transported up steep canyons where Apaches and Navajos sought refuge.

Marksmanship came to the forefront of fights against Indians in New Mexico as the Army made improvements in the types of muskets and rifles it used. Particularly prevalent in Santa Fe newspaper reports were the exploits of Mounted Riflemen and details about their comings and goings noted. For example, the *Santa Fe Weekly Gazette* in October 1856 noted the arrival of a regiment and their assignments at 14 posts.

In 1858, Col. William Loring commanded an expedition from Albuquerque that included

> **Santa Fe Weekly Gazette.**
> VOLUME V.] SANTA FE, NEW MEXICO, OCTOBER 4, 1856. [NUMBER 35
>
> The regiment of mounted riflemen under Brevet Colonel Loring, has arrived in this department, and is assigned to stations as follows:
> Head quarters and two companies, Jones and Ruffs, at Fort Union.
> Maj. Crittenden assigned to Fort Craig.
> Capt. Duncan's, Capt. Burgwin,
> " Roberts Los Lunas,
> " Porter's Fort Craig,
> " Lindsey's Fort Stanton,
> " Claiborne's Fort Thorn,
> " Rhetts Fort Fillmore,
> " Walker's Fort Bliss,
> And " Elliott to report to department Head quarters for field service.
> Company D. 2nd artillery, from Fort Massachusetts to Fort Stanton. Maj. Holms 8th infantry to the command of Fort Stanton.
> Maj. Van Horn assigned to the command of Alburquerque.

Newspapers in New Mexico reported constantly on military movements. Reports like the one above reveal a large presence of troops in the area.

> **Santa Fe Weekly Gazette.**
> VOLUME 1.] Santa Fe, New Mexico, July 24, 1858. [NUMBER 30
>
> We learn from Mr. Clever, U.S. Marshal, that Lieut. Wm. H. Averelle of the Rifle Regiment, passed Socorro with his company on the 3rd of this month, en route for Fort Defiance. The company, consisting of fifty men, were well mounted—the horses in very good order, the men in fighting spirits, and anxious to see the Navajoes; and we further learn from a letter from the Fort that the company had arrived safely at its destination.

Mounted Riflemen to fight Apaches. The Mounted Riflemen chased after the Natives in the south and killed Chief Cuchillo Negro (Black Knife). "The families of the Indians were taken prisoners, their camp equipment captured, and a flock of about a thousand sheep taken," noted an 1865 *"History of the U.S. Cavalry."* It detailed another attack by a detachment of Mounted Riflemen near Fort Craig, N.M. that year when soldiers captured a group of Natives. "They attempted to escape, when the lieutenant [William Averell] and his men fired upon them, killing all of them. They had been committing various depredations, and merited their fate."

Navajos were the unsuspecting targets of the first Army experiment of signal communications in a field expedition with Lieut. Albert James Myer, the father of the U.S. Signal Corps. Back in 1860, he was a surgeon assigned to New Mexico. He developed an idea to enhance warfare operations by waving flags for long-distance communications. He was given permission and resources to test his theories on Navajos.

Assigned for several months to Col. Edward Canby's expedition against the Navajos, Myer was so successful in his use of signals that his abstract concept became standard military practice. Messages were transmitted as far away as from 5 to 20 miles.

Albert James Myer, father of the U.S. Signal Corps., who tested his battle ideas on Navajos in New Mexico.

"The various columns of the expedition were kept in constant communication, and scout service was so completely executed that Col. Canby was able to report to the commanding officer of the Dept. of New Mexico (Dec. 14, 1860) 'that the guides and spies, with few exceptions, have been discharged and it will not be necessary to replace them,' " remarked an 1896 book called, *"The Signal Corps, U.S.A. in the War of the Rebellion."*

Given the numerous military advantages the Army had over the nomadic Natives, it is no wonder there were so many orphaned Indian battlefield babies like the Navajo child who would become Maria (Mary) Carleton. She was given the surname of General James Carleton after she was found lying next to her slain mother.

The military wasn't equipped to care for Native foundlings. Scant writings about these incidents indicate it was up to the discretion of the soldier who found the child to decide what to do.

Dolores Perea, one of my relatives, was an early student of the Sisters of Loretto in Santa Fe. She joined the order, took the religious name Lucia and became the first Hispanic native New Mexican superior of the order. She used her inheritance from her wealthy Perea family, who helped found the Santa Fe Trail, to build religious schools in Santa Fe and Las Vegas.

"In 1872, the soldiers found an Indian baby left to die beside the trail. The Indians had been in a combat with a wagon train and the party had all been killed. The baby was the only one of the group that escaped. The soldiers picked up the Indian child and took him in with them to the Mimbres. There the John Miller family took the child to raise," noted a N.M. oral history with J.C. Brock in 1938. "The boy proved to be an intelligent child, but cruel. When he was 12 years old he was caught in the act of dashing the brains in one of the Miller children with a hatchet. The child was at once returned to the San Carlos [Apache] reservation, after having been with an American family for 11 years."

There were no orphanages in New Mexico for 20 years after the Army began fighting Indians there. Two religious orders of Catholic nuns made the dangerous journey on wagons across the plains into Santa Fe to become established. They soon began to take in orphaned Native children.

The Sisters of Loretto at the Foot of the Cross, founded in Kentucky, arrived in New Mexico in 1852 to start a school. One case was briefly discussed by the order in their centennial book called, *Light in Yucca Land.* It mentioned how Sister Rosanna raised an orphaned Native boy while at their convent in Taos, which was established in 1884. As she aged and her health deteriorated, she moved to the Santa Fe convent. One day in 1914 a Native man and his two children came to see her. Sister Rosanna came downstairs on her crutches, put her arms around the man's neck and kissed him. A new arrival from the Kentucky motherhouse looked shocked. "Why she kissed that Indian!" The Mother Superior replied, "Yes, and she should have, for that is Indian Joe, and Sister Rosanna is the only mother the boy ever knew. He would not understand if Sister treated him

This N.M. state historical marker about the Sisters of Loretto and Lucia Perea is located near Loretto Chapel next to the historic plaza in downtown Santa Fe. Photo by Noël Fletcher.

in any other way."

Little Maria Carleton found herself turned over to four nuns from Ireland: Sisters Catherina, Pauline, Theodosia, and Vincent. The order was called the Sisters of Charity of Cincinnati. They arrived in Santa Fe in 1865 to open a hospital, but quickly responded to the need to care for orphans in their St. Vincent facility (called a hospital and asylum).

"The number of patients and orphans increased steadily, and in a few years as many as 73 patients and 60 children received shelter at once under their hospitable roof," stated the *"Historical Sketch of the Catholic Church in New Mexico"* in 1887.

Illustration from the 1800s of a Sister of Charity. Courtesy of the Library of Congress.

Although it is known in local newspapers even today that the Sisters of Charity took in the Navajo baby from the battlefield, there is little recorded information about her.

I stumbled across perhaps the only detailed information about Maria Carleton published Dec. 26, 1890 in *The Daily Optic* newspaper from Las Vegas, N.M. under the title: *"A Passion Flower—A Christmas Story."* A woman calling herself "Hawthorne" wrote it especially for the newspaper. At first, I thought it was fiction. But I was able to verify the names of all the people involved. I even found an 1870 census record that shows Maria, described as disabled, still living with the nuns. (The child is called Maria in the article and in the census even though modern references refer to her as Mary.)

"On many a battlefield babes were found dabbling in a dead mother's blood, for the Navajo [mother] was oftener by the side of her warrior husband than in her [hogan home], and little children were found wandering about the slain," wrote Hawthorne, whose husband was a lieutenant.

She described holding her baby son while standing one Christmas morning outside under the portal at the military headquarters in Santa Fe. They were listening to music in the distance played by the 3rd Cavalry band at Fort Marcy when she became aware of the sound of General Carleton pacing back and forth inside. He ventured outside holding "a moving bundle of partially colored rags from out which gleamed two great black eyes, utterly void of all expression, save what the shadow of the long heavy lashes gave them—all expression incomprehensible to me, then and ever after."

General Carleton announced he was giving the woman the Navajo child as a Christmas present.

"She was picked up on the battlefield asleep in the arms of her mother. She was an Amazon, madam—an Amazon, for she lay where dead men were thickest." He went on to explain that the girl's dead mother was carrying a musket in one hand and the baby in her other arm. "Poor little one! Her fate has been a hard one for she fell into cruel hands. Her half-starved little body is marked with her owner's whip and she has never known the sound of a kindly voice. God only knows what she has suffered. Will you take her and care for her—for me?" asked Carleton. "She has no one to claim her, for her name even is lost. She was about three when captured; she is 6 now and she has never spoken to anyone; fear has made her dumb. The people who had her said she would talk to herself—or to something they could not see—in a language they could not understand, but threats or blows failed to bring a sound from her. Her language was baby Navajo, I presume, but her captors insisted that she is a *bruja* [witch]. I only hope she has bewitched you into taking her," Carleton said.

Two women and a child sit outside a house among the officer's quarters in Santa Fe during the mid-1800s. Photo courtesy of the National Archives and Records Administration.

The woman spoke about how much she disliked, feared and wanted to refuse the child with "the wicked blood" of the "hated Navajo." Yet, she told Carleton she would "take the wretched little creature and try not to murder her." She described how a shivering Maria "squatted like a veritable pixie" while stretching her "grimy, claw-like hands" to the warmth of a fireplace.

Hawthorne said she applied balm to festering welts and scars that covered Maria's body.

"For the next few days, the whole of our Army family—commandant, staff officers, orderlies and the baby [her son], were absorbed in entertaining the stranger. Major DeForrest rummaged the shelves at Seligman's and Spiegelberg's and Delgado's for toys; quiet [Alfred] Merrill brought in an outlandish Navajo god made of leather; Ennis presented her with a pair of gaudily beaded moccasins and the baby heroically patted with his 'teething ring.' My sitting room looked like a holiday time shop and, amidst it all, sat my sphinx-like Indian, neither accepting nor refusing but altogether ignoring. She was obedient in everything, sullen in nothing, and she drove me to the verge of frenzy."

One day, a neighbor's daughter left behind a dirty rag doll. Maria discovered the doll, made crooning sounds, and squeezed the doll next to her heart. The woman was astonished to hear the child, who rarely made a sound. "The doll passed into Maria's possession and became the only thing that could unlock her silent heart."

Two events caused Maria to be passed over to the Sisters of Charity: the woman's husband had orders to move and Carleton was leaving for New York.

"Sister, maybe you can make her alive. I cannot," said the woman. "That horrid doll she holds is the only thing she will talk to and what that talk is only she and the doll seem to understand."

Unhappy with the woman's characterization of Maria, Carleton said, "'She has the soul of a saint, Sister, and the body of a martyr."

Sister Vincent replied: "'It will be with her as God wills. We will do for her all we can, and sure it would be a hard heart that had no pity in it for her.'"

Hawthorne left Santa Fe. Returning 20 years later, she visited the Sisters of Charity to ask about Maria and if she child ever talked or gave up the rag doll. Sister Catherine told Hawthorne she believed Maria was among "the Saints" in heaven.

"Sister took my hand and led me to the south wall of the parlor where hung an exquisite flower piece (embroidery). Buds of roses that seemed just bursting in creamy richness, violets faintly purple, lilies waxen petalled and one intense crimson-tinted passion flower over which hovered a white dove of peace. 'Maria did that with the bits of silk Sister Augustine threw aside," the nun replied."

Hawthorne asked how such a "stupid, passive Indian" could create such wonders. Instead, Sister Catherine described Maria as "a wonderful child" with her own story.

"Sister Vincent did not know what to do with the queer little thing when we got her so we left her to herself to see if she would show any desire for any one thing. All during the cold days of spring, she sat in a corner near the fire with her doll in her arms, singing half to herself in her heathenish songs, till sore my flesh would creep at the hearing of them. With every May, as the years rolled by, we would make an added effort to get the *niña* to understand that it was the month of the Blessed Mother and her month [since her name was Maria], too, but there she would stand, like a stone, and never say a word. Until one May, when she had grown into a slim bit of a girl, but yet tugged her doll. When the children were brought into our chapel for vespers, Maria was with the little ones and Sister Louise put them near one beautiful white altar. We had no flowers in those days, you know, but we had made lovely lilies and roses and the statue of our Blessed Lady shone like the stars under the soft wax lights. Sister Louis held Maria's hand as they knelt before the shrine. All at once, the child began to tremble and cried out in Spanish: 'Oh, the beautiful flowers, the beautiful Christ child!' and fell on the floor in a dead faint. For hours we thought her dead, indeed, but she came back and you never heard a tongue talk as did hers. All she had ever heard seemed to have been treasured up and pour out that night. She had been to the Christ child's garden and seen the beautiful flowers Sister Augustine so longed for as she stitched her canvas, and she joyfully cried: 'I am to make them just as my Sister August does.' And she did."

In the high desert of Santa Fe where Maria lived, there was an absence of flowers and color in the landscape. The beauty and wonder of flowers seemed to have touched her soul very deeply.

Maria sat with her favorite nun and "they created beauty on canvas" embroidering flowers as the Sister told Maria religious stories. According to the Sisters, Maria longed to have the Blessed Mother bring her a single rose or lily.

"Sister gave her bits of thread and canvas and the child made flowers that Sister Louise said smelled like the blossoms at the dear motherhouse among the Ohio hills."

That winter Maria became restless and developed a fever and cough.

"Scarcely a day passed that she did not express a longing to see flowers that grew out of the ground and blossomed under the sunshine and dews of heaven. We had planted and cared for many kinds and while some rewarded us with blooms, we had not succeeded in bringing forth lily, violet or roses and these were the only *flores* [flowers] to our child. The railroad had come and we sent away back to the beautiful gardens of the motherhouse for the blossoms, but when they came they were lifeless and scentless and less to her than those fashioned out of her silken threads."

Maria became weaker with each passing day as the nuns took turns attending the dying child. On Christmas Eve, the nuns were tired from many nights of watching and waiting around Maria, "whose little life had been so pure and gentle." The nuns left one by one for their evening meditation until an older Sister remained at Maria's side to watch but fell asleep. Sister Catherine was kneeling in the church and saw a white-clad figure pass by and kneel before the altar, which was decorated for Christmas.

"'It was Maria and for the life of me I could not move but just knelt here...watching her. High above her swung the gold star before the [tabernacle] host and the faint light of the tapers dimly outlined her face. With her face upturned to the body of our Lord and her hands clasped before her, she looked the angel I know she is. Suddenly she stooped, put out one hand between the chapel rails and with a faint scream of wonder or delight or fright, I didn't then know which, she hugged something to her breast. She just swayed back and forth a bit like a poor broken lily, and I had sense enough by that time to run to her side."

Fort Marcy stood in defense on a hilltop in Santa Fe, which is covered by purple wildflowers. As she lay dying, Maria hoped to see luscious flowers (lilies, violets, and roses) that were not readily available or grown in New Mexico's high desert climate of Santa Fe. Photo by Noël Fletcher.

Sister Catherine rushed to Maria and the alarmed nuns upstairs realized the child was missing from her room. "We carried her to her cot and unclosed the little hand fast growing cold in death and there we found a fresh, half-blown [bloomed] snow-white rosebud. Once she opened her eyes that were even then shining with the light of eternity and looked around till she saw Sister Augustine. We knew she wanted to speak to her and drew back a few steps whilst the Sister knelt by her 'The Christ child told me that before the Blessed Sacrament I would find the way that leads to his garden, and *Hermana mia* [my Sister], I found it, and this.' As she laid the bud in the hands of the Sister her sweet young sinless soul entered the path that led to him."

Hawthorne said Sister Catherine wiped away a tear at the end of the narrative. Feeling reverent and struck with awe, Hawthorne closed her story by telling how she went that June to visit Maria's grave where she placed roses, violets, lilies and a pale passion flower. "And

I thought of that other grave in some faraway spot, a soldier's grave where brave, great-hearted Carleton had made his last camp. 'The soul of a saint and the body of a martyr,' he had said, and perhaps his eyes looked deeper into the heart of the child than even he knew."

It is unknown when Maria died. I could find no listing for Maria in the 1880 Census among the nuns. In the 1870 Census record, it lists her age as 6, says she was born in Navajo Country, and attests that she attended school that year. There is an "X" marked in the column to list if the person is "deaf and dumb, insane or idiotic." This notation supports Hawthorne's claim that Maria was unable to fully speak until the events Sister Catherine described. She likely suffered from some type of psychological trauma.

Italian-born Sister Blandina Segale is among the most famous Sisters of Charity. The cause for canonization has been put forth to make her a saint.

Some of her writings reflect what today are shades of racism in referring to Hispanics and Natives. In a January 1877 letter to Sister Justina, she briefly mentioned Maria.

"General Carleton sent a little papoose, which was found on a battlefield, to the Orphan Asylum. The Sisters named her Mary Carleton. Were I to guess to what tribe she belongs I would say, 'Navajo.' She is a *'Chato,'* (Flat Nose)."

Sr. Blandina Segale (1850–1941)

Later she again says General Carleton himself brought the battlefield baby Maria to the convent, which he did, according to Hawthorne. But there is no mention of Maria being taken in by a Hispanic family who beat her and then passed her over to Hawthorne. The military wife must have made Maria suffer emotionally due to her ill will towards the child. It would seem that Army officers found Maria in the arms of her dead mother given Carleton's detailed account. Somehow the Army passed the baby to the Hispanics and later retrieved her following the abuse.

It is unknown how Maria would have done if she had been turned over to her tribe. Being among her own Navajo people may have enabled her to recover faster from her psychological trauma. Clearly she was a bright, loving and creative child. If Hawthorne's narrative is true, which it seems to be, it shows that Maria found warmth and affection during her life among nuns who provided her with some solace for her great sufferings.

An 1870 census from the Territory of New Mexico shows Maria Carleton, the Navajo baby found on the battlefield beside her dead mother. It also indicates that she had some disability since she was described as being almost mute and unable to speak.

When learning of the fate of Native captives such as Maria, I notice what short lives they lived away from their people. They died at such young ages. Even Pease Ross is thought to only have reached about 33 years old when he passed away. At best, these captive children coped rather than thrived in their new lives among people of different races with foreign ways.

It is also obvious that when a family wanted to rid itself of a captive Native child under the same roof, that child quickly found itself turned over to an Indian reservation. Why, then, weren't more children repatriated to their own people immediately after hostilities ceased? If the tribe and Army were still involved with hostilities, other Native communities were within reach that could have taken in the orphaned children.

In New Mexico, there are 19 Pueblos who remained at peace in their sovereign lands while the U.S. military waged war on nomadic neighboring tribes. Also, the military used Native scouts from various tribes in their operations. There were plenty of options available to the military and others to find homes for the battlefield babies among other Native peoples, where they most certainly would have lived happier lives. The only reason I can think of that prevented this solution to the problem of finding homes for these children is a prevailing view of racial superiority over indigenous peoples. The Anglos and Hispanics who kept these children did so for their own gain. They made money selling the children. They gained conversation pieces with war trophies. They acquired slaves/servants. They sought to enforce their "better" ways of life over a different race of subjugated people. In the end, though, it was the innocent children who were most often destroyed.

One of the few exceptions may be found in the case of a young Apache boy who found a home with an eccentric Italian photographer.

Chapter 23: Carlos Montezuma: An Apache Warrior of A Different Type

When an Apache boy was born in central Arizona around 1869, he was given a name Wassaja (Signaling). This name signified his life's mission to advance Native rights and to forever enlighten the lives of those who knew him. His legacy lives on after his death on Jan. 31, 1923 at age 54.

He endured many obstacles in his youth. His early childhood was spent with his tribe as the Apaches moved from one location to another while under siege by the Army. Enemies lurked everywhere. One place that seemed like a safe haven proved otherwise. That was the case at Camp Grant in May 1871. It also occurred inside a different cave a year later when Wassaja's life forever changed as he was taken captive.

Waging war against Natives included the indiscriminate killing of women and children in tactical operations. Describing this type of behavior as a horror he first encountered directed at Seminoles in Florida and later at Natives in the Southwest was General Oliver Otis Howard, called the "Christian General" for trying to incorporate his religious beliefs about morality into his work.

"The idea prevails today in a large portion of our country that to carry on war with any success whatever against Indian tribes it is necessary to come upon them by surprise and to fire directly into camps containing women and children as well as men," General Howard said to a Board of Indian Commissioners in 1873. "That massacre of Camp Grant—that horrible massacre which created a shudder not only throughout our county, but

Wassaja (center) holds the hands of his two sisters in this photo taken in 1872, two weeks after the children were captured and their mother murdered in a cave massacre by the 5th Cavalry in Arizona. The name of the eldest sister (left) is written in as "Co-Wow-Se-Puchia" and the youngest as "Ho-Lac-Ca". In 1875, the boy was interviewed for the *Chicago Tribune*. He told the reporter his sisters names were: Wasiputa and Uhlackkah. The photographer Carlos Gentile bought the boy and named him Carlos Montezuma, while his friend bought the girls. The sisters were never seen or heard from again after this photo was taken. Image courtesy of The Smithsonian Institution.

throughout the world, where so large a number of women and children were slain and so many children were carried away captives and sold into slavery, a large number of them still being in Mexico, and unrecovered by our government—was only an instance that was told. Nearly every massacre had been of a similar character. It is the way that our people have dealt with the Indians."

Arizona massacres of Indians were happening, according to General Howard: "Where exasperated whites form volunteer forces, or where they spur on the soldiers to do the work for them, excesses always follow." Anti-Native hostilities could be so great that killings were seen as justifiable. In one instance, Howard described to the Indian Commissioners how a contract Army doctor decided to poison a chief who came to Fort Reno to make peace. The Indian survived when he vomited the arsenic.

In February 1871, two Apache women decided to stay at Camp Grant in Arizona after they were treated well during a visit to seek a captured boy. Other Apaches sought to make peace and joined them after one officer said he would protect them as prisoners until he received instructions. The Natives were counted daily and on good terms with locals. The group rose to 500 Apaches who congregated a half-mile from the military post. "They were very destitute and almost naked but it was found that they were willing to work to obtain clothing, so they were set to gathering hay. They cut it with their knives and brought it on their backs but by this slow method they furnished the post with 150 tons in less than 2 months, besides gathering large quantities of mescal for their own use," journalist/historian Jacob Piatt Dunn wrote in his 1886 book, *"Massacres of the Mountains: A History of the Indian Wars of the Far West."*

On the morning of April 30, 1871, a group of nearly 150 American, Hispanic and Papago Indians left Tucson to kill the Apaches at Camp Grant. Of the 125 killed and missing during the surprise attack, only 8 were men, with majority of the victims being women and children. Their limbs had been hacked off, their heads smashed with rocks or clubs, and their bodies

General Oliver Otis Howard (1830–1909) won a Medal of Honor during the Civil War in an action against Confederate forces and lost his right arm. He helped found Howard University and was known as the "Christian General" for his moral convictions. Photo courtesy of the Library of Congress.

bore gunshot wounds. Surviving children were abducted and sold as slaves in Mexico. Although a Grand Jury issued criminal indictments, no one was convicted.

A letter to the *Arizona Miner* newspaper published May 27, 1871 summed up prevailing views. It said those slain "deserved a 'little killing'" and the "killing of those subsidized murderers and thieves near Camp Grant constitutes an act which is well worthy of imitation elsewhere throughout the Territory, and which should be repeated every time that opportunity offers."

A year later, another Arizona massacre of Apaches occurred but would remain largely unknown for 34 years until headlines in 1906 blared about a ghastly discovery: *"Found Cave Full of Dead Indians in Arizona—Cattleman discovers scene of slaughter of 'Seventy-two'"* and *"Found 200 Skeletons in Cave—Four men discover bones of Indians shot down in bloody battle in 1872."*

Rising from the tragedy of that massacre, little Apache captive Wassaja transformed into Carlos Montezuma—a world-renowned medical doctor, statesman for Native rights, author/publisher, and peacemaker respected among Indians and whites.

Jeff Adams, a prominent rancher, rode his horse into Phoenix on Feb. 2, 1906 telling a tale of his gruesome find in a cave where the bones of skeletons lay in heaps within a 35-by-100-foot area, noted the *Albuquerque Morning Journal* on Feb. 7. It termed the site as the place where the "5th Cavalry accomplished the greatest job of Indian killing in the history of the army."

"Grim and ghastly was the sight that met the eyes" of Adams and Ivy Grabtree and his two sons "when they entered a cave on Fish Creek last Sunday afternoon and there discovered the whitened skeletons of 200 Indian men, women and children," declared T*he Bisbee Daily Review* newspaper on Feb. 16.

The "sepulcher" site, described as located in Arizona's roughest terrains, had been lost as years passed.

"One of Arizona's bloodiest Indian fights is recalled by this important discovery—bloody for the Indians, all of whom were caught like rats in a trap and remorselessly shot to death

Soldiers fire to repulse an Apache attack. The gun battle took place in a rocky ravine in the Canyon of Gold near Tucson, Ariz. around 1871, which is about the same time Carlos Montezuma was captured after the massacre in the cave. Photo courtesy of the Library of Congress.

by Capt. James Burns and his command of soldiers in 1872," the *Review* stated.

Adams described the skeletons as belonging to men, women and children as young as 6 found lying on the cave floor "in all sorts of shapes, in heaps and singly." The only other objects were pieces of clothing, saddle blankets, several bundles of baskets, wood, and straw from weaving.

Capt. Burns, a native of Ireland, and a column of five Cavalry troops, and 100 Pima and Maricopa Indian scouts were hunting down a group of Apaches, who had hidden themselves 40 miles east of Phoenix in the western foothills of the Superstition Mountains, near old cliff dwellings. A trail stopped along a granite ridge nestled among numerous canyons. The soldiers had no idea where the Apaches could be until one Native scout found a footprint. It belonged to a small boy, about 8 years old, who had been out with his uncle keeping watch. The uncle escaped, but soldiers captured the boy (Wassaja's cousin) and forced the child to show them where his tribe was hidden.

"The cold, gray dawn of that chill December morning was sending its first rays above the horizon and looking down upon one of the worst bands of Apaches in Arizona, caught like wolves in a trap," recalled Capt. John G. Bourke in 1891. He said the Apaches rejected an order to surrender because they thought there was no way the soldiers could venture onto the narrow open trail to attack them without being shot.

"They rejected with scorn our summons to surrender, and defiantly shrieked that not one of our party should escape from that canyon. We heard their death song chanted, and then out of the cave and over the great pile of rock which protected the entrance like a parapet, swarmed

Charles (Carlo) Gentile (1835-1893) immigrated from Italy to America and adopted the captive Apache boy he named Carlos Montezuma. Gentile was an eccentric adventurer and roving photographer. He was active in many photography organizations and the Press Club of Chicago. Gentile also was involved with artists. Photo courtesy of Wikimedia Commons.

the warriors," Bourke said, adding that the soldiers outnumbered the Natives by three to one.

Then one soldier had an idea about how to shoot at the Indians, who were located in a cave and shielded by a granite wall. If aimed in certain places around the cave, the bullets would ricochet into the interior.

Bourke said the soldiers "poured in lead by the bucketful," with bullets hitting the roof and mouth of the cave. The sound of screams "filled the air" enabling the military to know their gunfire was striking the Apaches. "During the heaviest part of the firing a little boy, not more than four years old, absolutely naked, ran out at the side of the parapet and stood dumbfounded between the two fires," he continued. An Indian scout grabbed the baby out of harm's way and placed him among the soldiers. "A bullet, probably deflected from the rocks, had struck the boy on the top of the head and plowed round to the back of the neck, leaving a welt an 8th of an inch thick, but not injuring him seriously."

He said the Apaches refused a final offer to surrender, which ensured their demise.

"Every warrior died at his post. The women and children had hidden themselves in the inner recesses of the cave, which was of no great depth, and were captured and taken to Camp McDowell. A number of them had been struck by glancing bullets or fragments of falling rock. As soon as our pack trains could be brought up, we mounted the captives on our horses and mules and started for the nearest military station, the one

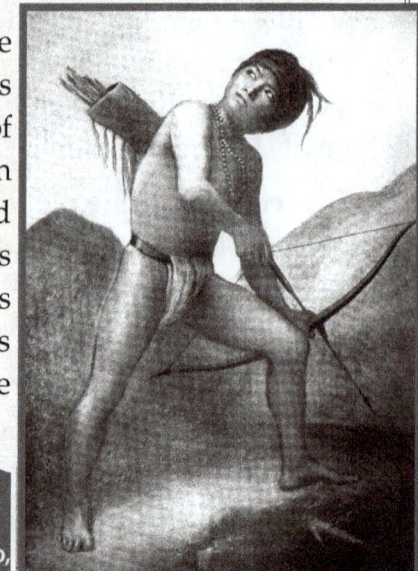

As a boy, Carlos Montezuma posed for an oil painting by J. Roy Robertson called "The Eagle's Last Flight," shown in a 1901 magazine. The painting was given to the Press Club of Chicago and hung in prominence in the reception room during the early 1900s. The club, now called the International Press Club of Chicago, no longer has the painting, which has gone missing over the years.

just named, over 50 miles away. This was the worst blow ever received by hostile Indians in America: in their chosen fortress, red-handed with plunder and blood, the whole band was wiped out of existence, with a loss to us of only one killed."

A soldier who took part in the massacre revealed more details after the skeletons were discovered. J.D. Green, of Tennessee, was stationed at Fort McDowell. He told *The Arizona Republican* on March 28, 1908 that the mass murder was "the most heartbreaking job" he ever did in the Army.

"The firing lasted 3 hours and at the end of that time one side of the face of every man was raw from contact with the lava bed, for under orders, all threw themselves on the ground, only raising their heads to fire. Mr. Green said it is to the shame of the government that those skeletons have been left unburied all these years."

The boy who told the officers the location of his tribe found his parents among the dead and threw himself on their bodies. Capt. Burns felt sorry for the child and "adopted" him immediately, calling him Mike Burns. When the captain died two years later, the boy was taken in by General Wesley Merritt of the 5th Cavalry and passed over to Capt. Edward Dravo before being placed at the Indian school in Carlisle. (Mike Burns returned to live in Arizona and had a government job there.)

This family (above) is from the Pima tribe that helped the 5th Cavalry in the cave massacre and sold Wassaja and his sisters. The captive Apache woman (below) was sold for 40 yards of *manta* (muslin) cloth at Camp Grant. These photos, courtesy of the Library of Congress, were taken by Carlo Gentile at the time he rescued Wassaja.

Wassaja, who somehow survived the gunfire in the cave, was also captured after the massacre. His path would cross decades later with his cousin Mike Burns, as both captive boys returned to their tribe later in life to reconnect with lost relatives.

In 1889, while in medical school, Carlos Montezuma drafted this speech he gave in Illinois about his early life.

"I am a full-blooded Apache of Arizona, was captured by the Pima tribe in 1871. They were friendly to the whites. I remained with them

The adobe house (left, shown in 1905) believed to be where Wassaja was sold to Charles Gentile. The Pima warrior (right, photographed in 1871 by Gentile) is thought to be the man who captured Wassaja from the cave and sold him to Gentile. It has been reported that Monty, as an adult, sought out this Pima man, who feared an act of revenge. Instead, Monty forgave the man and thanked him for taking him captive and selling him to Gentile. Monty was grateful for what he saw as an opportunity to advance himself in white civilization away from the poverty and limited chances of achievement on a segregated reservation. Photos courtesy of The Smithsonian Institution.

a few days when I was carried from village to village and offered for sale. In one place they offered a horse for me, but my captors thought I was worth more. Towards evening we came to a village where I was sold for $30 to Mr. Gentile, formerly a photographer of Chicago. He was taking landscapes in that region and at the same time collecting curiosities. Having the chance, he thought he would get a live one. We subsequently started East and visited Washington; Grand Rapids, Michigan; Chicago; and New York."

Charles (Carlo in his native Italian) Gentile bestowed his own first name on Wassaja. Instead of giving the boy his surname, he chose the grand name of the famous indigenous chief Montezuma, which showed his recognition and appreciation of the boy's cultural diversity. Then Gentile had a Catholic priest baptize the boy as Carlos Montezuma, a name for which he is known even today.

In 1872, the pair moved to Chicago, where Gentile had previously established a photo studio and was involved in both the art scene and the local Press Club.

Three years later, they sat down for an interview with the *Chicago Tribune*. By then, Gentile nicknamed the boy "Monty" and revealed that he convinced a friend to buy the boy's two sisters, who also survived the massacre.

Monty said his mother was murdered in the cave, but his father was away at another village. He recalled being terrified at seeing Gentile (the first white man he'd ever encountered) because he thought Gentile wanted to kill him and his camera was a cannon for shooting.

"Monty fraternizes amicably with boys of his age, and is expert at all games. In marbles, he is so successful as to accumulate them by hundreds. He can play cards, chess and checkers with remarkable skill and is very quick at mental calculation. He does not exhibit any of the vindictive traits of the Indian character, and Mr. Gentile says he is unique among Indians. He is good-natured and obliging, is perfectly truthful and honest. He does not suffer at all from any prejudice against him, as his force of character soon commands the respect of his schoolfellows. He is bold as a lion, and can thrash the average boy of 13 so that he is not imposed on. His vocabulary is larger than that of children his age and the quickness of his parts is such that he is considered a boy of bright promise," declared the newspaper in an article called, *"Montezuma: Gentile's little Indian Protégé."*

Monty dressed in a costume in 1872 soon after he went with Gentile. Photo by Napoleon Sarony, courtesy of the National Archives.

Monty attended school while moving around to various states with Gentile—who with the boy was said to have briefly joined Buffalo Bill's theatrical group, where Monty acted as the son of Cochise while Gentile took souvenir photos to sell. Despite Gentile's roving nature and lack of money, he tried to ensure Monty was provided for and placed the boy with others while they maintained periodic contact. In Monty's early writings, he mentions suffering from health problems while living in urban areas and having to spend more time in a rural Illinois climate to recuperate.

His spirit, ambition and determination to better himself is shown in an October 1887 letter he wrote to encourage other Native students at the Carlisle school in Pennsylvania, where Indian children had been taken from their tribes all over the country to be placed in a boarding school environment to educate them, teach them skills, and take away their prior Native ways from them.

Ever committed to his Native people no matter what tribal affiliation, Monty penned an uplifting story of his struggles to be educated. He walked to school at age 9 to earn his keep, studied harder at night than others, and performed manual labor on a farm during college.

"During these years I never have doubted that the great problem of the Indian question is capable of solution if the advantages which were open to me could be extended to all Indian youth," Monty told the Native students.

Dr. William H. Stedman (1840–1923), a Baptist preacher, took Monty into his home to live among his family. He may have had a positive influence on the youth because Monty's funeral was conducted at a Baptist church in Arizona.

An 1880 census shows that by age 16, Monty was with the young family of 39-year-old Dr. William H. Stedman (a Baptist preacher from Pennsylvania), his wife Belle, their four children (ranging from age 10 to 1 year), and Belle's sister Nellie (a 21-year-old teacher).

Monty graduated from Urbana High School followed by the University of Illinois in 1884 where he completed his Bachelor of Science degree in chemistry. Next he worked in a drug store to help fund his studies at Northwestern University's Chicago Medical College, earning his medical degree in 1889.

Before graduation to become a doctor, Monty focused on positive aspects of his life in his notes for the 1889 speech: "During these 15 years as an orphan among the whites I have been treated in a friendly manner and have had equal privileges with the palefaces," he stated, adding that in the future he hoped "to be able to lend my services wherever they may be needed."

This speech also provided a glimpse of his never-ending commitment as an activist for better treatment of Natives and advancements for their causes. At a time when few voices were critical of the U.S. government's actions towards Indians and even fewer publicly voiced such sentiments, Monty never missed an opportunity to say what he thought. His notes below from that early speech provide one such example.

"There never was in the history of our country a subject that demands more attention to than the study of the Indian nation; [when] America was first discovered, they were called Indians and were treated as such. Time brought different nationalities, [these land] claims among Indians were not understood so there was war between them….[dividing] the tribes according to their localities. From this on they were called savages. As savages among civilized nation the same privileges were not given to them. Year after year friendship [between whites and Natives] lengthened as well as distance; bloodshed was the result."

After medical school, Monty became a doctor for the Office of Indian Affairs and treated Natives until 1896 when he returned to Chicago to establish a private practice. He became a world-renowned specialist in stomach disorders and, at the same time, lent his expertise to teach medical students.

To the Students of Carlisle Indian School,

I have been thinking what would be best to write that might be a help and encouragement to your in your studies this year. I have concluded to relate to you briefly my early schooling and graduation to the degree of Bachelor of Science.

Now, imagine a small Apache boy in the wilds of Arizona, just as happy as a bird, free from every thought of danger.

How little did I think one night would separate me from my mother, father, sisters, and brother to live among strangers and be no more free! How little did I realize that this horrid prison life was but the stepping stone to a better and nobler aim! A brighter morning dawned at last! So with you all.

In the year 1871 I was taken from the most warlike tribe in America and placed in the midst of civilization in Chicago. My greatest wish was to understand the paper talking, as it was interpreted to me. I often saw boys and girls go to and from the schoolhouse. I had no idea that they all had to be taught, but I had a suspicious idea of the house. One morning, in April, the boy with whom I had associated, persuaded me to come into the schoolyard to play marbles by saying that 'I could win piles of marbles if I did!' So I consented.

The bell rang for school to begin. I went in and took a seat. The teacher came forward and asked me if I wanted to attend school. I could not speak English; all I could say was. 'Yes.'

Of course, I naturally said yes to every question. I was taken up to the principal. Here I was questioned and given a small note. This note specified what books I was to get. I left the school feeling as big as ever, and took the note to my guardian. He gave me a few pieces of money to purchase what was necessary. This was the beginning of my education.

At this time I did not know my A,B,C's. I could not count nor understand letters. It was but a few months before I could repeat the Lord's prayer, sing 'Precious Jewels' with the scholars, say my A,B,C's and count 100, besides write and describe different objects.

I learned as fast as any of the whites, for the reason that the teacher delighted to instruct me.

I left this school and went to another one. Here was the best teacher I ever had in a public school. This lady seemed to comprehend the nature of my circumstances and aided me all she could. I made good advancement in my first reader by taking my books home at night, so that I could be instructed there also.

Most of the reading I committed to memory.

On account of ill health I left this city and went into the country where for two years I walked two and a half miles to school, and worked to earn my board. This was when I was only nine years of age.

In the spring [of 1877], I went to Brooklyn to school. I was by this time sufficiently advanced to study grammar, arithmetic and history. At this school I always stood at the head of my class. I did this by staying at home nights to study; not by standing at corners as did some of white children.

In the fall of 1877, I returned to Urbana, Ill., where I was assisted in my studies with the view of preparing me for the State University. Inside of one year I passed an examination in geometry, algebra, philosophy, bookkeeping, botany, composition and physiology.

I made my way in College by paying and by working for my board.

In summer I worked on a farm. This I continued for four years, when I graduated with the degree of Bachelor of Science in the School of Chemistry.

During these years I never have doubted that the great problem of the Indian question is capable of solution if the advantages which were open to me could be extended to all Indian youth.

So with you all. Take care! You are being watched, and time will prove whether you are worthy of being protected and educated.

Carlos Montezuma
Medical College, Chicago, Ill. Oct. 1887

Monty in 1891. Courtesy of The Smithsonian Institution.

At the age of 35 in 1900, he still lived as a boarder in a household run by middle-aged Mary Johnson, her 3 daughters (aged 26 to 15), and 2 sons (both privates in the Army).

Three years later, Monty married Marie Keller, a 25-year-old immigrant from Germany. Not content to merely work as a doctor, Monty increasingly became a champion for Native rights. He opposed the concept of segregation by placing Indians on reservations, which he saw as isolating them and preventing them from making the same accomplishments in the same environment as white people. He used his brilliance as a communicator to publicly decry injustices to Natives and influence policy to protect their rights.

Dr. Carlos Montezuma in 1893 at the Carlisle Indian School. Nurses are thought to be seated around him. Photo by John Choate, courtesy of The Smithsonian Institution. He was the 2nd Native to earn a medical degree.

His most famous slogan, "with the spirit of Moses," was: "Let My People Go." In 1916, he began publishing a magazine under his native Apache name, Wassaja, and used that platform to rally against the abuse of having governmental bureaucracy (the Office of Indian Affairs) act as a go-between for Natives, who he believed should be free to act on their own behalf without an agency over them and dictating what it presumed was in their best interests.

He was a prolific writer and passionate orator who left behind a large body of work. In an opinion piece called *"How America has Betrayed the Indian,"* Monty voiced many daring and harsh sentiments in the *Chicago Tribune* on Oct. 4, 1903.

"Reservations are prisons, the fiendish device of so-called civilization for the Indians; while the prisoner is kept in his cell, the mere placing of furniture therein and supplying him with necessary food and raiment leave him none the less a prisoner still. No! you must first get him out of his prison cell. Make him know that he is a free man and then surround him with good environments. The law of nature is expansion and growth. The first step towards civilization of the Indian is to place him geographically so that he can commingle with the conquering race…I would not object to remain as an Indian and live as an Indian for ages to come were you to agree to take my ways and let me lead the trail of life. But when you monopolize all and leave me nothing, I object…Does not the Great Spirit say today, as of old, 'Let my people go'?"

His views for that time were extremely radical. Newspapers back then referred to Natives in derogatory terms like "redskins" and women were unable to vote until 1920. Yet, he remained fearless in acting on his convictions.

The Lexington Intelligencer.

Blockades to Indian Civilization

By DR. CARLOS MONTEZUMA,
An Indian Physician Practicing in Chicago.

THE SHOW MAN AND THE ANTHROPOLOGIST.—"Leave the Indians alone. It is beautiful to preserve the true children of nature as object lessons to study from." By blinding the Indians Buffalo Bill has wrongly educated the public. To leave the Indians alone as curiosities and studies may be well enough for the show man and the anthropologist. But what about the Indian? The standard of a splendid race is degraded by it. He deserves a better fate than to be decked with savage attire, only to be ridiculed and jeered at for mercenary and scientific purposes. Do away with your ignorance of the Indian. Help him to escape the deadly fate of the reservation system. Learn of him, as he will of you. Then you will develop the man and not the savage, the citizen and not the pauper. This is all I have to say for my people.

Carlos Montezuma

When Monty wrote this column that appeared in a Missouri newspaper May 10, 1902 there was much discussion in the nation about Natives being uncivilized and speculation about what to do with them. Indian children were being taken away and placed into distant boarding schools. Geronimo was living the final chapter of his life as a prisoner of war on a reservation. In fact, Indians were not given full U.S. citizenship until 1924. Monty sought for Natives to have equal rights. The fact that this column discusses how Natives were viewed in costumes as denigrating is poignant especially since Monty experienced this.

Although his views may have brought discomfort to some, Monty met with great admiration. An Arizona newspaper in 1896 reported on a talk given in San Francisco contrasting the outlaw Apache Kid with Monty. "Of his tribe it has been said that they were no more capable of civilization than the rattlesnakes upon which they feed," it noted, while adding that not only was Monty exceptional, but he proved Apaches could make great achievements.

For decades, his accomplishments and praises were published continuously in newspapers across the United States for decades. The *Washington Times* noted in June 1911 that Monty, a member of both the University Club of Chicago and Chicago Press Club, was consulted by "specialists the world over on intestinal troubles."

In November of that year, Monty championed his views about Natives in *Arizona Republican* newspaper. "My belief is that the sooner they [Indians] co-mingle with the people of the country and take on the new mode of living, the better it will be for them. …we are looked

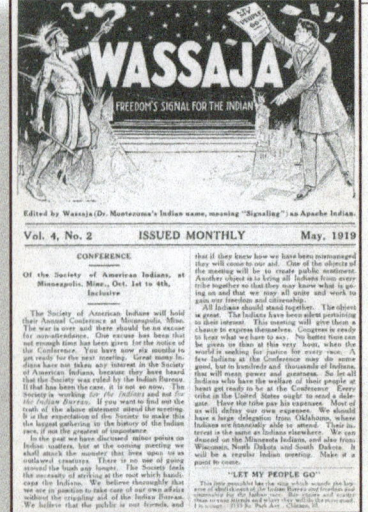

A copy of the *"Wassaja"* newsletter Monty published to champion his views on Native rights.

upon as curiosities and not human beings. I despise this brand, this infernal stigma that relegates my people to nonentity. The very depth of human anguish cries out against these intolerable daggers that thrust our very inner souls."

A critic of segregating Natives on reservations and in special Indian-only schools, Monty discussed the contrast of his life's accomplishments against those of a non-Native named Mickey Free, a boyhood friend who had been captured by the Apaches. Mickey, half-Irish and half-Hispanic, had grown up with the tribe and stayed with them when they were sent to a reservation. By contrast, Monty had been raised outside a reservation among whites.

A Washington, D.C. newspaper, the *Sunday Star*, remarked in August 1911, that an encounter between Mickey and Monty when adults became one of Monty's "favorite stories [that] strongly illustrates the mental equality of the Indian and white man."

Three decades after Gentile rescued Monty, the doctor returned to his people on the San Carlos reservation. "There he noticed a man whose parentage was evidently white, but who lived the life of the reservation Indian. Dr. Montezuma approached this man and spoke to him in English." However, Mickey indicated he didn't understand. "Dr. Montezuma investigated the history of this man and traced him back to the captive boy of his youth. He had spent his life among the Indians as an Indian and showed no more intelligence, energy or desire for better living than the other people of the wigwam. The interchange in racial surroundings of these two boys reflects more credit unto the Indian than upon the white."

Monty returned to his ancestral homelands in Arizona many times. There are varying accounts of the fate of his sisters who were bought at the same time as Monty by an acquaintance of Gentile

Mickey Free, a half-Irish and Hispanic, was captured by Apaches as a boy and became a childhood friend of Monty. Mickey grew up to be an Indian scout and remained with the Apaches.

named Charlie Mason. The price has been described as being two cows for both girls. It is said Mason and his Mexican wife took the girls over the border into Sonora, Mexico and the girls died sometime after the couple divorced.

Monty did have many interactions with his cousins, Charley and George Dickens. Monty's aunt (his mother's sister) and George were able to escape from the massacre. It has been mentioned that because Monty never forgot his Apache name it became a valuable link that enabled him to locate his Apache relatives, who lived at Fort McDowell in Arizona.

As his health declined due to tuberculosis, Monty wanted to die at his ancestral homeland. He left Chicago for Arizona, with his wife joining him later to be at his side. On Jan. 31, 1923 he succumbed to the disease. His death certificate said he contracted it in Chicago and had been suffering from TB for 5 years. His funeral was held at First Baptist Church, with burial following at Fort McDowell.

His papers were retained by his widow (who remarried and became Mary Keller Montezuma Moore) until her death in 1956. Monty's papers have been acquired by the State Historical Society of Wisconsin. Today, he continues to inspire scholars, the medical community, and people of all races. Buildings have been named in his honor. His efforts to help found the Society of American Indians, as a first national entity of Natives to work for their rights, has been a role model for other such efforts.

Monty's gifted character and life's work in overcoming adversity is one of the rare good stories about the fate of captive Native children. The next tale is also one of triumph about how a strong-willed Apache mother scaled a 10,600-foot-tall mountain range to reach freedom after becoming a captured servant in Santa Fe.

Monty (upper row, second right) poses among his former students at the 1921 reunion of the "Class of 1888" at Northwestern University Medical School.

Chapter 25: Geronimo's Cousin Nah-thle-tla: A Determined Mother

Unlike most stories of Native captives, the seizing of Nah-thle-tla was told from an Indian perspective. Her son Jason Betzinez (1860–1960) co-wrote his autobiography, *"I Fought with Geronimo."* It provides details about his mother's plight, how she was treated, and how other captives fared who were taken with her.

Nah-thle-tla and Geronimo were among the grandchildren of Apache chief Mahko, who has been described as peace loving. Her son placed her birthday near 1823. She called "The Night the Stars Fell" as one of her earliest memories. This experience she witnessed was probably Halley's Comet, which splashed across New Mexico's skies in late 1835.

Jason Betzinez in 1889. Courtesy of The Smithsonian Institution.

Her family of Warm Springs Apaches came from an area that included southern New Mexico. In her lifetime, she was captured twice after coming of age.

Her first husband was Shnowin. "Like all young Indians in love, Shnowin was full of love songs which he sang early in the morning and late in the evening. In spite of the intensity of his affection, the young man was too bashful to tell Nah-thle-tla about it, while she, because of tribal tradition, could not show in the slightest that she was aware of his feelings or that she returned them."

Before marrying, Shnowin's parents had to approve. The next step was for them to meet her parents to formally negotiate a marriage

A young Apache couple, Bonie Tela (left) and Hattie Tom in 1898. Photo by Frank A. Rinehart, courtesy of Wikimedia Commons.

Captives of the Southwest

price, "which usually consisted of one or more good horses." During the bargaining, conducted at the prospective bride's home, Shnowin had to wait outside while protocol dictated that Nah-thle-tla sat in silence behind her mother. "And after the marriage was arranged, the young people still were kept apart and the coming ceremony was not disclosed to the rest of the tribe. Meantime a strict watch was kept over the girl lest her reputation be tarnished."

Life went well for the young couple, who had two children, until a series of tragedies struck in 1855. That year, Shnowin joined other warriors in the tribe who rode across the border into Mexico to raid a community south of Casas Grandes in the state of Chihuahua.

Under the terms at the end of the U.S. war with Mexico, no military members from either country were allowed to cross each other's borders without prior government approval. So Apaches could raid in one country and flee across the border into safety without fear of reprisals.

While Shnowin and the other warriors were away, his wife and children stayed with her parents at their camp in the mountains near Fort Cummings, N.M. The Apaches felt safe there due to their close proximity to U.S. soldiers; the Army would unknowingly provide a buffer from any reprisals for the raid.

"When the Indians saw a body of men approaching their camp, they did not realize that these were Mexican soldiers, but thought

Chief Geronimo (1829–1909), who shared the same grandfather as Nah-thle-tla). This image of the famous warrior was taken in Arizona in 1886 at his campsite before he surrendered. Photo by C.S. Fly, courtesy of the Library of Congress.

A painting of Fort Cummings in 1867 by unknown, in *"Annals of Old Fort Cummings, New Mexico 1867-8,"* by William Thornton Parker (1916).

Warm Springs Apache chief Ka-ya-ten-na in 1884. His name can be translated to mean "Fights without Arrows" and "Cartridges all Gone." He was from the same tribe as Nah-thle-tla. Photo courtesy of the Library of Congress.

that they were their own warriors returning from the raid. No preparations were made to flee. No men of fighting age were in camp and no one had any firearms. Therefore the camp was virtually defenseless. Following the first burst of fire from the enemy, the camp was quickly overrun. The Mexicans again without mercy killed indiscriminately—women, children, old men, and boys. The survivors were seized as prisoners, among these being Nah-thle-tla and her two small children."

She would discover that her beloved Shnowin had been fatally wounded during the fierce battle in which the Apaches claimed victory.

With her little ones, Nah-thle-tla and the other captives were assembled by the Mexicans, who proceeded to destroy everything in the campsite except dried venison, which they stole and carried away to use for their rations. All of this occurred without any apparent knowledge from the American soldiers at Fort Cummings—which is astounding because the Mexican forces had to cross the U.S. border and travel some 50 miles inland to reach the Apache camp.

"Nah-thle-tla told me in later years that during the march toward Chihuahua the Mexican commander, whom she described as being a general, was kind to most of his prisoners. He was a bit harsh with one Indian woman who boasted that her husband was one of the fighters who had made the recent raid to Namiquipa. The general forced this woman to walk all the way to Casas Grandes, a distance of a hundred miles, instead of riding a horse or a mule like the other captives. He didn't realize that such a hike was no hardship to an Apache woman."

The Namiquipa raid had also been conducted in the state of Chihuahua and was nearly 90 miles from the Casas Grandes attack.

Nah-thle-tla and the other captives were unable to escape since soldiers guarded them closely at night. When the party reached Casas Grandes, they stopped to rest for two days before being loaded onto two-wheeled carts to veer east to Galeana in the state of Nuevo León, near the Gulf of Mexico.

"This stage of the journey, though only 25 miles long, required two days because of the slow pace of the carts. The route continued southeast up the Santa Maria River some 60 miles to Namiquipa. Here the inhabitants, still in a fury over the recent Indian attack, urged the general to turn over his prisoners to be slaughtered. The commander refused, so as the column pulled out, the Mexican women ran alongside the vehicles screaming curses and throwing rocks."

An Apache woman and baby (circa 1900). Photo by Edward Curtis, courtesy of the Library of Congress.

Several days later, the group reached their final destination in Mexico where the captive Apache women and children were dispersed and distributed to Mexican families. Nah-thle-tla never saw her children again.

She worked there for several months as a slave in a Mexican family until they sold her to a wealthy Hispanic man from Santa Fe, N.M. He also purchased another young captive Apache woman from New Mexico to accompany them. Both women were loaded onto an oxcart bound for Santa Fe in a journey that could take at least three months.

"The cart, webbed up with rope like a cage, was drawn by four oxen who moved quite slowly. Tied to a pole at the front of the cart trotted a large, mean dog to assist in preventing the escape of the prisoners."

The group passed from Juarez, Mexico and crossed the Rio Grande into El Paso, Texas. Their next destination was Albuquerque. While passing through Nah-thle-tla's ancestral lands of the Warm Springs Apaches, the other Native captive started to weep. "'What are you crying for?' asked Nah-thle-tla. "Don't you know that we are close to our homeland, that if we should manage to escape we would find our own people? Cheer up!' but they found no chance to slip away."

Once in Santa Fe, Nah-thle-tla was separated from the other captive, who entered into service for another family. Rarely did their paths cross from that point onward. Nah-thle-tla found herself "well received by the wife and children of the wealthy" Hispanic family.

Mountains rise in southern New Mexico near the ancestral homelands of the Warm Springs Apaches. This scenery has remained unchanged since the time Nah-thle-tla and her fellow captive would have seen it as they traveled the road to the homes of their new owners in Santa Fe. Photo by Noël Fletcher.

"She did her best to be a good houseworker, grinding corn for tortillas and doing the cooking and laundry for the family. The whole family was kind to her. For example, they often gave her some kind of fruit for breakfast. One day, not receiving fruit, she asked for it. The man replied that it was all gone but since she liked it so much he would make a trip of some four days over the mountains to obtain a new supply. Fruits in those days were mostly imported from Sonora [Mexico]."

When the man left, the young people in his family decided to hold a big dance party in his absence. They held a large dance that lasted so long throughout that night that it left them tired the next day. When night came, the family slept so soundly that Nah-thle-tla seized a chance to escape.

"She wrapped in a cloth some food and other things which she would need, climbed through a window to the wall surrounding the house and garden, and lowered herself by a rope to the ground. Then she fled to the outskirts of the town. As it was beginning to get light she concealed herself under a pile of brush, where some woodcutters had been at work, to wait through the day until darkness. No one disturbed her and her only danger came from dogs sniffing around where she was."

She traveled after nightfall and headed south "toward the mountains as the Apaches always did when in flight. At first she traveled only at night, hiding during the daytime. Several times she saw Mexican *vaqueros* riding near her place of concealment but she was not found."

Once she reached the high Sandia mountains, she moved during the daylight since she

These photos show the route Nah-thle-tla took to freedom. She had to cross the plains outside of Santa Fe (upper left) and descend rocky cliffs (middle left). As she approached the highest range (the Sandia Mountains outside Albuquerque), she had to cross harsh terrain with rattlesnakes and other dangers (top right). To gain the highest vantage point to find her way home, she climbed to the top of the Sandias, whose crest is the highest point at 10,678 feet. Photo top left by Zita Fletcher. All other photos by Noël Fletcher.

thought should wouldn't be discovered. "Though her only weapon was a butcher knife and there were wolves, mountain lions, and grizzlies in the range, she was not afraid. Once she saw the tracks of a large bear at a waterhole with the rocks still wet from water he had splashed, but never met any creature large enough to be dangerous."

She survived on nuts, seeds and berries. "She was a wiry, well-built young woman, accustomed to walking long distances. The trip over steep mountains, cliffs, canyons and rough lava beds was tiring but she stood up well under the hardships."

After traveling for more than a week, she reached the top of the mountains from where she spotted a high southern peak she recognized due to its unique shape. It was the Magdalena Mountains where her family lived. "Then at last she began to cry for the first time since she had been captured months before. But it was for gladness that soon she might see her mother again."

She waited for the sun to set before venturing into the lowlands near Isleta Pueblo where she must cross the Rio Grande. "When she came to its banks in the darkness she was afraid to cross, not knowing how deep the water might be. She moved back a few yards and hid in the weeds. About noon the next day she saw some Hispanics fording the river on foot, which showed her where it was possible to cross. After dark when she was sure that the Hispanics in the nearby farmhouse were asleep, she waded down into the water, holding her bundle on her head. In its deepest place the river came up to her armpits but it was a half-mile wide."

An Apache woman fills her pot with water. Photo (circa 1900) by Edward Curtis, courtesy of the Library of Congress.

A military map from New Mexico in 1861 shows the how far Nah-thle-tla traveled when she fled her captivity as a slave in Santa Fe and walked most of the way to her Apache homeland.

Reaching the banks safely, Nah-thle-tla noticed a pony in a cornfield. She created a bridle out of the rope she carried, stole the horse and rode south across the plains towards the mountains. Three days later, she was resting on a hilltop when she noticed a trio of Native warriors coming nearby. "She was afraid that they might be Navajos, with whom the Warm Springs Apaches were not friendly at that time. As the strangers came nearer, she saw from their clothing and the bands around their hair that they were Apaches. She called out to them whereupon they at once vanished. Since hostile Indians often used women as decoys, these Apaches would not show themselves unless they were sure that no danger existed. So she called out more loudly giving her name and telling that she had just escaped from Mexican captivity."

Two Navajo warriors pause on horseback. Photo (circa 1900) by Edward Curtis, courtesy of the Library of Congress.

The warriors carefully approached. She recognized "with great joy" that her chief, named Loco, was among that hunting party. She joined them and reunited with her mother and other family members at the hunting party's campsite.

Jason was proud his mother had escaped and by her strong willpower had walked 250 miles in such an arduous and dangerous journey to rejoin her family.

Chief Loco (1823–1905) with a knife tucked inside his gun belt in 1886. His Apache name was Jlin-tay-i-tith (Stops his Horse) and he was born about the same year as Nah-thle-tla. He was known as a peacemaker who tried to avoid war at all costs. Loco was also an early advocate for education and sent his children to school before many other Apaches did. Photo by Frank A. Randall, courtesy of The Smithsonian Institution.

Two years later, she married his father, Tudeevia. Her new husband's father was Chief Tudeevia, who succeeded Baishan after the Battle of Ramos [in Mexico], but died before his namesake was of age to be his successor. Instead, the Warm Springs Apaches elected Victorio and Loco as dual leaders. "Both were experienced fighters, very able men. Victorio being the more warlike of the two. I became well acquainted with both of them," Jason said.

Nah-thle-tla was captured again soon after her second marriage. Instead of using her for a slave, her new captors were residents of the town of Monticello, some 20 miles away "who were to become good friends." They took her as a pawn to make peace with her tribe. "They sent her to tell Chief Loco that they would like to make peace with the Indians. Loco, always peaceably inclined, was quite willing. The resulting 'treaty' between our band and Monticello was never broken not even during the reigns of terror which resulted successively from the outbreaks of Cochise, Victoria, Nana, Chato and Geronimo."

Nah-thle-tla at 105 years old. Photo courtesy of the Oklahoma Historical Society.

Not only did Nah-thle-tla survive captivity twice, but she lived to witness a great many changes that happened to her people. Her cousin Geronimo turned himself into military authorities following unsuccessful attempts to maintain their nomadic lifestyle after Apaches were put on a reservation. Geronimo and her son Jason were shipped to the East Coast. Jason eventually attended the Carlisle Indian School and became successful in Oklahoma. She moved to Fort Sill, Oklahoma in 1894. Geronimo died as a prisoner of war there in 1909.

She is shown in photos at an advanced age visiting his grave. In 1932, she was declared America's oldest living mother when she reached 110 years of age. Two years later she died. Her son Jason also attained longevity. He reached the age of 100 before he passed away in 1960.

Indian Woman Dies At Ripe Old Age—110

LAWTON, Okla., June 7. (AP)—The 110-year-old Nah-Thle-Tla, who as a child played with Geronimo, fierce Apache chieftain, is dead.

The Apache woman, who never until the past year was seriously ill, was named America's oldest living mother by the national federation of Women's clubs in 1932.

Conclusion

A common thread that weaves the stories of all the captives together is race—one racial group attacking another. Many innocent people were simply trying to live their ordinary lives when another group decided it was justifiable to use violence to rob, beat, murder, kidnap, sometimes mutilate, and enslave others and their loved ones. The victors in these acts also found reasons to justify their brutality and lack of humanity. They used these reasons to justify the use of military force against civilians and defenseless people. This created an atmosphere that made many people favorable to the idea of genocide.

The Rio Grande snakes through a cottonwood forest in Albuquerque, N.M. as the majestic Sandia Mountains keep their ever-watchful eyes on the inhabitants below. Photo by Noël Fletcher.

When someone looks at a person of a different race as inferior, great harm is possible. No one has the moral superiority or inherent authority to abuse another. Yet, horrendous acts were done to each other by all three major ethnicities of New Mexico including Anglos, Hispanics and Natives.

Despite it all, there were heroes who rose above their circumstances. Those who reached out to people of another race with compassion and even love. Those who stood up to object to the wrongs and try to make positive changes. The cases that come to mind are the Native boy Juan Jose Gabaldon from San Ildefonso Pueblo who saved Jane Adeline Wilson, Andres Martinez who spent his adult life in service to his Kiowa saviors, Capt. Silas Stillman Soule who was murdered after testifying against another officer for massacring peaceful Indians, Sister Rosanna who provided a mother's love to a captive Native orphaned boy, and Dr. Carlos Montezuma who lived his life without bitterness, and opted for courage and conviction to bridge racial divides.

Although many tragedies have filled these pages, let us remember the worth of every human being and the lasting power that one person can have through acts of respect and compassion for one another.

About Noël Fletcher

Noël Fletcher is a journalist, author and photographer of Hispanic and English descent. She is from New Mexico, a land rich in rugged beauty and the Southwestern cultural blend of Native Americans, Hispanics, and Anglos. Her Hispanic ancestors came as Conquistadors to the Rio Grande valley and settled there. Among them were the Perea family of Spanish-Arab origin, who helped found the famed Santa Fe Trail and served in government roles under the Spanish crown, the Mexican era, and the American acquisition. On her father's side, her Fletcher and Ballinger relatives were early East Coast settlers from England; some from Virginia served in a volunteer militia under the Continental Army during the Revolutionary War.

Early in her career as a journalist, Noël worked through the trenches of daily news coverage at the *Desert Sun* newspaper in Palm Springs, an interesting locale of intrigue and affluence.

A few years later, she left on a whim to Hong Kong—with one suitcase in hand, $200, and the names of four people she'd never met—to become a foreign correspondent in Asia. Within two weeks, she landed a job at the *Hongkong Standard* newspaper covering the Supreme Court, a.k.a. the "High Court." She learned the ropes of the British legal system by reporting on a world populated by red-coated High Court justices, wigged barristers, black-frocked solicitors, and prisoners in the dock. She covered white-collar crime and sensational murder trials as well as the Court of Appeals.

Noël's foreign correspondent credentials in Beijing.

Noël presented information on her Perea family during the Santa Fe Trail Travelers and Descendants Conference.

Moving up the ranks as a foreign correspondent, Noël focused on business and financial news, thereby becoming part of an elite American press corps. Her beat was Asia.

She lived and worked in China, Hong Kong, and traveled through many other Asian countries including South Korea and Singapore. She was posted in Beijing as a prestigious "China correspondent" and became fluent in Mandarin. She delved deeper into the art, culture and history of Asia.

Noël experienced a poignant chapter in China's history during the events of the Tiananmen Square Massacre, which took place a few miles from the diplomatic compound where she lived. One of the few American women journalists there, she was on the last U.S. flight evacuated from Beijing and returned to China two weeks later to continue reporting.

Her work as an author, artist and book publisher reflects her interests in art, history, and diverse cultures. Her books often involve investigative research. She seeks to blend visual imagery with writing, including her own artwork and historical images.

Taking a break from her interviews as a financial journalist in Nanjing, Noël visited the mausoleum of Sun Yat-Sen, China's first president and founding father.

Noël's other Books

River of My Ancestors: The Rio Grande in Pictures by Noël Fletcher

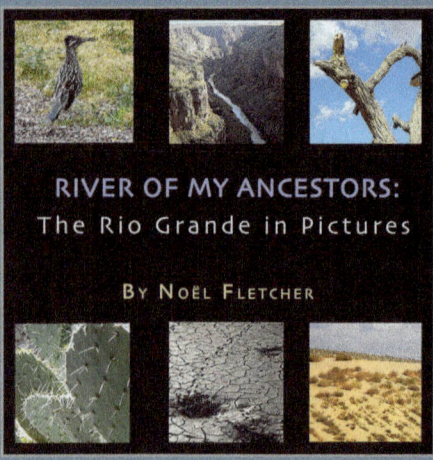

Take a journey along the wild and rugged Rio Grande. Beautiful pictures capture the essence of the famous river and its importance in the arid Southwest. Native New Mexican author and photographer Noël Fletcher provides family stories and insights about frontier life.

Follow the Rio Grande through deserts, wetlands, and rocky cliffs. Experience natural wonders, including volcanic lands and river rapids, and encounter wildlife such as snakes, wolves, cranes, and bighorn sheep.

With 180+ striking color photos, the book features:

- Author biography
- Wild West history
- the world's largest cottonwood forest
- the legendary Rio Grande Gorge
- Spanish colonial irrigation systems
- Bosque del Apache National Wildlife Refuge
- Unique wildlife and plants
- Oral tradition from Spanish settlers and family stories
- Interesting facts about New Mexico, local culture, and life along the Rio Grande

This captivating book combines vivid photos and the written word to tell a living history of the famous Rio Grande and the beautiful desert land of New Mexico.

The Strange Side of War *by* Sarah Macnaughtan & Noël Fletcher

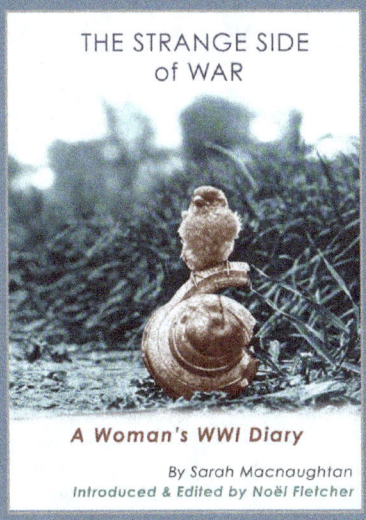

Take a journey across the dangerous battlefields of a world at war. Accompany Scottish novelist Sarah Macnaughtan as she volunteers alongside British humanitarian groups to alleviate the suffering in war-torn lands. Her many adventures tell unique stories of tragedy and triumph, taking readers on an unforgettable journey from the trenches of Belgium to the distant frontiers of Persia and tsarist Russia.

Author/editor Noël Fletcher provides new historical context that brings Sarah's story to life and helps readers to remember the bravery and sacrifice of those who died. Illustrated with 130+ rare photos and propaganda posters from World War I, this important work features historical insights about the people and places involved in the conflict.

Two Years in the Forbidden City *by* Princess Der Ling

This true story was the first eyewitness account of the Imperial Court written by a Chinese aristocrat for Western readers. It provides an up-close view of the notorious Dowager Empress Tzu-hsi in her final years. Enhanced with rich imagery and additional historical notes, it includes interesting historical details and photos about China's infamous Dowager Empress, the Boxer Rebellion and the Imperial Court. It is illustrated with 100+ historical photographs, illustrations, and paintings from the late 1800s to early 1900s. Author/editor Noël Fletcher that provides context for this book in modern Chinese history.

More Books from Fletcher & Co. Publishers

Every book is a journey. Fletcher & Co. Publishers is an independent, art-house publishing company. We use new media and graphic design techniques to transport you into the world of the novel.

Our books aren't just written words. They're experiences: international cultures, art, suspense, history, and adventure.

Watch our video trailers on YouTube and Vimeo to preview each book, see interesting images, and learn more about our newest releases.

Visit us our website to find out about our latest news.

Edge of Suspicion *by* Zita Steele

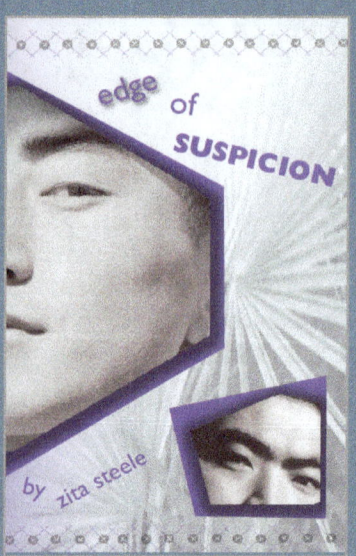

Justin Moon of South Korea is the world's top private eye. He travels to Singapore to catch an elusive cybercriminal. The pay is lucrative. His client is an attractive blonde CEO. It should be the easiest job in his career. Things get complicated with the arrival of Okada, a mysterious drifter with a mission of revenge. As Moon tries to solve the mystery, he uncovers a tangled maze of deceit. Each new clue leads him in an unpredictable direction. A deadly game of cat-and-mouse begins. Featuring over 100 photos, *Edge of Suspicion* is both an exciting story and a work of art.

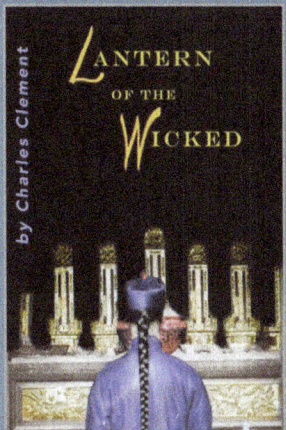

Lantern of the Wicked *by* CHARLES CLEMENT

In the decadent and dangerous Shanghai of 1929, someone is spying for the Japanese, and the International Settlement's British police are on the hunt. Now, in the midst of the Mid-Autumn Moon Festival, American aviator Jack "Ace" Jordan becomes the prime suspect. A thrilling narrative blending fact, fiction and rare photographs, *Lantern of the Wicked* creates an atmospheric window into the complexity and dark grandeur of the colonial Orient in this gripping historical mystery.

Envoy: Rule of Silence *by* ZITA STEELE

Take a journey into a thrilling world of secrets and lies in modern-day Europe. Polish ex-secret policeman Michal Krynski is tired of working as a double agent for France's security bureau. His last mission - to track down a runaway DJ. As he travels to the strange island of Malta, Krynski plots revenge against the system that ruined his life. Will he catch the DJ or kill him? Zita Steele is a novelist and artist. She writes with an expertise in criminology, cybercrime, and international relations. She creates her own illustrations.

New Mexico Ghosts and Haunting Images *by* ARIELA DESOLINA

Let explorer-photographer Ariela Desolina spirit you away to New Mexico, where haunting ruins - some with ghostly inhabitants - will capture your imagination. With photos from the St. James Hotel, a notorious hangout of Western outlaws and gamblers, and other mysterious locations. Mysterious shapes and ghostly forms (undetected when the pictures were taken) sometimes appear in her photos. Includes photos of the haunted ruins of the Kelly Mine, once among the richest old gold & silver mines in the Southwest.

The Spy *by* JAMES FENIMORE COOPER

During the dark days of the Revolutionary War, America struggles for nationhood. Meanwhile, in the shadows, a spy is trading secrets of vital importance to the cause – but for whose side? Colonials and loyalists play a game of cloak and daggers in America's first spy novel. Our edition features 30+ color photographs, chapter titles, and illuminating notations, designed to give you a front-seat experience. This was the first major fiction novel on espionage ever written and published in America.

Mystery of the Yellow Room *by* GASTON LEROUX

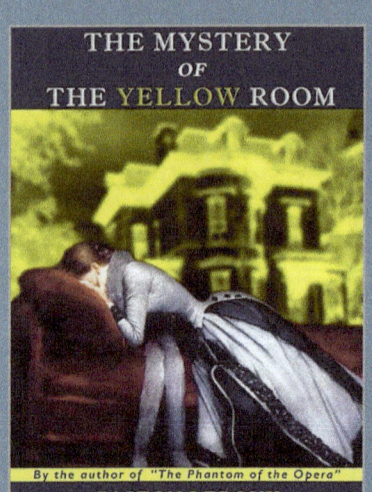

News of a strange crime spreads like wildfire in Paris. Someone has attempted to murder the daughter of a brilliant scientist. But nobody can explain how the murderer got in and out of the locked room of her isolated country home. Only Joseph Rouletabille, an impatient young journalist, has the genius to solve this crime. Written by the author of *"The Phantom of the Opera,"* this novel was published in 1907 as France's reply to Sherlock Holmes. Our edition has adapted text from archaic Victorian to standard English. It also features updated maps and is illustrated with 30+ historical paintings and illustrations from 19th century France.

Erwin Rommel Photographer–Vol. 1 A Survey *by* **Erwin Rommel and Zita Steele**

Take a journey behind the camera of a world-famous military commander. Experience WWII firsthand from Field Marshal Rommel's private photo collection, seized by U.S. forces in 1945. View 340+ images, including photos Rommel took during campaigns in France and North Africa and others he collected. Included are Rommel's personal photos of family and friends. The photos are digitally restored for detail. Some are accompanied by Rommel's own handwritten photo captions. Author/artist Zita Steele uses her knowledge of German language and culture, with in-depth research about Rommel and his campaigns, to provide context for the photos. Zita also analyzes patterns in Rommel's photography to shed a light on the artistic personality of this notable military leader.

Vol. 2 Rommel & His Men

by **Erwin Rommel and Zita Steele**

Experience life on the frontlines with Field Marshal Erwin Rommel. View 200+ images from Rommel's private photo collection, seized by U.S. forces in 1945. Join Rommel as he interacts with his German and Italian troops. See him and his men at work, at rest, and on the move. View Rommel's mementos of his men and military leaders. This book provides a candid view of Rommel as an ordinary soldier rather than a general. The photos are digitally restored and enhanced for detail. Some are accompanied by Rommel's own handwritten photo captions.

Vol. 3 Adventures in Color

by **Erwin Rommel and Zita Steele**

Join Field Marshal Erwin Rommel in WWII through his rare color photographs. View 130 color images from Rommel's private photo collection, seized by U.S. forces in 1945, and a selection of Rommel's hand-drawn sketches of his war experiences. Join Rommel as he travels across vast and colorful terrains, flies a dive bomber plane, drives across desert battlefields and explores North African villages. The photos and sketches are digitally restored and enhanced for detail. Also included are 10 original sketches by Rommel as well as historical facts and analysis.

www.ingramcontent.com/pod-product-compliance
Lightning Source LLC
Chambersburg PA
CBHW080430230426
43662CB00015B/2234